To Joyce
God Bless!

Dave

ON KILLING

The Psychological Cost of Learning
to Kill in War and Society

by Lieutenant Colonel Dave Grossman

BACK
BAY
BOOKS

Little, Brown and Company
Boston   New York   London

Copyright © 1995, 1996 by David A. Grossman

First Paperback Edition

Permissions to use previously published material appear on pages 352–53.

Library of Congress Cataloging-in-Publication Data

Grossman, Dave.
On killing : the psychological cost of learning to kill in war and
society / Dave Grossman. — 1st ed.
   p. cm.
  Includes index.
  ISBN 0-316-33000-0 (hc)   0-316-33011-6 (pb)
   1. Combat — Psychological aspects. 2. Psychology, Military.
3. Homicide — Psychological aspects. 4. Violence — Social aspects.
5. Violence — Psychological aspects. I. Title.
U22.3.G76 1995
355'.0019 — dc20   95-13888

Illustrations by Mary Reilly

10   9

MV-NY

Printed in the United States of America

Dedication

Not of the princes and prelates with periwigged charioteers
Riding triumphantly laureled to lap the fat of the years,
Rather the scorned — the rejected — the men hemmed in with spears;

The men in tattered battalion which fights till it dies,
Dazed with the dust of the battle, the din and the cries,
The men with the broken heads and the blood running into their eyes.

Not the be-medalled Commander, beloved of the throne,
Riding cock-horse to parade when the bugles are blown,
But the lads who carried the hill and cannot be known.

Others may sing of the wine and the wealth and the mirth,
The portly presence of potentates goodly in girth; —
Mine be the dirt and the dross, the dust and scum of the earth!

Theirs be the music, the colour, the glory, the gold;
Mine be a handful of ashes, a mouthful of mould.
Of the maimed, of the halt and the blind in the rain and the cold —

Of these shall my songs be fashioned, my tale be told. Amen.

— John Masefield
  "A Consecration"

Contents

Acknowledgments

War has always interested me; not war in the sense of maneuvers devised by great generals ... but the reality of war, the actual killing. I was more interested to know in what way and under the influence of what feelings one soldier kills another than to know how the armies were arranged at Austerlitz and Borodino.

— Leo Tolstoy

I have been assisted in this study by a host of great men and women who have stood beside me and gone before me in this endeavor. These I do now gratefully acknowledge.

To my wonderful and infinitely patient wife, Jeanne, for her staunch support; to my mother, Sally Grossman; and to Duane Grossman, my father and co-conspirator, whose many hours of help in research and concept made this book possible.

To the Indian Battalion of Arkansas State University, the finest ROTC battalion in the U.S. Army. To my fellow soldier-scholars among the ROTC cadre, to all my dear friends among the staff and faculty at Arkansas State University, and particularly to Jan Camp, who helped much with preparing the final draft and getting quotation authorizations. And most of all to my young ROTC cadets at Arkansas State; it is currently my privilege to teach them, and my honor to initiate them into the way of the warrior.

To Major Bob Leonhard, Captain Rich Hooker, Lieutenant Colonel Bob Harris, Major/Dr. Duane Tway, and that indomitable team, Harold Thiele and Elantu Viovoide: peers, friends, and fellow believers who have endured many a crude draft and contributed much time and effort to assisting and supporting me in this work.

To Richard Curtis, my literary agent, who contributed significantly and then waited long and patiently for the completion of this work. And to Roger Donald and Geoff Kloske, my editors at Little, Brown and Company, who had faith in this book and then worked long and hard to help me to fine-tune it into a professional product. And to Becky Michaels, my publicist, a true professional who has been faithful during the hard part.

To that magnificent group of soldier-scholars at the U.S. Military Academy whom I had the privilege of working with: Colonel Jack Beach, Colonel John Wattendorf, Lieutenant Colonel Jose Picart, and all the gang in the PL100 committee. And to that superb group of West Point cadets who volunteered to spend their summer conducting interviews, testing some of the theories presented in this book.

To my fellow students at the British Army Staff College at Camberley, England, who provided me with one of the finest and most intellectually stimulating years of my life.

To all of those remarkable soldiers who have molded, mentored, befriended, and commanded me, patiently giving of their wisdom and experiences over twenty years: First Sergeant Donald Wingrove, Sergeant First Class Carmel Sanchez, Lieutenant Greg Parlier, Captain Ivan Middlemiss, Major Jeff Rock, Lieutenant Colonel Ed Chamberlain, Lieutenant Colonel Rick Everett, Colonel George Fisher, Major General William H. Harrison, and countless others to whom I owe so much. And to Chaplain Jim Boyle: Ranger buddy, friend, and true brother. For most of these this is not their current rank, but that was what they were when I needed them most.

To Dr. John Warfield and Dr. Phillip Powell, at the University of Texas at Austin, who gave unselfishly of their wealth of wisdom and knowledge, while trusting me and letting me do it my way. And to Dr. John Lupo and Dr. Hugh Rodgers at Columbus College, in Columbus, Georgia, from whom I learned to love history.

I also need to make special acknowledgment of the extensive use I have made of the recent and excellent books by Paddy Griffith, Gwynne Dyer, John Keegan, Richard Gabriel, and Richard Holmes. Paddy Griffith was a boon mentor, friend, and companion during my stay in England, and along with Richard Holmes and John Keegan he is one of the world's true giants in this field today. And I particularly want to note that this study would have been much more difficult to complete without drawing on the tremendous body of insight and personal narratives collected in Richard Holmes's book *Acts of War*. Holmes's superb book will be *the* primary reference source for generations of scholars who study the processes of men in battle. My correspondence with him has confirmed that he is a gentleman, a gentle man, and a soldier-scholar of the highest order.

And I need to recognize that one of this study's most valuable and unusual sources of individual narratives has been the pages of *Soldier of Fortune* magazine. The image of the traumatized Vietnam veteran being spit upon, insulted, and degraded upon return to the United States is not mythical, but based upon literally thousands of such incidents — as chronicled in Bob Greene's excellent book, *Homecoming*. In this environment of condemnation and accusation, many Vietnam veterans felt that they had only one national forum in which they could attain some degree of closure by writing of their experiences in a sympathetic and nonjudgmental environment, and that forum was *Soldier of Fortune* magazine. To those who would prejudge this material and automatically reject anything coming from this quarter as mindless machismo, I ask that you read these narratives first. I am particularly indebted to Colonel Harris for his recommendation of this novel resource, and for the loan of his personal collection of these magazines. Most of all I need to thank Colonel (retired) Alex McColl, at *Soldier of Fortune,* for his support in using these quotes. It is good to know that there are still places where an officer is a gentleman, his word is his bond, and that is all that is required.

Last, and *most important,* to all the veterans throughout history who have recorded their responses to killing, and to those in my own life who permitted me to interview them. To Rich, Tim, Bruce, Dave, "Sarge" (Arf!), the Sheepdog Committee (who still share a wonderful secret with me), and a hundred others who have shared secrets with me. And to their wives, who sat beside them and held their hands while they wept and told of things they had never told before. To Brenda, Nan, Lorraine, and dozens of others. All those who spoke with me have been promised anonymity in return for their secret thoughts, but my debt to them is such that it can never be paid.

To all of these I wish to say thank you. I do truly stand on the shoulders of giants. But the responsibility for the report given from this august height is strictly my own. Thus, the views presented here do not necessarily represent the views of the Department of Defense or its components, the U.S. Military Academy at West Point, or Arkansas State University.

David A. Grossman
Arkansas State University
Jonesboro, Arkansas

A Brief Note Concerning Gender

War has often been a sexist environment, but death is an equal opportunity employer. Gwynne Dyer tells us:

> Women have almost always fought side by side with men in guerrilla or revolutionary wars, and there isn't any evidence they are significantly worse at killing people — which may or may not be comforting, depending on whether you see war as a male problem or a human one.

With but one exception, all of my interviewees have been male, and when speaking of the soldier the words of war turn themselves easily to terms of "he," "him," and "his"; but it could just as readily be "she," "her," and "hers." While the masculine reference is used throughout this study, it is used solely out of convenience, and there is no intention to exclude the feminine gender from any of the dubious honors of war.

Introduction to the Paperback Edition

If you are a virgin preparing for your wedding night, if you or your partner are having sexual difficulties, or if you are just curious . . . then there are hundreds of scholarly books available to you on the topic of sexuality. But if you are a young "virgin" soldier or law-enforcement officer anticipating your baptism of fire, if you are a veteran (or the spouse of a veteran) who is troubled by killing experiences, or if you are just curious . . . then, on *this* topic, there has been absolutely nothing available in the way of scholarly study or writing.

Until now.

Over a hundred years ago Ardant du Picq wrote his *Battle Studies,* in which he integrated data from both ancient history and surveys of French officers to establish a foundation for what he saw as a major nonparticipatory trend in warfare. From his experiences as the official historian of the European theater in World War II, Brigadier General S. L. A. Marshall wrote *Men Against Fire,* in which he made some crucial observations on the firing rates of men in war. In 1976 John Keegan wrote his definitive *Face of Battle,* focusing again exclusively on war. With *Acts of War,* Richard Holmes wrote a key book exploring the nature of war. But the link between killing and war is like the link between sex and relationships. Indeed, this last analogy applies across the board. All previous authors have written books on relationships (that is, war), while this is a book on the act itself: on killing.

These previous authors have examined the general mechanics and nature of war, but even with all this scholarship, no one has looked into the specific nature of the act of killing: the intimacy and psychological impact of the act, the stages of the act, the social and psychological implications and repercussions of the act, and the resultant disorders (including impotence and obsession). *On Killing* is a humble attempt to rectify this. And in doing so, it draws a novel and reassuring conclusion about the nature of man: despite an unbroken tradition of violence and war, man is not by nature a killer.

The Existence of the "Safety Catch"

One of my early concerns in writing *On Killing* was that World War II veterans might take offense at a book demonstrating that the vast majority of combat veterans of their era would not kill. Happily, my concerns were unfounded. Not one individual from among the thousands who have read *On Killing* has disputed this finding.

Indeed, the reaction from World War II veterans has been one of consistent confirmation. For example, R. C. Anderson, a World War II Canadian artillery forward observer, wrote to say the following:

> I can confirm many infantrymen never fired their weapons. I used to kid them that we fired a hell of a lot more 25-pounder [artillery] shells than they did rifle bullets.
>
> In one position . . . we came under fire from an olive grove to our flank.
>
> Everyone dived for cover. I was not occupied, at that moment, on my radio, so, seeing a Bren [light machine gun], I grabbed it and fired off a couple of magazines. The Bren gun's owner crawled over to me, swearing, "Its OK for you, you don't have to clean the son of a bitch." He was really mad.

Colonel (retired) Albert J. Brown, in Reading, Pennsylvania, exemplifies the kind of response I have consistently received while speaking to veterans' groups. As an infantry platoon leader and company commander in World War II, he observed that "Squad leaders and platoon sergeants had to move up and down the firing line kicking men to get them to fire. We felt like we were doing good to get two or three men out of a squad to fire."

There has been a recent controversy concerning S. L. A. Marshall's World War II firing rates. His methodology appears not to have met modern scholarly standards, but when faced with scholarly concern about a researcher's methodology, a scientific approach involves replicating the research. In Marshall's case, every available parallel scholarly study replicates his basic findings. Ardant du Picq's surveys and observations of the ancients, Holmes's and Keegan's numerous accounts of ineffectual firing, Holmes's assessment of Argentine firing rates in the Falklands War, Griffith's data on the extraordinarily low killing rates among Napoleonic and American Civil War regiments, the British Army's laser reenactments of historical battles, the FBI's studies of nonfiring rates among law-enforcement officers in the 1950s and 1960s, and countless other individual and anecdotal observations all confirm Marshall's conclusion that the vast majority of combatants throughout history, at the moment of truth when they could and should kill the enemy, have found themselves to be "conscientious objectors."

Taking Off the Safety Catch

Slightly more controversial than claims of *low* firing rates in World War II have been observations about *high* firing rates in Vietnam resulting from training or "conditioning" techniques designed to enable killing in the modern soldier. From among thousands of readers and listeners, there were two senior officers with experience in Vietnam who questioned R. W. Glenn's finding of a 95 percent firing rate among American soldiers in Vietnam. In both cases their doubt was due to the fact that they had found a lack of ammunition expenditure among some soldiers in the rear of their formations. In each instance they were satisfied when it was pointed out that both Marshall's and Glenn's data revolved around two questions: "Did you see the enemy?" and "Did you fire?" In the jungles of Vietnam there were many circumstances in which combatants were completely isolated from comrades who were only a short distance away; but among those who did see the enemy, there appears to have been extraordinarily consistent high firing rates.

High firing rates resulting from modern training/conditioning techniques can also be seen in Holmes's observation of British firing rates in the Falklands and in FBI data on law-enforcement firing rates since the introduction of modern training techniques in the late 1960s. And initial reports from researchers using formal and informal surveys to replicate Marshall's and Glenn's findings all indicate universal concurrence.

A Worldwide Virus of Violence

The observation that violence in the media is causing violence in our streets is nothing new. The American Psychiatric Association and the American Medical Association have both made unequivocable statements about the link between media violence and violence in our society. The APA, in its 1992 report *Big World, Small Screen,* concluded that the "scientific debate is over."

There are people who claim that cigarettes don't cause cancer, and we know where their money is coming from. There are also people who claim that media violence does not cause violence in society, and we know which side of *their* bread is buttered. Such individuals can always get funding for their research and are guaranteed coverage by the media that they protect. But these individuals have staked out the same moral and scientific ground as scientists in the service of cigarette manufacturers.

On Killing's contribution to this debate is its explanation as to *how* and *why* violence in the media and in interactive video games is causing violence in our streets, and the way this process replicates the conditioning used to enable killing in soldiers and law-enforcement officers . . . but without the safeguards.

An understanding of this "virus of violence" must begin with an assessment of the magnitude of the problem: ever-increasing incidence of violent crime, in spite of the way that medical technology is holding down the murder rate, and in spite of the role played by an ever-growing number of incarcerated violent criminals and an aging population in holding down the violence.

It is not just an American problem, it is an international phenomenon. In Canada, Scandinavia, Australia, New Zealand, and all across Europe, assault rates are skyrocketing. In countries like India,

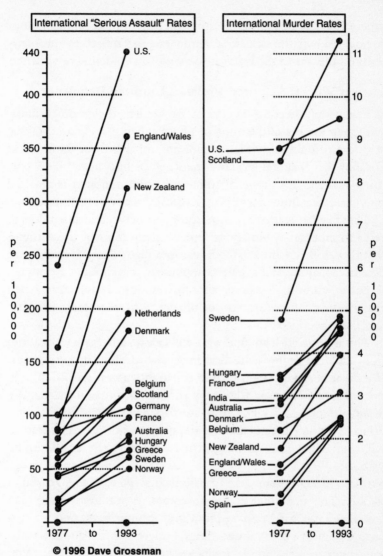

© 1996 Dave Grossman
As reported by each nation to Interpol offices, and published in Interpol's
biannual *International Crime Statistics.*

Note that what a nation elects to report under the headings of "murder" and "assault" can vary from nation to nation. For example, Scotland's totals include acts that the United States might classify as "manslaughter," thereby inflating its numbers. Therefore, comparisons between nations are of limited value. What is important is the *increase* in violent crime within each nation, and the fact that this is occurring in all the indicated countries.

where there is no significant infrastructure of medical technology to hold it down, the escalating murder rate best reflects the problem. Around the world the result is the same: an epidemic of violence.

How It Works: Acquired Violence Immune Deficiency

When people become angry, or frightened, they stop thinking with their forebrain (the mind of a human being) and start thinking with their midbrain (which is indistinguishable from the mind of an animal). *They are literally "scared out of their wits."* The only thing that has any hope of influencing the midbrain is also the only thing that influences a dog: classical and operant conditioning.

That is what is used when training firemen and airline pilots to react to emergency situations: precise replication of the stimulus that they will face (in a flame house or a flight simulator) and then extensive shaping of the desired response to that stimulus. Stimulus-response, stimulus-response, stimulus-response. In the crisis, when these individuals are scared out of their wits, they react properly and they save lives.

This is done with anyone who will face an emergency situation, from children doing a fire drill in school to pilots in a simulator. We do it because, when people are frightened, it works. We do not *tell* schoolchildren what they should do in case of a fire, we *condition* them; and when they are frightened, they do the right thing. Through the media we are also conditioning children to kill; and when they are frightened or angry, the conditioning kicks in.

It is as though there were two filters that we have to go through to kill. The first filter is the forebrain. A hundred things can convince your forebrain to put a gun in your hand and go to a certain point: poverty, drugs, gangs, leaders, politics, and the social learning of violence in the media — which is magnified when you are from a broken home and are searching for a role model. But traditionally all these things have slammed into the resistance that a frightened, angry human being confronts in the midbrain. And except with sociopaths (who, by definition, do not have this resistance), the vast, vast majority of circumstances are not sufficient to overcome this midbrain safety net. But if you are conditioned to overcome these midbrain inhibitions, then you are a walking time bomb, a pseudosociopath, just waiting for the random factors of social interaction and forebrain rationalization to put you at the wrong place at the wrong time.

Another way to look at this is to make an analogy with AIDS. AIDS does not kill people; it simply destroys the immune system and makes the victim vulnerable to death by other factors. The "violence immune system" exists in the midbrain, and conditioning in the media creates an "acquired deficiency" in this immune system. With this weakened immune system, the victim becomes more vulnerable to violence-enabling factors, such as poverty, discrimination, drug addiction (which can provide powerful motives for crime in order to fulfill real or perceived needs), or guns and gangs (which can provide the means and "support structure" to commit violent acts).

Canada is an example of a nation that we have always considered to be relatively crime-free and stable. Stringent gun laws, comparatively intact family structure, beloved and paternalistic government. But (surprise!) Canada has the exact same problem that we do. According to the Canadian Center for Justice, since 1964 the number of murders has doubled per capita, and "attempted murders" increased from 6 per million in 1964 to 40 per million in 1992. And assaults went up from 209 per 100,000 in 1964 to 940 per 100,000 in 1992. This is almost exactly the same ratio as the increase in violent crime in the United States. Vast numbers of Canadians have caught the virus of violence, the "acquired violence immune deficiency," and as they ingest America's media violence, they are paying the inevitable price.

This process is occurring around the world in nations that are exposed to media violence. The one exception is Japan.

If you have a destroyed immune system, your only hope is to live in a "bubble" that isolates you from potential contagions. Japan is an example of a nation living in a "violence bubble." In Japan we see a powerful family and social structure; a homogeneous society with an intact, stable, and relatively homogeneous criminal structure (which has a surprisingly "positive" group and leadership influence, at least as far as sanctioning freelancers); and an island nation with draconian control of not just guns but many other aspects of life.

Thus, the Japanese have very few cultural, social, "forebrain" violence-enabling factors working against them, so we do not see nearly as much violence in their society. But they (like any nation that has a significant number of citizens with "acquired violence immune deficiency") are like weapons, sitting loaded with the safety off, just waiting for someone (another Tojo?) to pull the trigger.

The bottom line is that Japan can "accept" a higher degree of midbrain violence-enabling in the media because that variable is being held down by all the other factors. For a while.

But this restraint can defy gravity for only so long. Certainly their recent terrorist nerve-gas attacks have been sufficient to cause some soul-searching as Japan examines the degree to which media violence is causing its citizens to accept violence as a viable alternative.

Most of the world has *not* been able to protect its citizens. Governments around the globe, try as they might, have not been able to keep their immune-deficient citizens in a bubble. And they will never truly be able to control violent crime unless they stop infecting their children.

"Just Turn It Off," or "Let Them Eat Cake"

One common response to any concern about media violence is, "We *have* adequate controls. They are called the 'off' switch. If you don't like it, just turn it off."

Unfortunately, this is a tragically inadequate response to the problem. In today's society the family structure is breaking down and even in intact families there is enormous economic and social pressure for mothers to work. Single mothers, broken homes, latchkey kids, and parental neglect are increasingly the norm. Through herculean effort, parents *might* be able to protect their own kids in today's world, but that doesn't do much good if the kid next door is a killer.

The worst thing about the "off switch" solution is that it is so blatantly, profoundly racist in its effect, if not its intent, because the black community in America is the "culture" or "nation" that has borne the brunt of the electronic media's violence-enabling. In this case, poverty, drugs, gangs, discrimination, and the availability of firearms all predispose more blacks than whites toward violence. These factors defeat the first filter; then the absence of the second, midbrain filter becomes noticeable.

Bronson James, a black Texas-based radio commentator whose show I was on, observed that this is identical to the genocidal process in which for centuries the white man used alcohol in a systematic policy to destroy the culture of the American Indian. For a variety of cultural and genetic reasons, the Indians were predisposed toward alcoholism, and we dumped it into them as a crucial part of the process that ultimately destroyed their civilization.

The pumping of media violence into the ghettos today is equally genocidal. Media violence-enabling in the ghetto is the moral equivalent of shouting, "FIRE!" in a crowded theater. As a result, murder is the number-one cause of death among black male teens, and 25 percent of all black males in their twenties are in jail, on probation, or on parole.

If this isn't genocide, then it is close.

What makes the "off switch" solution so racist is that, if these murders and incarceration rates were happening to the sons of white upper- and middle-class America, you can bet that we would have seen some drastic action by now. Viewed in this light, I think that most individuals would agree that the "just turn it off" solution probably rates right up there with "let them eat cake" and "I was just following orders" as all-time offensive statements.

In developmental psychology there is a general understanding that an individual must master the twin areas of sexuality and aggression (Freud's Eros and Thanatos) in order to have truly achieved adulthood. In the same way, the maturation of the human race necessitates our collective mastery of these two areas. In recent years we have made significant progress in the field of sexology, and this book is dedicated to the creation and exploration of the equivalent field of "killology."

After nuclear holocaust, the next major threat to our existence is the violent decay of our civilization due to violence-enabling in the electronic media. This book appears to be well on its way to making a difference in the desperate worldwide battle against the virus of violence.

May it be so, and may you, the reader, find what you seek in these pages.

Introduction

Killing and Science: On Dangerous Ground

This is the time of year when people would slaughter, back when people did that — Rollie and Eunice Hochstetter, I think, were the last in Lake Wobegon. They kept pigs, and they'd slaughter them in the fall when the weather got cold and the meat would keep. I went out to see them slaughter hogs once when I was a kid, along with my cousin and my uncle, who was going to help Rollie.

Today, if you are going to slaughter an animal for meat, you send it in to the locker plant and pay to have the guys there do it. When you slaughter pigs, it takes away your appetite for pork for a while. Because the pigs let you know that they don't care for it. They don't care to be grabbed and dragged over to where the other pigs went and didn't come back.

It was quite a thing for a kid to see. To see living flesh, and the living insides of another creature. I expected to be disgusted by it, but I wasn't — I was fascinated. I got as close as I could.

And I remember that my cousin and I sort of got carried away in the excitement of it all and we went down to the pigpen and we started throwing little stones at pigs to watch them jump and squeal and run. And all of a sudden, I felt a big hand on my shoulder, and I was spun around, and my uncle's face was three inches away from mine. He said "If I ever see you do that again I'll beat you 'til you can't stand up, you hear?" And we heard.

I knew at the time that his anger had to do with the slaughter, that it was a ritual and it was done as a Ritual. It was done swiftly, and there was no foolishness. No joking around, very little conversation. People went about their jobs — men and women — knowing exactly what to do. And always with respect for the animals that would become our food. And our throwing stones at pigs violated this ceremony, and this ritual, which they went through.

Rollie was the last one to slaughter his own hogs. One year he had an accident; the knife slipped, and an animal that was only wounded got loose and ran across the yard before it fell. He never kept pigs after that. He didn't feel he was worthy of it.

It's all gone. Children growing up in Lake Wobegon will never have a chance to see it.

It was a powerful experience, life and death hung in the balance.

A life in which people made do, made their own, lived off the land, lived between the ground and God. It's lost, not only to this world: but also to memory.

— Garrison Keillor
  "Hog Slaughter"

Why should we study killing? One might just as readily ask, Why study sex? The two questions have much in common. Richard Heckler points out that "it is in the mythological marriage of Ares and Aphrodite that Harmonia is born." Peace will not come until we have mastered both sex and war, and to master war we must study it with at least the diligence of Kinsey or Masters and Johnson. Every society has a blind spot, an area into which it has great difficulty looking. Today that blind spot is killing. A century ago it was sex.

For millennia man sheltered himself and his family in caves, or huts, or one-room hovels. The whole extended family — grandparents, parents, and children — all huddled together around the warmth of a single fire, within the protection of a single wall. And for thousands of years sex between a husband and wife could generally only take place at night, in the darkness, in this crowded central room.

I once interviewed a woman who grew up in an American Gypsy family, sleeping in a big communal tent with aunts, uncles, grandparents, parents, cousins, brothers, and sisters all around her. As a young child, sex was to her something funny, noisy, and slightly bothersome that grown-ups did in the night.

In this environment there were no private bedrooms. Until very recently in human history, for the average human being, there was no such luxury as a bedroom, or even a bed. Although by today's sexual standards this situation may seem awkward, it was not without its advantages. One advantage was that sexual abuse of children could not happen without at least the knowledge and tacit consent of the entire family. Another, less obvious benefit of this age-old living arrangement was that throughout the life cycle, from birth to death, sex was always before you, and no one could deny that it was a vital, essential, and a not-too-mysterious aspect of daily human existence.

And then, by the period that we know as the Victorian era, everything had changed. Suddenly the average middle-class family lived in a multiroom dwelling. Children grew up having never witnessed the primal act. And suddenly sex became hidden, private, mysterious, frightening, and dirty. The era of sexual repression in Western civilization had begun.

In this repressed society, women were covered from neck to ankle, and even the furniture legs were covered with skirts, since the sight of these legs disturbed the delicate sensitivities of that era. Yet at the same time that this society repressed sex, it appears to have become obsessed by it. Pornography as we know it blossomed. Child prostitution flourished. And a wave of sexual child abuse began to ripple down through the generations.[1]

Sex is a natural and essential part of life. A society that has no sex has no society in one generation. Today our society has begun the slow, painful process of escaping from this pathological dichotomy of simultaneous sexual repression and obsession. But we may have begun our escape from one denial only to fall into a new and possibly even more dangerous one.

A new repression, revolving around killing and death, precisely parallels the pattern established by the previous sexual repression.

Throughout history man has been surrounded by close and personal death and killing. When family members died of disease, lingering injury, or old age they died in the home. When they died anywhere close to home, their corpses were brought to the house — or cave, or hut, or hovel — and prepared for burial by the family.

Places in the Heart is a movie in which Sally Field portrays a woman on a small cotton farm early in this century. Her husband has been shot and killed and is brought to the house. And, repeating a Ritual that has been enacted for countless centuries by countless millions of wives, she lovingly washes his naked corpse, preparing it for burial as tears streak down her face.

In that world each family did its own killing and cleaning of domestic animals. Death was a part of life. Killing was undeniably essential to living. Cruelty was seldom, if ever, a part of this killing. Mankind understood its place in life, and respected the place of the creatures whose deaths were required to perpetuate existence. The American Indian asked forgiveness of the spirit of the deer he killed, and the American farmer respected the dignity of the hogs he slaughtered.

As Garrison Keillor records in "Hog Slaughter," the slaughter of animals has been a vital Ritual of daily and seasonal activity for most people until this last half century of human existence. Despite the rise of the city, by the opening of the twentieth century the majority of the population, even in the most advanced industrial societies, remained rural. The housewife who wanted a chicken dinner went out and wrung the chicken's neck herself, or had her children do it. The children watched the daily and seasonal killings, and to them killing was a serious, messy, and slightly boring thing that everyone did as a part of life.

In this environment there was no refrigeration, and few slaughterhouses, mortuaries, or hospitals. And in this age-old living arrangement, throughout the life cycle, from birth to death, death and killing were always before you — either as a participant or a bored spectator — and no one could deny that it was a vital, essential, and common aspect of daily human existence.

And then, in just the last few generations, everything began to change. Slaughterhouses and refrigeration insulated us from the necessity of killing our own food animals. Modern medicine began to cure diseases, and it became increasingly rare for us to die in the youth and prime of our lives, and nursing homes, hospitals, and mortuaries insulated us from the death of the elderly. Children began to grow up having never truly understood where their food came from, and suddenly Western civilization seemed to have decided that killing, killing anything at all, was increasingly hidden, private, mysterious, frightening, and dirty.

The impact of this ranges from the trivial to the bizarre. Just as the Victorians put skirts around their furniture to hide the legs, now mousetraps come equipped with covers to hide the killer's handiwork. And laboratories conducting medical research with animals are broken into, and lifesaving research is destroyed by animal-rights activists. These activists, while partaking of the medical fruits of their society — fruits based upon centuries of animal research — attack researchers. Chris DeRose, head of the Los Angeles–based activist group Last Chance for Animals, says: "If the death of one rat cured all diseases it wouldn't make any difference to me. In the scheme of life we're equal."

Any killing offends this new sensibility. People wearing fur or leather coats are verbally and physically attacked. In this new order people are condemned as racists (or "speciests") and murderers when they eat meat. Animal-rights leader Ingrid Newkirk says, "A rat is a pig is a boy," and compares the killing of chickens to the Nazi Holocaust. "Six million people died in concentration camps," she told the *Washington Post*, "but six billion broiler chickens will die this year in slaughterhouses."

Yet at the same time that our society represses killing, a new obsession with the depiction of violent and brutal death and dismemberment of humans has flourished. The public appetite for violence in movies, particularly in splatter movies such as *Friday the 13th, Halloween,* and *The Texas Chainsaw Massacre*; the cult status of "heroes" like Jason and Freddy; the popularity of bands with names like Megadeth and Guns N' Roses; and skyrocketing murder and violent crime rates — all these are symptoms of a bizarre, pathological dichotomy of simultaneous repression and obsession with violence.

Sex and death are natural and essential parts of life. Just as a society without sex would disappear in a generation, so too would a society without killing. Every major city in our nation must exterminate millions of rats and mice each year or become uninhabitable. And granaries and grain elevators must exterminate millions of rats and mice each year. If they fail to do this, instead of being the world's breadbasket the United States would be unable to feed itself, and millions of people around the world would face starvation.

Certain genteel sensitivities of the Victorian era are not without value and benefit to our society, and few would argue for a return to communal sleeping arrangements. In the same way, those who hold and espouse modern sensibilities about killing are generally gentle and sincere human beings who in many ways represent the most idealistic characteristics of our species, and their concerns have great potential value once we bring them into perspective. As technology enables us to butcher and exterminate whole species (including our own), it is vital that we learn restraint and self-discipline. But we must also remember that death has its place in the natural order of life.

It seems that when a society does not have natural processes (such as sex, death, and killing) before it, that society will respond by denying and warping that aspect of nature. As our technology insulates us from a specific aspect of reality, our societal response seems to be to slip deep into bizarre dreams about that which we flee. Dreams spun from the fantasy stuff of denial. Dreams that can become dangerous societal nightmares as we sink deeper into their tempting web of fantasy.

Today, even as we waken from the nightmare of sexual repression, our society is beginning to sink into a new denial dream, that of violence and horror. This book is an attempt to bring the objective light of scientific scrutiny into the process of killing. A. M. Rosenthal tells us:

The health of humankind is not measured just by its coughs and wheezes but by the fevers of its soul. Or perhaps more important yet, by the quickness and care we bring against them.

If our history suggests unreason's durability, our experience teaches that to neglect it is to indulge it and that to indulge it is to prepare hate's triumph.

"To neglect it is to indulge it." This is, therefore, a study of aggression, a study of violence, and a study of killing. Most specifically, it is an attempt to conduct a scientific study of the act of killing within the Western way of war and of the psychological and sociological processes and prices exacted when men kill each other in combat.

Sheldon Bidwell held that such a study would by its very nature lay on "dangerous ground because the union between soldier and scientist has not yet passed beyond flirtation." I would seek to go in harm's way and effect not just a serious union between soldier and scientist, but a tentative *ménage à trois* between soldier, scientist, and historian.

I have combined these skills to conduct a five-year program of research into the previously taboo topic of killing in combat. In this study it is my intention to delve into this taboo subject of killing and to provide insight into the following:

- The existence of a powerful, innate human resistance toward killing one's own species and the psychological mechanisms that have been developed by armies *over the centuries* to overcome that resistance
- The role of atrocity in war and the mechanisms by which armies are both empowered and entrapped by atrocity
- What it feels like to kill, a set of standard response stages to killing in combat, and the psychological price of killing
- The techniques that have been developed and applied with tremendous success in *modern* combat training in order to condition soldiers to overcome their resistance to killing
- How the American soldier in Vietnam was first psychologically enabled to kill to a far greater degree than any other soldier in history, then denied the psychologically essential purification

xxxINTRODUCTION

ritual that exists in every warrior society, and finally condemned
and accused by his own society to a degree that is unprecedented
in Western history. And the terrible, tragic price that America's
three million Vietnam veterans, their families, and our society
are paying for what we did to our soldiers in Vietnam

• Finally, and *perhaps most important,* I believe that this study will
provide insight into the way that rifts in our society combine
with violence in the media and in interactive video games to
indiscriminately condition our nation's children to kill. In a fashion very similar to the way the army conditions our soldiers. But
without the safeguards. And we will see the terrible, tragic price
that our nation is paying for what we are doing to our children.

A Personal Note

I am a soldier of twenty years' service. I have been a sergeant in
the 82d Airborne Division, a platoon leader in the 9th (High Tech
Test Bed) Division, and I have been a general staff officer and a
company commander in the 7th (Light) Infantry Division. I am a
parachute infantryman and an army Ranger. I have been deployed
to the Arctic tundras, the Central American jungles, NATO headquarters, the Warsaw Pact, and countless mountains and deserts.
I am a graduate of military schools ranging from the XVIII Airborne
Corps NCO Academy to the British Army Staff College. I graduated summa cum laude from my undergraduate training as a historian, and Kappa Delta Pi from my graduate training as a psychologist. I have had the privilege of being a cospeaker with General
Westmoreland before the national leadership of the Vietnam Veterans Coalition of America, and I have served as the keynote speaker
for the Sixth Annual Convention of the Vietnam Veterans of
America. I have served in academic positions ranging from a junior-
high-school counselor to a West Point psychology professor. And
I am currently serving as the Professor of Military Science and Chair
of the Department of Military Science at Arkansas State University.

But for all this experience, I, like Richard Holmes, John Keegan,
Paddy Griffith, and many others who have gone before me in
this field, have not killed in combat. Perhaps I could not be as
dispassionate and objective as I need to be if I had to carry a load

of emotional pain myself. But the men whose words fill this study *have* killed.

Very often what they shared with me was something that they had never shared with anyone before. As a counselor I have been taught, and I hold it to be a fundamental truth of human nature, that when someone withholds something traumatic it can cause great damage. When you share something with someone it helps to place it in perspective, but when you hold it inside, as one of my psychology students once put it, "it eats you alive from the inside out." Furthermore, there is great therapeutic value in the catharsis that comes with lancing these emotional boils. The essence of counseling is that pain shared is pain divided, and there was much pain shared during these periods.

The ultimate objective of this book is to uncover the dynamics of killing, but my prime motivation has been to help pierce the taboo of killing that prevented these men, and many millions like them, from sharing their pain. And then to use the knowledge gained in order to understand first the mechanisms that enable war and then the cause of the current wave of violent crime that is destroying our nation. If I have succeeded, it is because of the help given to me by the men whose tales are told herein.

Many copies of early drafts of this work have been circulating among the Vietnam veterans' community for several years now, and many veterans have carefully edited and commented on those drafts. Many of these vets read this book and shared it with their spouses. Then those wives shared it with other wives, and these wives shared it with their husbands. And so on. Many times the veterans and/or their wives contacted me and let me know how they were able to use this book to communicate and understand what had happened in combat. Out of their pain has come understanding, and out of that understanding has come the power to heal lives and, perhaps, to heal a nation that is being consumed with violence.

The men whose personal narratives appear in this study are noble and brave men who trusted others with their experiences in order to contribute to the body of human knowledge. Many killed in combat. But they killed to save their lives and the lives of their comrades, and my admiration and affection for them and their brothers are very real. John Masefield's poem "A Consecration" serves as a better dedication than any I could write. The exception to this admiration is, of course, addressed in the section "Killing and Atrocities."

If in my absence of euphemisms and my effort to clearly and clinically speak of "killers" and "victims," if in these things the reader senses moral judgment or disapproval of the individuals involved, let me flatly and categorically deny it.

Generations of Americans have endured great physical and psychological trauma and horror in order to give us our freedoms. Men such as those quoted in this study followed Washington, stood shoulder to shoulder with Crockett and Travis at the Alamo, righted the great wrong of slavery, and stopped the murderous evil of Hitler. They answered their nation's call and heeded not the cost. As a soldier for my entire adult life, I take pride in having maintained in some small way the standard of sacrifice and dedication represented by these men. And I would not harm them or besmirch their memory and honor. Douglas MacArthur said it well: "However horrible the incidents of war may be, the soldier who is called upon to offer and give his life for his country, is the noblest development of mankind."

The soldiers whose narratives form the heart and soul of this work understood the essence of war. They are heroes as great as any found in the *Iliad,* yet the words that you will read here, their own words, destroy the myth of warriors and war as heroic. The soldier understands that there are times when all others have failed, and that then he must "pay the butcher's bill" and fight, suffer, and die to undo the errors of the politicians and to fulfill the "will of the people."

"The soldier above all other people," said MacArthur, "prays for peace, for they must suffer and bear the deepest wounds and scars of war." There is wisdom in the words of these soldiers. There is wisdom in these tales of a "handful of ashes, a mouthful of mould. / Of the maimed, of the halt and the blind in the rain and the cold." There is wisdom here, and we would do well to listen.

Just as I do not wish to condemn those who have killed in lawful combat, nor do I wish to judge the many soldiers who chose *not* to kill. There are many such soldiers; indeed I will provide evidence that in many historical circumstances these non-firers represented the majority of those on the firing line. As a soldier who may have stood beside them I cannot help but be dismayed at their failure to support their cause, their nation, and their fellows; but as a human being who has understood some of the burden that they have borne, and the sacrifice that they have made, I cannot help but be proud of them and the noble characteristic that they represent in our species.

The subject of killing makes most healthy people uneasy, and some of the specific subjects and areas to be addressed here will be repulsive and offensive. They are things that we would rather turn away from, but Carl von Clausewitz warned that "it is to no purpose, it is even against one's better interest, to turn away from the consideration of the affair because the horror of its elements excites repugnance." Bruno Bettelheim, a survivor of the Nazi death camps, argues that the root of our failure to deal with violence lies in our refusal to face up to it. We deny our fascination with the "dark beauty of violence," and we condemn aggression and repress it rather than look at it squarely and try to understand and control it.

And, finally, if in my focus on the pain of the killers I do not sufficiently address the suffering of their victims, let me apologize now. "The guy pulling the trigger," wrote Allen Cole and Chris Bunch, "never suffers as much as the person on the receiving end." It is the existence of the victim's pain and loss, echoing forever in the soul of the killer, that is at the heart of his pain.

Leo Frankowski tells us that "cultures all develop blind spots, things that they don't even think about because they *know* the truth about them." The veterans quoted in this study have had their faces rubbed in this cultural blind spot. We are truly, as one veteran put it to me, "virgins studying sex," but they can teach us what they have learned at such a dear price. My objective is to understand the psychological nature of killing in combat and to probe the emotional wounds and scars of those men who answered their nation's call and meted out death — or chose to pay the price for not doing so.

Now more than ever we must overcome our revulsion and understand, as we have never understood before, why it is that men fight and kill. And equally important, why it is that they will not. Only on the basis of understanding this ultimate, destructive aspect of human behavior can we hope to influence it in such a way as to ensure the survival of our civilization.[2]

SECTION I

Killing and the Existence of Resistance: A World of Virgins Studying Sex

It is therefore reasonable to believe that the average and healthy individual — the man who can endure the mental and physical stresses of combat — still has such an inner and usually unrealized resistance towards killing a fellow man that he will not of his own volition take life if it is possible to turn away from that responsibility. . . . At the vital point he becomes a conscientious objector.

— S. L. A. Marshall
   Men Against Fire

Then I cautiously raised the upper half of my body into the tunnel until I was lying flat on my stomach. When I felt comfortable, I placed my Smith Wesson .38-caliber snub-nose (sent to me by my father for tunnel work) beside the flashlight and switched on the light, illuminating the tunnel.

There, not more than 15 feet away, sat a Viet Cong eating a handful of rice from a pouch on his lap. We looked at each other for what seemed to be an eternity, but in fact was probably only a few seconds.

Maybe it was the surprise of actually finding someone else there, or maybe it was just the absolute innocence of the situation, but neither one of us reacted.

After a moment, he put his pouch of rice on the floor of the tunnel beside him, turned his back to me and slowly started crawling away. I, in turn, switched off my flashlight, before slipping back into the lower tunnel and making my way back to the entrance. About 20 minutes later, we received word that another squad had killed a VC emerging from a tunnel 500 meters away.

I never doubted who that VC was. To this day, I firmly believe that grunt and I could have ended the war sooner over a beer in Saigon than Henry Kissinger ever could by attending the peace talks.

— Michael Kathman
"Triangle Tunnel Rat"

Our first step in the study of killing is to understand the existence, extent, and nature of the average human being's resistance to killing his fellow human. In this section we will attempt to do that.

When I started interviewing combat veterans as a part of this study, I discussed some of the psychological theories concerning the trauma of combat with one crusty old sergeant. He laughed scornfully and said, "Those bastards don't know anything about it. They're like a world of virgins studying sex, and they got nothing to go on but porno movies. And it *is* just like sex, 'cause the people who *really* do it just don't talk about it."

In a way, the study of killing in combat is very much like the study of sex. Killing is a private, intimate occurrence of tremendous intensity, in which the destructive act becomes psychologically very much like the procreative act. For those who have never experienced it, the depiction of battle that Hollywood has given us, and the cultural mythology that Hollywood is based upon, appear to be about as useful in understanding killing as porno-graphic movies would be in trying to understand the intimacy of a sexual relationship. A virgin observer might get the mechanics of sex right by watching an X-rated movie, but he or she could never hope to understand the intimacy and intensity of the procreative experience.

As a society we are as fascinated by killing as we are by sex — possibly more so, since we are somewhat jaded by sex and have a fairly broad base of individual experience in this area. Many children, upon seeing that I am a decorated soldier, immediately ask "Have you ever killed anyone?" or "How many people have you killed?"

Where does this curiosity come from? Robert Heinlein once wrote that fulfillment in life involved "loving a good woman and killing a bad man." If there is such a strong interest in killing in our society, and if it equates in many minds to an act of manhood equivalent to sex, then why hasn't the destructive act been as specifically and systematically studied as the procreative act?

Over the centuries there have been a few pioneers who have laid the foundation for such a study, and in this section we will attempt to look at them all. Probably the best starting point is with S. L. A. Marshall, the greatest and most influential of these pioneers.

Prior to World War II it had always been assumed that the average soldier would kill in combat simply because his country and his leaders have told him to do so and because it is essential to defend his own life and the lives of his friends. When the point came that he didn't kill, it was assumed that he would panic and run.

During World War II U.S. Army Brigadier General S. L. A. Marshall asked these average soldiers what it was that they did in battle. His singularly unexpected discovery was that, of every hundred men along the line of fire during the period of an encounter, an average of only 15 to 20 "would take any part with their weapons." This was consistently true "whether the action was spread over a day, or two days or three."

Marshall was a U.S. Army historian in the Pacific theater during World War II and later became the official U.S. historian of the European theater of operations. He had a team of historians working for him, and they based their findings on individual and mass interviews with thousands of soldiers in more than four hundred infantry companies, in Europe and in the Pacific, immediately after they had been in close combat with German or Japanese troops. The results were consistently the same: only 15 to 20 percent of the American riflemen in combat during World War II would fire at the enemy. Those who would not fire did not run or hide (in many cases they were willing to risk great danger to rescue comrades, get ammunition, or run messages), but they simply would not fire their weapons at the enemy, even when faced with repeated waves of banzai charges.[1]

The question is why. Why did these men fail to fire? As I examined this question and studied the process of killing in combat from the standpoints of a historian, a psychologist, and a soldier, I began to realize that there was one major factor that was missing from the common understanding of killing in combat, a factor that answers this question and more. That missing factor is the simple and demonstrable fact that there is within most men an intense resistance to killing their fellow man. A resistance so strong that, in many circumstances, soldiers on the battlefield will die before they can overcome it.

To some, this makes "obvious" sense. "Of course it is hard to kill someone," they would say. "I could never bring myself to do it." But they would be wrong. With the proper conditioning and the proper circumstances, it appears that almost anyone can and will kill. Others might respond, "Any man will kill in combat when he is faced with someone who is trying to kill him." And they would be even more wrong, for in this section we shall observe that throughout history the majority of men on the battlefield would *not* attempt to kill the enemy, even to save their own lives or the lives of their friends.

Chapter One

Fight or Flight, Posture or Submit

The notion that the only alternatives to conflict are fight or flight are embedded in our culture, and our educational institutions have done little to challenge it. The traditional American military policy raises it to the level of a law of nature.

— Richard Heckler
In Search of the Warrior Spirit

One of the roots of our misunderstanding of the psychology of the battlefield lies in the misapplication of the fight-or-flight model to the stresses of the battlefield. This model holds that in the face of danger a series of physiological and psychological processes prepare and support the endangered creature for either fighting or fleeing. The fight-or-flight dichotomy is the appropriate set of choices for any creature faced with danger *other* than that which comes from its own species. When we examine the responses of creatures confronted with aggression from their own species, the set of options expands to include posturing and submission. This application of animal kingdom intraspecies response patterns (that is, fight, flee, posture, and submit) to human warfare is, to the best of my knowledge, entirely new.

The first decision point in an intraspecies conflict usually involves deciding between fleeing or posturing. A threatened baboon or rooster who elects to stand its ground does not respond to aggression from one of his own kind by leaping instantly to the enemy's throat. Instead, both creatures instinctively go through a series of posturing actions that, while intimidating, *are almost always harmless.* These actions are designed to convince an opponent, through both sight and sound, that the posturer is a dangerous and frightening adversary.

When the posturer has failed to dissuade an intraspecies opponent, the options then become fight, flight, or submission. When the fight option is utilized, it is *almost never to the death.* Konrad Lorenz pointed out that piranhas and rattlesnakes will bite anything and everything, but among themselves piranhas fight with raps of their tails, and rattlesnakes wrestle. Somewhere during the course of such highly constrained and nonlethal fights, one of these intraspecies opponents will usually become daunted by the ferocity and prowess of its opponent, and its only options become submission or flight. Submission is a surprisingly common response, usually taking the form of fawning and exposing some vulnerable portion of the anatomy to the victor, in the instinctive knowledge that the opponent will not kill or further harm one of its own kind once it has surrendered. The posturing, mock battle, and submission process is vital to the survival of the species. It prevents needless deaths and ensures that a young male will live through early confrontations when his opponents are bigger and better prepared. Having been outpostured by his opponent, he can then submit and live to mate, passing on his genes in later years.

There is a clear distinction between actual violence and posturing. Oxford social psychologist Peter Marsh notes that this is true in New York street gangs, it is true in "so-called primitive tribesmen and warriors," and it is true in almost any culture in the world. All have the same "patterns of aggression" and all have "very orchestrated, highly ritualized" patterns of posturing, mock battle, and submission. These rituals restrain and focus the violence on relatively harmless posturing and display. What is created is a "perfect illusion of violence." Aggression, yes. Competitiveness, yes. But only a "very tiny, tiny level" of actual violence.

"There is," concludes Gwynne Dyer, "the occasional psychopath who really wants to slice people open," but most of the

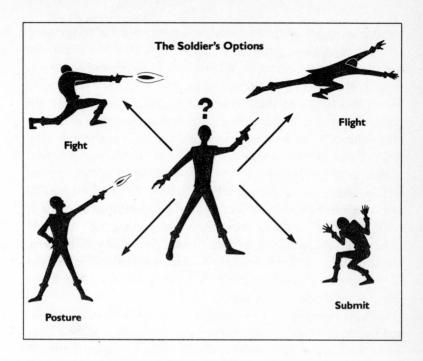

The Soldier's Options

Fight

Flight

Posture

Submit

participants are really interested in "status, display, profit, and damage limitation." Like their peacetime contemporaries, the kids who have fought in close combat throughout history (and it is kids, or adolescent males, whom most societies traditionally send off to do their fighting), killing the enemy was the very least of their intentions. In war, as in gang war, posturing is the name of the game.

In this account from Paddy Griffith's *Battle Tactics of the Civil War,* we can see the effective use of verbal posturing in the thick woods of the American Civil War's Wilderness campaign:

> The yellers could not be seen, and a company could make itself
> sound like a regiment if it shouted loud enough. Men spoke later
> of various units on both sides being "yelled" out of their positions.

In such instances of units being yelled out of positions, we see posturing in its most successful form, resulting in the opponent's selection of the flight option without even attempting the fight option.

Adding the posture and submission options to the standard fight-or-flight model of aggression response helps to explain many of the actions on the battlefield. When a man is frightened, he literally stops thinking with his forebrain (that is, with the mind of a human being) and begins to think with the midbrain (that is, with the portion of his brain that is essentially indistinguishable from that of an animal), and in the mind of an animal it is the one who makes the loudest noise or puffs himself up the largest who will win.

Posturing can be seen in the plumed helmets of the ancient Greeks and Romans, which allowed the bearer to appear taller and therefore fiercer to his foe, while the brilliantly shined armor made him seem broader and brighter. Such plumage saw its height in modern history during the Napoleonic era, when soldiers wore bright uniforms and high, uncomfortable shako hats, which served no purpose other than to make the wearer look and feel like a taller, more dangerous creature.

In the same manner, the roars of two posturing beasts are exhibited by men in battle. For centuries the war cries of soldiers have made their opponents' blood run cold. Whether it be the battle cry of a Greek phalanx, the "hurrah!" of the Russian infantry, the wail of Scottish bagpipes, or the Rebel yell of our own Civil War, soldiers have always instinctively sought to daunt the enemy through nonviolent means prior to physical conflict, while encouraging one another and impressing themselves with their own ferocity and simultaneously providing a very effective means of drowning the disagreeable yell of the enemy.

A modern equivalent to the Civil War occurrence mentioned above can be seen in this Army Historical Series account of a French battalion's participation in the defense of Chipyong-Ni during the Korean War:

> The [North Korean] soldiers formed one hundred or two hundred yards in front of the small hill which the French occupied, then launched their attack, blowing whistles and bugles, and running with bayonets fixed. When this noise started, the French soldiers began cranking a hand siren they had, and one squad started running toward the Chinese, yelling and throwing grenades far to the front

and to the side. When the two forces were within twenty yards of each other the Chinese suddenly turned and ran in the opposite direction. It was all over within a minute.

Here again we see an incident in which posturing (involving sirens, grenade explosions, and charging bayonets) by a small force was sufficient to cause a numerically superior enemy force to hastily select the flight option.

With the advent of gunpowder, the soldier has been provided with one of the finest possible means of posturing. "Time and again," says Paddy Griffith,

> we read of regiments [in the Civil War] blazing away uncontrollably, once started, and continuing until all ammunition was gone or all enthusiasm spent. Firing was such a positive act, and gave the men such a physical release for their emotions, that instincts easily took over from training and from the exhortations of officers.

Gunpowder's superior *noise*, its superior *posturing* ability, made it ascendant on the battlefield. The longbow would still have been used in the Napoleonic Wars if the raw mathematics of killing effectiveness was all that mattered, since both the longbow's firing rate and its accuracy were *much* greater than that of a smoothbore musket. But a frightened man, thinking with his midbrain and going "ploink, ploink, ploink" with a bow, doesn't stand a chance against an equally frightened man going "BANG! BANG!" with a musket.

Firing a musket or rifle clearly fills the deep-seated need to posture, and it even meets the requirement of being relatively harmless when we consider the consistent historical occurrences of firing over the enemy's head, and the remarkable ineffectiveness of such fire.

Ardant du Picq became one of the first to document the common tendency of soldiers to fire harmlessly into the air simply for the sake of firing. Du Picq made one of the first thorough investigations into the nature of combat with a questionnaire distributed to French officers in the 1860s. One officer's response to du Picq stated quite frankly that "a good many soldiers fired into the air at long distances," while another observed that "a certain number of our soldiers fired almost in the air, without aiming, seeming to want to stun themselves, to become drunk on rifle fire during this gripping crisis."

Paddy Griffith joins du Picq in observing that soldiers in battle have a desperate urge to fire their weapons even when (perhaps especially when) they cannot possibly do the enemy any harm. Griffith notes:

> Even in the noted "slaughter pens" at Bloody Lane, Marye's Heights, Kennesaw, Spotsylvania and Cold Harbor an attacking unit could not only come very close to the defending line, but it could also stay there for hours — and indeed for days — at a time. Civil War musketry did not therefore possess the power to kill large numbers of men, even in very dense formations, at long range. At short range it could and did kill large numbers, *but not very quickly* [emphasis added].

Griffith estimates that the average musket fire from a Napoleonic or Civil War regiment (usually numbering between two hundred and one thousand men) firing at an exposed enemy regiment at an average range of thirty yards, would usually result in hitting *only one or two men per minute!* Such firefights "dragged on until exhaustion set in or nightfall put an end to hostilities. Casualties mounted because the contest went on so long, not because the fire was particularly deadly."

Thus we see that the fire of the Napoleonic- and Civil War–era soldier was incredibly ineffective. This does not represent a failure on the part of the weaponry. John Keegan and Richard Holmes in their book *Soldiers* tell us of a Prussian experiment in the late 1700s in which an infantry battalion fired smoothbore muskets at a target one hundred feet long by six feet high, representing an enemy unit, which resulted in 25 percent hits at 225 yards, 40 percent hits at 150 yards, and 60 percent hits at 75 yards. This represented the potential killing power of such a unit. The reality is demonstrated at the Battle of Belgrade in 1717, when "two

Imperial battalions held their fire until their Turkish opponents were only thirty paces away, but hit only thirty-two Turks when they fired and were promptly overwhelmed."

Sometimes the fire was completely harmless, as Benjamin McIntyre observed in his firsthand account of a totally bloodless nighttime firefight at Vicksburg in 1863. "It seems strange . . . ," wrote McIntyre, "that a company of men can fire volley after volley at a like number of men at not over a distance of fifteen steps and not cause a single casualty. Yet such was the facts in this instance." The musketry of the black-powder era was not always so ineffective, but over and over again the average comes out to only one or two men hit per minute with musketry.

(Cannon fire, like machine-gun fire in World War II, is an entirely different matter, sometimes accounting for more than 50 percent of the casualties on the black-powder battlefield, and artillery fire has consistently accounted for the majority of combat casualties in this century. This is largely due to the group processes at work in a cannon, machine-gun, or other crew-served-weapons firing. This subject is addressed in detail later in this book in the section entitled "An Anatomy of Killing.")

Muzzle-loading muskets could fire from one to five shots per minute, depending on the skill of the operator and the state of the weapon. With a potential hit rate of well over 50 percent at the average combat ranges of this era, the killing rate should have been hundreds per minute, instead of one or two. The weak link between the killing potential and the killing capability of these units was the soldier. The simple fact is that when faced with a living, breathing opponent instead of a target, a significant majority of the soldiers revert to a posturing mode in which they fire over their enemy's heads.

Richard Holmes, in his superb book *Acts of War,* examines the hit rates of soldiers in a variety of historical battles. At Rorkes Drift in 1897 a small group of British soldiers were surrounded and vastly outnumbered by the Zulu. Firing volley after volley into the massed enemy ranks at point-blank range, it seems as if no round could have possibly missed, and even a 50 percent hit rate would seem to be low. But Holmes estimates that in actuality approximately thirteen rounds were fired for each hit.

In the same way, General Crook's men fired 25,000 rounds at Rosebud Creek on June 16, 1876, causing 99 casualties among the Indians, or 252 rounds per hit. And in the French defense from fortified positions during the Battle of Wissembourg, in 1870, the French, shooting at German soldiers advancing across open fields, fired 48,000 rounds to hit 404 Germans, for a hit ratio of 1 hit per 119 rounds fired. (And some, or possibly even the majority, of the casualties *had* to have been from artillery fire, which makes the French killing rate even more remarkable.)

Lieutenant George Roupell encountered this same phenomenon while commanding a British platoon in World War I. He stated that the only way he could stop his men from firing into the air was to draw his sword and walk down the trench, "beating the men on the backside and, as I got their attention, telling them to fire low." And the trend can be found in the firefights of Vietnam, when more than fifty thousand bullets were fired for every enemy soldier killed.[2] "One of the things that amazed me," stated Douglas Graham, a medic with the First Marine Division in Vietnam, who had to crawl out under enemy and friendly fire to aid wounded soldiers, "is how many bullets can be fired during a firefight without anyone getting hurt."

The focus of primitive tribesmen on posturing at the expense of fighting in times of war is usually blatant and obvious. Richard Gabriel points out that primitive New Guinea tribes were excellent shots with the bow and arrows they used while hunting, but when they went to war with each other they took the feathers off of the backs of their arrows, and it was only with these inaccurate and useless arrows that they fought their wars. In the same way, the American Indians considered "counting coup," or simply touching their enemy, to be far more important than killing.

This trend can be seen in the roots of the Western way of war. Sam Keen notes that Professor Arthur Nock at Harvard was fond of saying that wars between the Greek city-states "were only slightly more dangerous than American football." And Ardant du Picq points out that in all his years of conquest, Alexander the

Great lost only seven hundred men to the sword. His enemy lost many, many more, but almost all of this occurred *after* the battle (which appears to have been an almost bloodless pushing match), when the enemy soldiers had turned their backs and begun to run. Carl von Clausewitz makes the same point when he notes that the vast majority of combat losses historically occurred in the pursuit *after* one side or the other had won the battle. (Why this occurs is a subject that will be looked at in detail in the section "Killing and Physical Distance.")

As we shall see, modern training or conditioning techniques can partially overcome the inclination to posture. Indeed, the history of warfare can be seen as a history of increasingly more effective mechanisms for enabling and conditioning men to overcome their innate resistance to killing their fellow human beings. In many circumstances highly trained modern soldiers have fought poorly trained guerrilla forces, and the tendency of poorly prepared forces to instinctively engage in posturing mechanisms (such as firing high) has given a significant advantage to the more highly trained force. Jack Thompson, a Rhodesian veteran, observed this process in combat against untrained forces. In Rhodesia, says Thompson, their immediate action drill was to "shed our packs and assault into the fire . . . *always*. That was because the [guerrillas] were not able to deliver effective fire, and their bullets went high. We would quickly establish fire superiority, and rarely ever lost a man."

This psychological and technological superiority in training and killing enabling continues to be a vital factor in modern warfare. It can be seen in the British invasion of the Falklands and the 1989 United States invasion of Panama, where the tremendous success of the invaders and the remarkable disparity between the kill ratios can be at least partially explained by the degree and quality of training in the different forces.

Missing the target does not necessarily involve firing obviously high, and two decades on army rifle ranges have taught me that a soldier must fire unusually high for it to be obvious to an observer. In other words, the intentional miss can be a very subtle form of disobedience.

One of the best examples of an intentional miss was the experience of my grandfather John, who had been assigned to a firing squad during World War I. A major source of pride from his days as a veteran was that he was able to *not* kill while a member of that firing squad. He knew that the commands would be "Ready, aim, fire," and he knew that if he aimed at the prisoner on the command of "aim," he would hit the target he was aiming at on the command of "fire." His response was to aim slightly away from the prisoner on the command of "aim," enabling him to miss when he pulled the trigger on the command of "fire." My grandfather bragged for the rest of his life about outsmarting the army in this manner. Of course, others in the firing squad did kill the prisoner, but his conscience was clear. In the same way, generations of soldiers appear to have either intentionally or instinctively outwitted the powers that be by simply exercising the soldier's right to miss.

Another excellent example of soldiers exercising their right to miss is this mercenary-journalist's account of going with one of Eden Pastora's (a.k.a. Commandante Zero) Contra units on an ambush of a civilian river launch in Nicaragua:

I'll never forget Surdo's words as he gave his imitation of a Pastora harangue prior to going into battle, telling the entire formation, *"Si mata una mujer, mata una piricuaco; si mata un niño, mata un piricuaco."*

Piricuaco is a derogatory term, meaning rabid dog, we used for the Sandinistas, so in effect Surdo was saying "If you kill a woman, you're killing a Sandinista, if you kill a child, you're killing a Sandinista." And off we went to kill women and children.

Once again I was part of the 10 men who would actually perform the ambush. We cleared our fields of fire and settled back to await the arrival of women and children and whatever other civilian passengers there might be on this launch.

Each man was alone with his thoughts. Not a word was spoken among us regarding the nature of our mission. Surdo paced back and forth nervously some yards behind us in the protection of the jungle.

. . . The loud throb of the powerful diesels of the 70-foot launch preceded its arrival by a good two minutes. The signal to commence firing was given as it appeared in front of us and I watched the RPG-7 [rocket] arc over the boat and into the jungle on the opposite bank. The M60 [machine gun] opened up, I rattled off a 20-round burst from my FAL. Brass was flying as thick as the jungle insects as our squad emptied their magazines. *Every bullet sailed harmlessly over the civilian craft.*

When Surdo realized what was happening he came running out of the jungle cursing violently in Spanish and firing his AK [rifle] at the disappearing launch. Nicaraguan peasants are mean bastards, and tough soldiers. But they're not murderers. I laughed aloud in relief and pride as we packed up and prepared to move out.

— Dr. John
  "American in ARDE"

Note the nature of such a "conspiracy to miss." Without a word being spoken, every soldier who was obliged and trained to fire reverted — as millions of others must have over the centuries — to the simple artifice of soldierly incompetence. And like the firing-squad member mentioned earlier, these soldiers took a great and private pleasure in outmaneuvering those who would make them do that which they would not.

Even more remarkable than instances of posturing, and equally indisputable, is the fact that a significant number of soldiers in combat elect not even to fire over the enemy's head, but instead do not fire at all. In this respect their actions very much resemble the actions of those members of the animal kingdom who "submit" passively to the aggression and determination of their opponent rather than fleeing, fighting, or posturing.

We have previously observed General S. L. A. Marshall's findings concerning the 15 to 20 percent firing rates of U.S. soldiers in World War II. Both Marshall and Dyer note that the dispersion of the modern battlefield was probably a major factor in this low firing rate, and dispersion is indeed one factor in a complex equation of restraints and enabling mechanisms. Yet Marshall noted that even in situations where there were several riflemen together in a position facing an advancing enemy, only one was likely to fire while the others would tend to such "vital" tasks as running messages, providing ammo, tending wounded, and spotting targets. Marshall makes it clear that in most cases the firers were aware of the large body of nonfirers around them. The inaction of these passive individuals did not seem to have a demoralizing effect on actual firers. To the contrary, the presence of the nonfirers seemed to enable the firers to keep going.[3]

Dyer argues that all other forces on the World War II battlefield must have had somewhere near the same rate of nonfirers. If, says Dyer, "a higher proportion of Japanese or Germans had been willing to kill, then the volume of fire they actually managed to produce would have been three, four, or five times greater than a similar number of Americans — and it wasn't."[4]

There is ample supporting evidence to indicate that Marshall's observations are applicable not only to U.S. soldiers or even to the soldiers on all sides in World War II. Indeed, there are compelling data that indicate that this singular lack of enthusiasm for killing one's fellow man has existed throughout military history.

A 1986 study by the British Defense Operational Analysis Establishment's field studies division used historical studies of more than one hundred nineteenth- and twentieth-century battles and test trials using pulsed laser weapons to determine the killing effectiveness of these historical units. The analysis was designed (among other things) to determine if Marshall's nonfirer figures were correct in other, earlier wars. A comparison of historical combat performances with the performance of their test subjects (who were not killing with their weapons and were not in any physical danger from the "enemy") determined that the killing potential in these circumstances was much greater than the actual historical casualty rates. The researchers' conclusions openly supported Marshall's findings, pointing to "unwillingness to take part [in combat] as the main factor" that kept the actual historical killing rates significantly below the laser trial levels.

But we don't need laser test trials and battle reenactments to determine that many soldiers have been unwilling to take part in combat. The evidence has been there all along if we had only looked.

Chapter Two

Nonfirers Throughout History

Nonfirers in the Civil War

Imagine a new recruit in the American Civil War.

Regardless of the side he was on, or whether he came in as a draftee or a volunteer, his training would have consisted of mind-numbingly-repetitive drill. Whatever time was available to teach even the rawest recruit was spent endlessly repeating the loading drill, and for any veteran of even a few weeks, loading and firing a musket became an act that could be completed without thinking.

The leaders envisioned combat as consisting of great lines of men firing in unison. Their goal was to turn a soldier into a small cog in a machine that would stand and fire volley after volley at the enemy. Drill was their primary tool for ensuring that he would do his duty on the battlefield.

The concept of drill had its roots in the harsh lessons of military success on battlefields dating back to the Greek phalanx. Such drill was perfected by the Romans. Then, as firing drill, it was turned into a science by Frederick the Great and then mass-produced by Napoleon.

Today we understand the enormous power of drill to condition and program a soldier. J. Glenn Gray, in his book *The Warriors,* states that while soldiers may become exhausted and "enter into a dazed condition in which all sharpness of consciousness is lost" they can still "function like cells in a military organism, doing what is expected of them because it has become automatic."

One of the most powerful examples of the military's success in developing conditioned reflexes through drill can be found in John Masters's *The Road Past Mandalay,* where he relates the actions of a machine-gun team in combat during World War II:

> The No. 1 [gunner] was 17 years old — I knew him. His No. 2 [assistant gunner] lay on the left side, beside him, head toward the enemy, a loaded magazine in his hand ready to whip onto the gun the moment the No. 1 said "Change!" The No. 1 started firing, and a Japanese machine gun engaged them at close range. The No. 1 got the first burst through the face and neck, which killed him instantly. But he did not die where he lay, behind the gun. He rolled over to the right, away from the gun, his left hand coming up in death to tap his No. 2 on the shoulder in the signal that means *Take over.* The No. 2 did not have to push the corpse away from the gun. It was already clear.

The "take over" signal was drilled into the gunner to ensure that his vital weapon was *never* left unmanned should he ever have to leave. Its use in this circumstance is evidence of a conditioned reflex so powerful that it is completed without conscious thought as the last dying act of a soldier with a bullet through the brain.

Gwynne Dyer strikes right to the heart of the matter when he says, "*Conditioning,* almost in the Pavlovian sense, is probably a better word than *Training,* for what was required of the ordinary soldier was not thought, but the ability to . . . load and fire their muskets completely automatically even under the stress of combat." This conditioning was accomplished by "literally thousands of hours of repetitive drilling" paired with "the ever-present incentive of physical violence as the penalty for failure to perform correctly."

The Civil War weapon was usually a muzzle-loading, black-powder, rifled musket. To fire the weapon a soldier would take a paper-wrapped cartridge consisting of a bullet and some gunpowder. He would tear the cartridge open with his teeth, pour the powder down the barrel, set the bullet in the barrel, ram it home, prime the weapon with a percussion cap, cock, and fire. Since gravity was needed to pour the powder down the barrel, all of this was done from a standing position. Fighting was a stand-up business.

With the introduction of the percussion cap, and the advent of oiled paper to wrap the cartridge in, weapons had become generally quite reliable even in wet weather. The oiled paper around the cartridge prevented the powder from becoming wet, and the percussion cap ensured a reliable ignition source. In anything but a driving rainstorm, a weapon would malfunction *only* if the ball was put in before the powder (an extremely rare mistake given the drill the soldier had gone through), or if the hole linking the percussion cap with the barrel was fouled — something that *could* happen after a lot of firing, but that was easily corrected.

A minor problem could arise if a weapon was double loaded. In the heat of battle a soldier might sometimes be unsure as to whether a musket was loaded, and it was not uncommon to place a second load on top of the first. But such a weapon was still quite usable. The barrels of these weapons were heavy, and the black powder involved was relatively weak. Factory tests and demonstrations of weapons of this era often involved firing a rifle with various kinds of multiple loads in it, sometimes with a weapon loaded all the way to the end of the barrel. If such a weapon was fired, the first load would ignite and simply push all the other loads out of the barrel.

These weapons were fast and accurate. A soldier could generally fire four or five rounds a minute. In training, or while hunting with a rifled musket, the hit rate would have been at least as good as that achieved by the Prussians with smoothbore muskets when they got 25 percent hits at 225 yards, 40 percent hits at 150 yards, and 60 percent hits at 75 yards while firing at a 100-foot by 6-foot target. Thus, at 75 yards, a 200-man regiment should be able to hit as many as 120 enemy soldiers in the first volley. If four shots were fired each minute, a regiment could potentially kill or wound 480 enemy soldiers in the first minute.

The Civil War soldier was, without a doubt, the best trained and equipped soldier yet seen on the face of the earth. Then came the day of combat, the day for which he had drilled and marched for so long. And with that day came the destruction of all his preconceptions and delusions about what would happen.

At first the vision of a long line of men with every man firing in unison might hold true. If the leaders maintained control, and if the terrain was not too broken, for a while the battle could be one of volleys between regiments. But even while firing in regimental volleys, something was wrong. Terribly, frightfully wrong. An average engagement would take place at thirty yards. But instead of mowing down hundreds of enemy soldiers in the first minute, regiments killed only one or two men per minute. And instead of the enemy formations disintegrating in a hail of lead, they stood and exchanged fire for hours on end.

Sooner or later (and usually sooner), the long lines firing volleys in unison would begin to break down. And in the midst of the confusion, the smoke, the thunder of the firing, and the screams of the wounded, soldiers would revert from cogs in a machine to individuals doing what comes naturally to them. Some load, some pass weapons, some tend the wounded, some shout orders, a few run, a few wander off in the smoke or find a convenient low spot to sink into, and a few, a very few, shoot.

Numerous historical references indicate that, like their World War II equivalents, most soldiers of the muzzle-loading-musket era busied themselves with other tasks during battle. For example, the image of a line of soldiers standing and firing at the enemy is belied by this vivid account by a Civil War veteran describing the Battle of Antietam in Griffith's book: "Now is the pinch. Men and officers . . . are fused into a common mass, in the frantic struggle to shoot fast. Everybody tears cartridges, loads, passes guns, or shoots. Men are falling in their places or running back into the corn."

This is an image of battle that can be seen over and over again. In Marshall's World War II work and in this account of Civil War battle we see that only a few men actually fire at the enemy, while others gather and prepare ammo, load weapons, pass weapons, or fall back into the obscurity and anonymity of cover.

The process of some men electing to load and provide support for those who are willing to shoot at the enemy appears to have been the norm rather than the exception. Those who did fire, and were the beneficiary of all of this support, can be seen in countless reports collected by Griffith, in which individual Civil War soldiers fired one hundred, two hundred, or even an incredible four hundred rounds of ammunition in battle. This in a period when the standard issue of ammunition was only forty rounds, with a weapon that became so fouled as to be useless without cleaning after firing about forty shots. The extra ammunition and muskets *must* have been supplied and loaded by the firers' less aggressive comrades.

Aside from firing over the enemy's heads, or loading and supporting those who were willing to fire, there was another option well understood by du Picq when he wrote: "A man falls and disappears, who knows whether it was a bullet or the fear of advancing that struck him?" Richard Gabriel, one of the foremost writers in the field of military psychology in our generation, notes that "in engagements the size of Waterloo or Sedan, the opportunity for a soldier not to fire or to refuse to press the attack by merely falling down and remaining in the mud was too obvious for shaken men under fire to ignore." Indeed, the temptation must have been great, and many *must* have done so.

Yet despite the obvious options of firing over the enemy's head (posturing), or simply dropping out of the advance (a type of flight), and the widely accepted option of loading and supporting those who were willing to fire (a limited kind of fighting), evidence exists that during black-powder battles thousands of soldiers elected to passively submit to both the enemy and their leaders through fake or mock firing. The best indicator of this tendency toward mock firing can be found in the salvage of multiply-loaded weapons after Civil War battles.

The Dilemma of the Discarded Weapons

Author of the *Civil War Collector's Encyclopedia* F. A. Lord tells us that after the Battle of Gettysburg, 27,574 muskets were recovered from the battlefield. Of these, nearly 90 percent (twenty-four thousand) were loaded. Twelve thousand of these loaded muskets were found to be loaded more than once, and six thousand of the multiply loaded weapons had from three to ten rounds loaded in the barrel. One weapon had been loaded twenty-three times. Why, then, were there so many loaded weapons available on the battlefield, and why did at least twelve thousand soldiers misload their weapons in combat?

A loaded weapon was a precious commodity on the black-powder battlefield. During the stand-up, face-to-face, short-range battles of this era a weapon should have been loaded for only a fraction of the time in battle. More than 95 percent of the time was spent in loading the weapon, and less than 5 percent in firing it. If most soldiers were desperately attempting to kill as quickly and efficiently as they could, then 95 percent should have been shot with an empty weapon in their hand, and any loaded, cocked, and primed weapon available dropped on the battlefield would have been snatched up from wounded or dead comrades and fired.

There were many who were shot while charging the enemy or were casualties of artillery outside of musket range, and these individuals would never have had an opportunity to fire their weapons, but they hardly represent 95 percent of all casualties. If there is a desperate need in *all* soldiers to fire their weapon in combat, then many of these men should have died with an empty weapon. And as the ebb and flow of battle passed over these weapons, many of them should have been picked up and fired at the enemy.

The obvious conclusion is that most soldiers were *not* trying to kill the enemy. Most of them appear to have not even wanted to fire in the enemy's general direction. As Marshall observed, most soldiers seem to have an inner resistance to firing their weapon in combat. The point here is that the resistance appears to have existed long before Marshall discovered it, and this resistance is the reason for many (if not most) of these multiply loaded weapons.

The physical necessity for muzzle-loaders to be loaded from a standing position, combined with the shoulder-to-shoulder massed firing line so beloved of the officers of this era, presented a situation in which — unlike that studied by Marshall — it was very difficult for a man to disguise the fact that he was not shooting. And in this volley-fire situation, what du Picq called the "mutual surveillance" of authorities and peers must have created an intense pressure to fire.

There was not any "isolation and dispersion of the modern battlefield" to hide nonparticipants during a volley fire. Their every action was obvious to those comrades who stood shoulder to shoulder with them. If a man truly was not able or willing to fire, the only way he could disguise his lack of participation was to load his weapon (tear cartridge, pour powder, set bullet, ram it home, prime, cock), bring it to his shoulder, and then *not actually fire,* possibly even mimicking the recoil of his weapon when someone nearby fired.

Here was the epitome of the industrious soldier. Carefully and steadily loading his weapon in the midst of the turmoil, screams, and smoke of battle, no action of his was discernible as being something other than that which his superiors and comrades would find commendable.

The amazing thing about these soldiers who failed to fire is that they did so in direct opposition to the mind-numbingly repetitive drills of that era. How, then, did these Civil War soldiers consistently "fail" their drillmasters when it came to the all-important loading drill?

Some may argue that these multiple loads were simply mistakes, and that these weapons were discarded because they were misloaded. But if in the fog of war, despite all the endless hours of training, you do accidentally double-load a musket, you shoot it anyway, and the first load simply pushes out the second load. In the rare event that the weapon is actually jammed or nonfunctional in some manner, you simply drop it and pick up another. But that is not what happened here, and the question we have to ask ourselves is, Why was firing the only step that was skipped? How could at least twelve thousand men from both sides and all units make the exact same mistake?

Did twelve thousand soldiers at Gettysburg, dazed and confused by the shock of battle, accidentally double-load their weapons, and then were all twelve thousand of them killed before they could fire these weapons? Or did all twelve thousand of them discard these weapons for some reason and then pick up others? In some cases their powder may have been wet (even through their oiled-paper coating), but that many? And why did six thousand more go on to load their weapons yet again, and still not fire? Some may have been mistakes, and some may have been caused by bad powder, but I believe that the only possible explanation for the vast majority of these incidents is the same factor that prevented 80 to 85 percent of World War II soldiers from firing at the enemy. The fact that these Civil War soldiers overcame their powerful conditioning (through drill) to fire clearly demonstrates the impact of powerful instinctive forces and supreme acts of moral will.

If Marshall had not asked the soldiers immediately after battle in World War II, we would have never known the amazing ineffectiveness of our fire. In the same way, since no one asked the soldiers of the Civil War, or any other war prior to World War II, we cannot know the effectiveness of their fire. What we can do is extrapolate from the available data, and the available data indicate that at least half of the soldiers in black-powder battles did not fire their weapons, and only a minute percentage of those who did fire aimed to kill the enemy with their fire.

Now we can begin to fully understand the reasons underlying Paddy Griffith's discovery of an average regimental hit rate of one or two men per minute in firefights of the black-powder era. And we see that these figures strongly support Marshall's findings. With the rifled muskets of that era, the *potential* hit rate was at least as high as that achieved by the Prussians with smoothbore muskets when they got 60 percent hits at seventy-five yards. But the *reality* was a minute fraction of this.

Griffith's figures make perfect sense if during these wars, as in World War II, only a small percentage of the musketeers in a regimental firing line were actually attempting to shoot at the enemy while the rest stood bravely in line firing above the enemy's heads or did not fire at all.

When presented with this data, some respond that they are specific to a civil war in which "brother fought brother." Dr. Jerome Frank answers such claims clearly in his book *Sanity and Survival in the Nuclear Age,* in which he points out that civil wars are usually more bloody, prolonged, and unrestrained than other types of war. And Peter Watson, in *War on the Mind,* points out that "deviant behavior by members of our own group is perceived as more disturbing and produces stronger retaliation than that of others with whom we are less involved." We need only look at the intensity of aggression between different Christian factions in Europe in the past and in Ireland, Lebanon, and Bosnia today, or the conflict between Leninist, Maoist, and Trotskyist Communists, or the horror in Rwanda and other African tribal battles, to confirm this fact.

It is my contention that most of these discarded weapons on the battlefield at Gettysburg represent soldiers who had been unable or unwilling to fire their weapons in the midst of combat and then had been killed, wounded, or routed. In addition to these twelve thousand, a similar proportion of soldiers must have marched off that battlefield with similarly multiloaded weapons.

Secretly, quietly, at the moment of decision, just like the 80 to 85 percent of World War II soldiers observed by Marshall, these soldiers found themselves to be conscientious objectors who were unable to kill their fellow man. This is the root reason for the incredible ineffectiveness of musket fire during this era. This is what happened at Gettysburg, and if you look deeply enough you will soon discover that this is also what happened in the other black-powder battles about which we do not necessarily have the same kind of data.

A case in point is the Battle of Cold Harbor.

"Eight Minutes at Cold Harbor"

The Battle of Cold Harbor deserves careful observation here, since it is the example that most casual observers of the American Civil War would hold up to refute an 80 to 85 percent nonfiring rate.

In the early morning hours of the third of June 1864, forty thousand Union soldiers under the command of Ulysses S. Grant attacked the Confederate army at Cold Harbor, Virginia. The Confederate forces under Robert E. Lee were in a carefully prepared system of trenches and artillery emplacements unlike anything that Grant's Army of the Potomac had ever encountered. A newspaper correspondent observed that these positions were "intricate, zig-zagged lines within lines . . . lines built to enfilade an opposing line, lines within which lies a battery [of artillery]." By the evening of the third of June more than seven thousand attacking Union soldiers were killed, wounded, or captured while inflicting negligible damage on the well-entrenched Confederates.

Bruce Catton, in his superb and definitive multivolume account of the Civil War, states, "Offhand, it would seem both difficult and unnecessary to exaggerate the horrors of Cold Harbor, but for some reason — chiefly, perhaps, the desire to paint Grant as a callous and uninspired butcher — no other Civil War battle gets as warped a presentation as this one."

Catton is referring largely to exaggerated accounts of Union casualties (usually claiming the thirteen thousand casualties of two weeks' fighting at Cold Harbor as the casualty rate for the one day's fighting), but he also debunks the very common misconception that seven thousand (or even thirteen thousand) casualties occurred in "Eight Minutes at Cold Harbor." This belief is not so much wrong as it is a gross oversimplification. It is quite correct that most of the isolated, disjointed Union charges launched at Cold Harbor were halted in the first ten to twenty minutes, but once the attackers' momentum was broken the attacking Union soldiers did not flee, and the killing did *not* end. Catton notes that "the most amazing thing of all in this fantastic battle is the fact that all along the front the beaten [Union soldiers] did not pull back to the rear." Instead they did exactly what Union and Confederate soldiers had done over and over again in that war: "They stayed where they were, anywhere from 40 to 200 yards from the confederate line, gouging out such shallow trenches as they could, and kept on firing." And the Confederates kept on firing at *them,* often with cannons firing from the flanks and rear at horrendously short range. "All day long," says Catton, "the terrible sound of battle continued. Only an experienced soldier could tell by the sound alone, that the pitch of the combat in midafternoon was any lower than it had been in the murky dawn when the charges were being repulsed."

It took over eight *hours,* not eight minutes, to inflict those horrendous casualties on Grant's soldiers. And as in most wars from the time of Napoleon on down to today, it was not the infantry but the *artillery* that inflicted most of these casualties.

Only when artillery (with its close supervision and mutual sur-veillance processes among the crew) is brought into play can any significant change in this killing rate be observed. (The greater distance that artillery usually is from its targets, as we will see, also increases its effectiveness.) The simple fact appears to be that, like S. L. A. Marshall's riflemen of World War II, the vast majority of the rifle- and musket-armed soldiers of previous wars were consis-tent and persistent in their psychological inability to kill their fellow human beings. Their weapons were technologically capable, and they were physically quite able to kill, but at the decisive moment each man became, in his heart, a conscientious objector who could not bring himself to kill the man standing before him.

This all indicates that there is a force in play here. A previously undiscovered psychological force. A force stronger than drill, stronger than peer pressure, even stronger than the self-preservation instinct. The impact of this force is not limited to only the black-powder era or only to World War II: it can also be seen in World War I.

Nonfirers of World War I

Colonel Milton Mater served as an infantry company commander in World War II and relates several World War II experiences that strongly support Marshall's observations. Mater also provides us with several instances in which World War I veterans warned him to expect that there would be many nonfirers in combat.

When he first joined the service in 1933, Mater asked his uncle, a veteran of World War I, about his combat experience. "I was amazed to find that the experience foremost in his mind was 'draftees who wouldn't shoot.' He expressed it something like this: 'They thought if they didn't shoot at the Germans, the Germans wouldn't shoot at them.'"

Another veteran of the trenches of World War I taught Mater in an ROTC class in 1937 that, based on his experiences, nonfirers would be a problem in any future war. "He took pains to impress us with the difficulty of making some men fire their rifles to avoid becoming sitting ducks for the fire and movement of the enemy."

There is ample indication of the existence of the resistance to killing and that it appears to have existed at least since the black-powder era. This lack of enthusiasm for killing the enemy causes many soldiers to posture, submit, or flee, rather than fight; it represents a powerful psychological force on the battlefield; and it is a force that is discernible throughout the history of man. The application and understanding of this force can lend new insight to military history, the nature of war, and the nature of man.

Chapter Three

Why Can't Johnny Kill?

Why did individual soldiers over hundreds of years refuse to kill the enemy, even when they knew that doing so would endanger their own lives? And why, if this has been so throughout history, have we not been fully aware of it?

Why Can't Johnny Kill?

Many veteran hunters, upon hearing accounts of nonfirers, might say, "Aha, buck fever," and they would be quite right. But what is buck fever? And why do men experience during the hunt that inability to kill that we call buck fever? (The relationship between the failures to kill on the battlefield and failures to kill in the hunt are explored more completely in a later section.) We must turn back to S. L. A. Marshall for the answer.

Marshall studied this issue during the entire period of World War II. He, more than any other individual prior to him, understood the thousands of soldiers who did not fire at the enemy, and he concluded that "the average and healthy individual . . . has such an inner and usually unrealized resistance towards killing a fellow man that he will not of his own volition take life if it is possible to turn away from that responsibility. . . . At the vital point," says Marshall, the soldier "becomes a conscientious objector."

Marshall understood the mechanics and emotions of combat. He was a combat veteran of World War I, asking the combat veterans of World War II about their responses to battle, and he understood, he had been there. "I well recall . . . ," said Marshall, "the great sense of relief that came to [World War I] troops when they were passed to a quiet sector." And he believed that this "was due not so much to the realization that things were safer there as to the blessed knowledge that for a time they were *not under the compulsion to take life*." In his experience that philosophy of the World War I soldier was "Let 'em go; we'll get 'em some other time."

Dyer also studied the matter carefully, building his knowledge on those who knew, and he too understood that "men will kill under compulsion — men will do almost anything if they know it is expected of them and they are under strong social pressure to comply — but the vast majority of men are not born killers."

The U.S. Army Air Corps (now the U.S. Air Force) ran head-on into this problem when it discovered that during World War II less than 1 percent of their fighter pilots accounted for 30 to 40 percent of all enemy aircraft destroyed in the air, and according to Gabriel, most fighter pilots "never shot anyone down or even tried to." Some suggest that simple fear was the force that prevented these men from killing, but these pilots usually flew in small groups led by proven killers who took the nonkillers into dangerous situations, and these men bravely followed. But when it came time to kill, they looked into the cockpit at another man, a pilot, a flier, one of the "brotherhood of the air," a man frighteningly like themselves; and when faced with such a man it is possible that the vast majority simply could not kill him. The pilots of both fighter and bomber aircraft faced the terrible dilemma of air combat against others of their own kind, and this was a significant factor in making their task difficult. (The matter of the mechanics of killing in air battles and the U.S. Air Force's remarkable discoveries in attempting to preselect "killers" for pilot training are addressed later in this study.)

That the average man will not kill even at the risk of all he holds dear has been largely ignored by those who attempt to understand the psychological and sociological pressures of the battlefield. Looking another human being in the eye, making an independent decision to kill him, and watching as he dies due to your action combine to form the single most basic, important, primal, and potentially traumatic occurrence of war. If we understand this, then we understand the magnitude of the horror of killing in combat.

The Israeli military psychologist Ben Shalit in his book *The Psychology of Conflict and Combat,* referring to Marshall's studies, says that it is "clear that many soldiers do not shoot directly at the enemy. Many reasons are given; one of them — *which, oddly enough, is not often discussed* — may be the reluctance of the individual to act in a direct aggressive way."

Why is this not often discussed? If Johnny can't kill, if the average soldier will not kill unless coerced and conditioned and provided with mechanical and mental leverage, then why has it not been understood before?

British field marshal Evelyn Wood has said that in war only cowards need lie. I believe that to call the men who did not fire in combat cowards is grossly inaccurate, but those who did not fire do, indeed, have something to hide. Or at the very least something that they would not be very proud of and would readily lie about in later years. The point is that (1) an intense, traumatic, guilt-laden situation will inevitably result in a web of forgetfulness, deception, and lies; (2) such situations that continue for thousands of years become institutions based on a tangled web of individual and cultural forgetfulness, deception, and lies tightly woven over thousands of years; and (3) for the most part there have been two such institutions about which the male ego has always justified selective memory, self-deception, and lying. These two institutions are sex and combat. After all, "All is fair in love and war."

For thousands of years we did not understand human sexuality. We understood the big things about sex. We knew that it made babies, and it worked. But we had no idea how human sexuality affected the individual. Until the studies of human sexuality by Sigmund Freud and researchers of this century we had not even begun to really understand the role that sex played in our lives. For thousands of years we did not truly study sex and therefore had no hope of ever understanding it. The very fact that in studying sex we were studying ourselves made impartial observation difficult. Sex was especially difficult to study because so much of the ego and self-esteem of each individual was invested in this area full of myths and misunderstanding.

If someone was impotent or frigid, would he or she let that be common knowledge? If the majority of the marriages of two centuries ago suffered problems with impotence or frigidity, would we have known? An educated man of two hundred years ago would have probably said, "They manage to make plenty of babies, don't they? They must be doing something right!"

And if one hundred years ago a researcher discovered that sexual abuse of children was rampant in society, how would such a discovery be treated? Freud made just such a discovery, and he was personally disgraced and professionally scorned by his peers and by society at large for even suggesting such a thing. It is only today, one hundred years later, that we have begun to accept and address the magnitude of sexual abuse of children in our society.

Until someone with authority and credibility asked individuals in privacy and with dignity, we had no hope of ever realizing what was occurring sexually in our culture. And even under such circumstances, society as a whole has to be sufficiently prepared and enlightened in order to throw off the blinders that limit its ability to perceive itself.

In the same way that we did not understand what was occurring in the bedroom, we have not understood what was occurring on the battlefield. Our ignorance of the destructive act matched that of the procreative act. If a soldier would not kill in combat, when it was his duty and responsibility to do so, would he let that be common knowledge? And if the majority of soldiers two hundred years ago did not fulfill their duties on the battlefield, would we have known? A general of the era would probably have said, "They manage to kill plenty of people don't they? They won the war for us didn't they? They must be doing something right!" Until S. L. A. Marshall asked the individuals involved, immediately after the fact, we had no hope of understanding what was occurring on the battlefield.

Philosophers and psychologists have long been aware of man's basic inability to perceive that which is closest to him. Sir Norman Angell tells us that "it is quite in keeping with man's curious intellectual history, that the simplest and most important questions are those he asks least often." And the philosopher-soldier Glenn Gray speaks from personal experience in World War II when he observes that "few of us can hold on to our real selves long enough to discover the real truths about ourselves and this whirling earth to which we cling. This is especially true," observes Gray, "of men in war. The great god Mars tries to blind us when we enter his realm, and when we leave he gives us a generous cup of the waters of Lethe to drink."

If a professional soldier were to see through the fog of his own self-deception, and if he were to face the cold reality that he can't do what he has dedicated his life to, or that many of his soldiers would rather die than do their duty, it would make his life a lie. Such a man would be apt to deny his weakness with all the energy he could muster. No, the soldiers are not apt to write of their failures or the failures of their men; with few exceptions, it is only the heroes and the glory that make their way into print.

Part of the reason for our lack of knowledge in this area is that combat is, like sex, laden with a baggage of expectations and myth. A belief that most soldiers will not kill the enemy in close combat is contrary to what we want to believe about ourselves, and it is contrary to what thousands of years of military history and culture have told us. But are the perceptions handed down to us by our culture and our historians accurate, unbiased, and reliable?

In *A History of Militarism,* Alfred Vagts accuses military history, as an institution, of having played a large part in the process of militarizing minds. Vagts complains that military history is consistently written "with polemic purpose for the justification of individuals or armies and with small regard for socially relevant facts."

He states, "A very large part of military history is written, if not for the express purpose of supporting an army's authority, at least with the intention of not hurting it, not revealing its secrets, avoiding the betrayal of weakness, vacillation, or distemper."

Vagts paints an image of military and historical institutions that for thousands of years have reinforced and supported each other in a process of mutual glorification and aggrandizement. To a certain extent, this is probably because those who are good at killing in war are quite often those who throughout history have hacked their way to power. The military and the politicians have been the same people for all but the most recent part of human history, and we know that the victor writes the history books.

As a historian, as a soldier, and as a psychologist, I believe that Vagts is quite correct. If for thousands of years the vast majority of soldiers secretly and privately were less than enthused about killing their fellow man on the battlefield, the professional soldiers and their chroniclers would be the last to let us know the inadequacies of their particular charges.

The media in our modern information society have done much to perpetuate the myth of easy killing and have thereby become part of society's unspoken conspiracy of deception that glorifies killing and war. There are exceptions — such as Gene Hackman's *Bat 21,* in which an air force officer has to kill people up close and personal for a change and is horrified at what he has done — but for the most part we are given James Bond, Luke Skywalker, Rambo, and Indiana Jones blithely and remorselessly killing off men by the hundreds. The point here is that there is as much disinformation and as little insight concerning the nature of killing coming from the media as from any other aspect of our society.

Even after Marshall's World War II revelations, the subject of nonfirers is an uncomfortable one for today's military. Writing in *Army* magazine — the U.S. Army's foremost military journal — Colonel Mater states that his experiences as an infantry company commander in World War II strongly supported Marshall's findings and noted several World War I anecdotes that suggest that the problem of nonfirers was just as serious in that war.

Mater then bitterly — and appropriately — complains that "thinking back over my many years of service, I cannot remember a single official lecture or class discussion of how to assure that your men will fire." This included "such formal schooling as the wartime Infantry Leadership and Battle School I attended in Italy and the Command and General Staff College at Ft. Leavenworth, Kansas, that I attended in 1966. Nor do I remember any articles on the subject in *Army* magazine or other military publications."[5] Colonel Mater concludes, "It is as if there were a conspiracy of silence around this subject: 'We don't know what to do about it — so let's forget it.'"

There does indeed seem to be a conspiracy of silence on this subject. In his book *War on the Mind,* Peter Watson observes that Marshall's findings have been largely ignored by academia and the fields of psychology and psychiatry, but they were very much taken to heart by the U.S. Army, and a number of training measures were instituted as a result of Marshall's suggestions. According to studies by Marshall, these changes resulted in a firing rate of 55 percent in Korea and, according to a study by Scott, a 90 to 95 percent firing rate was attained in Vietnam. Some modern soldiers use the disparity between the firing rates of World War II and Vietnam to claim that Marshall had to be wrong, for the average military leader has great difficulty in believing that any significant body of his soldiers will not do their job in combat. But these doubters don't give sufficient credit to the revolutionary corrective measures and training methods introduced since World War II.

The training methods that increased the firing rate from 15 pecent to 90 percent are referred to as "programming" or "conditioning" by some of the veterans I have interviewed, and they do appear to represent a form of classical and operant conditioning (à la Pavlov's dog and B. F. Skinner's rats), which is addressed in detail in the section "Killing in Vietnam." The unpleasantness of this subject, combined with the remarkable success of the army's training programs, and the lack of official recognition might imply that it is classified. But there is no secret master plan responsible for the lack of attention given to this subject. There is instead, in the words of philosopher-psychologist Peter Marin, "a massive unconscious cover-up" in which society hides itself from the true nature of combat. Even among the psychological and psychiatric literature on war, "there is," writes Marin, "a kind of madness at work." He notes, "Repugnance toward killing and the refusal to kill" are referred to as "acute combat reaction." And psychological trauma resulting from "slaughter and atrocity are called 'stress,' as if the clinicians . . . are talking about an executive's overwork." As a psychologist I believe that Marin is quite correct when he observes, "Nowhere in the [psychiatric and psychological] literature is one allowed to glimpse what is actually occurring: the real horror of the war and its effect on those who fought it."

It would be almost impossible to keep something of this nature classified for more than fifty years now, and those in the military who do understand — the Marshalls and the Maters — are crying out their messages, but no one wants to hear their truths.

No, it is not a military conspiracy. There is, indeed, a cover-up and a "conspiracy of silence," but it is a cultural conspiracy of forgetfulness, distortion, and lies that has been going on for thousands of years. And just as we have begun to wipe away the cultural conspiracy of guilt and silence concerning sex, we *must* now wipe away this similar conspiracy that obscures the very nature of war.

Chapter Four

The Nature and Source of the Resistance

Where does this resistance to killing one's fellow man come from? Is it learned, instinctive, rational, environmental, hereditary, cultural, or social? Or some combination thereof?

One of Freud's most valuable insights involves the existence of the life instinct (Eros) and the death instinct (Thanatos). Freud believed that within each individual there is a constant struggle between the superego (the conscience) and the id (that dark, lurking mass of destructive and animal urges residing within each of us), and that the struggle is mediated by the ego (the self). One wit once referred to this situation as "a struggle in a locked, dark basement; between a homicidal sex-crazed monkey and a puritanical old maid; being mediated by a timid accountant."

In battle we see the id, the ego, the superego, Thanatos, and Eros in turmoil within each soldier. The id wields the Thanatos like a club and screams at the ego to kill. The superego appears to have been neutralized, for authority and society say that now it is good to do what has always been bad. Yet something stops the soldier from killing. What? Could it be that Eros, the life force, is much stronger than ever before understood?

Much has been made of the obvious existence and manifestation of Thanatos in war, but what if there is within most men a stronger drive than Thanatos? What if there is within each person a force that understands at some gut level that all humanity is inextricably interdependent and that to harm any part is to harm the whole?

The Roman emperor Marcus Aurelius understood this force even as he fought desperate battles against the barbarians who would ultimately destroy Rome. "Every individual dispensation," wrote Marcus Aurelius, more than a millennia and a half ago, "is one of the causes of the prosperity, success, and even survival of That which administers the universe. To break off any particle, no matter how small, from the continuous concatenation — whether of causes or of any other elements — is to injure the whole."

Holmes records another veteran who, almost two millennia after Marcus Aurelius, grasped the same concept when he observed that some of the marines he was with in Vietnam reached a point of reflection after battle in which they "came to see the young Vietnamese they had killed as allies in a bigger war of individual existence, as young men with whom they were united throughout their lives against the impersonal 'thems' of the world." Holmes then makes a timeless and powerful perception about the psyche of the American soldier when he notes that "in killing the grunts of North Vietnam, the grunts of America had killed a part of themselves."

Perhaps this is why we avoid this truth. Perhaps to truly understand the magnitude of the resistance to killing is also to understand the magnitude of man's inhumanity to man. Glenn Gray, driven by his own personal guilt and anguish resulting from his World War II experiences, cries out with the pain of every self-aware soldier who has thought this matter through: "I, too, belong to this species. I am ashamed not only of my own deeds, not only of my nation's deeds, but of human deeds as well. I am ashamed to be a man.

"This," says Gray, "is the culmination of a passionate logic which begins in warfare with the questioning of some act the soldier has been ordered to perform contrary to his conscience." If this process continues, then "consciousness of failure to act in response to conscience can lead to the greatest revulsion, not only for oneself, but for the human species."

We may never understand the nature of this force in man that causes him to strongly resist killing his fellow man, but we can give praise for it to whatever force we hold responsible for our existence. And although military leaders responsible for winning a war may be distressed by it, as a race we can view it with pride.

There can be no doubt that this resistance to killing one's fellow man is there and that it exists as a result of a powerful combination of instinctive, rational, environmental, hereditary, cultural, and social factors. It is there, it is strong, and it gives us cause to believe that there may just be hope for mankind after all.

SECTION II

Killing and Combat Trauma:
The Role of Killing in Psychiatric Casualties

Nations customarily measure the "costs of war" in dollars, lost production, or the number of soldiers killed or wounded. Rarely do military establishments attempt to measure the costs of war in terms of individual human suffering. Psychiatric breakdown remains one of the most costly items of war when expressed in human terms.

— Richard Gabriel
  No More Heroes

Chapter One

The Nature of Psychiatric Casualties:
The Psychological Price of War

Richard Gabriel tells us that "in every war in which American soldiers have fought in this century, the chances of becoming a psychiatric casualty — of being debilitated for some period of time as a consequence of the stresses of military life — were greater than the chances of being killed by enemy fire."

During World War II more than 800,000 men were classified 4-F (unfit for military service) due to psychiatric reasons. Despite this effort to weed out those mentally and emotionally unfit for combat, America's armed forces lost an additional 504,000 men from the fighting effort because of psychiatric collapse — enough to man fifty divisions! At one point in World War II, psychiatric casualties were being discharged from the U.S. Army faster than new recruits were being drafted in.

In the brief 1973 Arab-Israeli War, almost a third of all Israeli casualties were due to psychiatric causes, and the same seems to have been true among the opposing Egyptian forces. In the 1982 incursion into Lebanon, Israeli psychiatric casualties were twice as high as the number of dead.

Swank and Marchand's much-cited World War II study determined that after sixty days of *continuous* combat, 98 percent of all

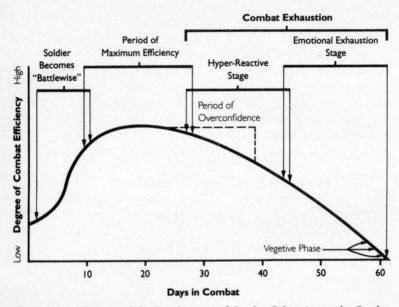

The Relation of Stress and the Development of Combat Exhaustion to the Combat Efficiency of the Average Soldier

Source: Swank and Marchand, 1946

surviving soldiers will have become psychiatric casualties of one kind or another. Swank and Marchand also found a common trait among the 2 percent who are able to endure sustained combat: a predisposition toward "aggressive psychopathic personalities."

The British in World War I believed that their soldiers were good for several hundred days before inevitably becoming a psychiatric casualty. But this was only made possible by the British policy of rotating men out of combat for four days of rest after approximately twelve days of combat, as opposed to America's World War II policy of leaving soldiers in combat for up to eighty days at a stretch.

It is interesting to note that spending *months* of *continuous* exposure to the stresses of combat is a phenomenon found only on the battlefields of this century. Even the years-long sieges of previous centuries provided ample respites from combat, largely due to limitations of artillery and tactics. The actual times of personal risk were seldom more than a few hours in duration. Some psychiatric casualties have always been associated with war, but it is only in this century that our physical and logistical capability to sustain combat has completely outstripped our psychological capacity to endure it.

The Manifestations of Psychiatric Casualties

In his book *No More Heroes* Richard Gabriel examines the many historical symptoms and manifestations of psychiatric casualties.[1] Among these are fatigue cases, confusional states, conversion hysteria, anxiety states, obsessional and compulsive states, and character disorders.

Fatigue Cases

This state of physical and mental exhaustion is one of the earliest symptoms. Increasingly unsociable and overly irritable, the soldier loses interest in all activities with comrades and seeks to avoid any responsibility or activity involving physical or mental effort. He becomes prone to crying fits or fits of extreme anxiety or terror. There will also be such somatic symptoms as hypersensitivity to sound, increased sweating, and palpitations. Such fatigue cases set the stage for further and more complete collapse. If the soldier is forced to remain in combat, such collapse becomes inevitable; the only real cure is evacuation and rest.

Confusional States

Fatigue can quickly shift into the psychotic dissociation from reality that marks confusional states. Usually, the soldier no longer knows who he is or where he is. Unable to deal with his environment, he has mentally removed himself from it. Symptoms include delirium, psychotic dissociation, and manic-depressive mood swings. One often noted response is Ganzer syndrome, in which the soldier will begin to make jokes, act silly, and otherwise try to ward off the horror with humor and the ridiculous.

The degree of affliction in confusional states can range from the merely neurotic to the overtly psychotic. The sense of humor exhibited in the movie and television series *M*A*S*H* is an excellent example of individuals mildly afflicted with Ganzer syndrome. And this personal narrative provides a look at a man severely afflicted with Ganzer syndrome:

> "Get that thing out of my face, Hunter, or I'll feed it to you with hot sauce."
>
> "C'mon, Sarge, don't you want to shake hands with 'Herbert'?"
>
> "Hunter, you're f——ed up. Anybody who'd bring back a gook arm is sick. Anybody who'd bring one in the tent is begging for extra guard. You don't know where that thing's been. QUIT PICKING YOUR NOSE WITH IT! OUT, HUNTER! OUT!"
>
> "Aw, Sarge, 'Herbert' just wants to make friends. He's lonely without his old friends, 'Mr. Foot' and 'Mr. Ballbag.' "
>
> "Double guard tonight, Hunter, and all week. Goodbye, sicko. Enjoy your guard."
>
> "Say good night to 'Herbert,' everyone."
>
> "OUT! OUT!"
>
> Black humor of course. Hard laughs for the hard guys. After a time, nothing was sacred. If Mom could only see what her little boy was playing with now.
>
> Or what they were paying him to do.
>
> — W. Norris
> "Rhodesia Fireforce Commandos"

Conversion Hysteria

Conversion hysteria can occur traumatically during combat or post-traumatically, years later. Conversion hysteria can manifest itself as an inability to know where one is or to function at all, often accompanied by aimless wandering around the battlefield with complete disregard for evident dangers. Upon occasion the soldier becomes amnesiatic, blocking out large parts of his memory. Often, hysteria degenerates into convulsive attacks in which the soldier rolls into the fetal position and begins to shake violently.

Gabriel notes that during both world wars cases of contractive paralysis of the arm were quite common, and usually the arm used to pull the trigger was the one that became paralyzed. A soldier may become hysterical after being knocked out by a concussion, after receiving a minor nondebilitating wound, or after experiencing a near miss. Hysteria can also show up after a wounded soldier has been evacuated to a hospital or rear area. Once he is there, hysteria can begin to emerge, most often as a defense against returning to fight. Whatever the physical manifestation, it is always the mind that produces the symptoms, in order to escape or avoid the horror of combat.

Anxiety States

These states are characterized by feelings of total weariness and tenseness that cannot be relieved by sleep or rest, degenerating into an inability to concentrate. When he can sleep, the soldier is often awakened by terrible nightmares. Ultimately the soldier becomes obsessed with death and the fear that he will fail or that the men in his unit will discover that he is a coward. Generalized anxiety can easily slip into complete hysteria. Frequently anxiety is accompanied by shortness of breath, weakness, pain, blurred vision, giddiness, vasomotor abnormalities, and fainting.

Another reaction, which is commonly seen in Vietnam veterans suffering post-traumatic stress disorder (PTSD), years after combat, is emotional hypertension, in which the soldier's blood pressure rises dramatically with all the accompanying symptoms of sweating, nervousness, and so on.[2]

Obsessional and Compulsive States

These states are similar to conversion hysteria, except that here the soldier realizes the morbid nature of his symptoms and that his fears are at their root. Even so, his tremors, palpitations, stammers, tics, and so on cannot be controlled. Eventually the soldier is likely to take refuge in some type of hysterical reaction that allows him to escape psychic responsibility for his physical symptoms.

Character Disorders

Character disorders include obsessional traits in which the soldier becomes fixated on certain actions or things; paranoid trends accompanied by irascibility, depression, and anxiety, often taking on the tone of threats to his safety; schizoid trends leading to hypersensitivity and isolation; epileptoid character reactions accompanied by periodic rages; the development of extreme dramatic religiosity; and finally degeneration into a psychotic personality. What has happened to the soldier is an altering of his fundamental personality.

These are only some of the possible symptoms of psychiatric casualties in war. Gabriel notes that "The mind has shown itself infinitely capable of bringing about any number of combinations of symptoms and then, to make matters worse, burying them deep in the soldier's psyche so that even the overt manifestations become symptoms of deeper symptoms of even deeper underlying causes." The key understanding to take away from this litany of mental illness is that within a few months of sustained combat *some symptoms of stress* will develop in almost all participating soldiers.

Treating the Mentally Maimed

Treatment for these many manifestations of combat stress involves simply removing the soldier from the combat environment. Until the post-Vietnam era, when hundreds of thousands of PTSD cases appeared, this was the only treatment believed necessary to permit the soldier to return to a normal life. But the problem is that the military does not want to simply return the psychiatric casualty to normal life, it wants to return him to combat! And he is understandably reluctant to go.

The evacuation syndrome is the paradox of combat psychiatry. A nation must care for its psychiatric casualties, since they are of no value on the battlefield — indeed, their presence in combat can have a negative impact on the morale of other soldiers — and they can still be used again as valuable seasoned replacements once they've recovered from combat stress. But if soldiers begin to realize that insane soldiers are being evacuated, the number of psychiatric casualties will increase dramatically. An obvious solution to this problem is to rotate troops out of battle for periodic rest and recuperation — this is standard policy in most Western armies — but this is not always possible in combat.

Proximity — or forward treatment — and expectancy are the principles developed to overcome the paradox of evacuation syndrome. These concepts, which have proved themselves quite effective since World War I, involve (1) treatment of the psychiatric casualty as far forward on the battlefield as possible — that is, in the closest possible *proximity* to the battlefield, often still inside enemy artillery range — and (2) constant communication to the casualty by leadership and medical personnel of their *expectancy* that he will be rejoining his comrades in the front line as soon as possible. These two factors permit the psychiatric casualty to get the much-needed rest that is the only current cure for his problem, while not giving a message to still-healthy comrades that psychiatric casualty is a ticket off of the battlefield.

Limited chemical treatments have been used in recent years to assist in the recovery process. According to Watson, "the so-called truth drugs have also been used near the front line to 'abreact' soldiers who are shell-shocked." Such drugs have reportedly been used with some success by the Israelis to induce psychiatric casualties to "talk through the circumstances leading to their reaction, an activity which appears to prevent their fears being 'bottled up' and so causing some other, long-term syndrome."

But the use of chemicals in combat may not be quite so benign in the future. Gabriel, a retired intelligence officer and consultant to both the House and Senate Armed Services Committees, provides a chilling note on the future of the treatment and prevention of combat psychiatric casualties. He believes that the armed forces of both the West and the East are searching for a chemical answer to this problem. Gabriel warns that the perfection of a "nondepleting neurotrop" to be given to soldiers prior to battle would result in "armies of sociopaths."

Gabriel concludes from his research that "one can but marvel at the inventiveness of the human psyche in its efforts to escape its surrounding horror." Similarly, we must marvel at the inventiveness of modern armies and nations in their efforts to ensure that they get full value from their soldiers. And we cannot help but come away with an image of war as one of the most horrifying and traumatic acts a human being can participate in. War is an environment that will psychologically debilitate 98 percent of all who participate in it for any length of time. And the 2 percent who are not driven insane by war appear to have already been insane — aggressive psychopaths — before coming to the battlefield.

Chapter Two

The Reign of Fear

> If I had time and anything like your ability to study war, I think
> I should concentrate almost entirely on the "actualities of war" —
> the effects of tiredness, hunger, fear, lack of sleep, weather. . . .
> The principles of strategy and tactics, and the logistics of war
> are really absurdly simple: it is the actualities that make war so
> complicated and so difficult, and are usually so neglected by his-
> torians.
>
> — Field Marshal Lord Wavell, in a letter to Liddell Hart

What goes on in the mind of a soldier in combat? What are the
emotional reactions and underlying processes that cause the vast
majority of those who survive sustained combat to ultimately slip
into insanity?

Let us use a model as a framework for the understanding and
study of psychiatric casualty causation, a metaphorical model representing and integrating the factors of fear, exhaustion, guilt and
horror, hate, fortitude, and killing. Each of these factors will be
examined and then integrated into the overall model to present a
detailed understanding of the combat soldier's psychological and
physiological state.

The first of these factors is Fear.

Research and the Reign of Fear

A variety of past investigators came up with an overly simplistic — yet widely accepted — explanation for psychiatric casualties when they declared that the cause of most trauma in war is the fear of death and injury. In 1946 Appel and Beebe held that the key to understanding the psychiatric problems of combat soldiers was the simple fact that the danger of being killed or maimed imposed a strain so great that it caused men to break down. And Watson, a London *Times* journalist who made a multiyear study of the application of psychology and psychiatry to war, concludes in his book *War on the Mind* that "combat stress, with its real fear of death, is quite different from other kinds of stress."

But clinical studies that tried to demonstrate that fear of death and injury are responsible for psychiatric casualties have been consistently unsuccessful. An example of such a study is Mitchell Berkun's 1958 research into the nature of psychiatric breakdown in combat. Berkun began with a concern for "the role played by fear, that, is by a concern about possible death or injury in the response to adverse environments." In one of his experiments soldiers on board a military transport aircraft were told that their pilot would soon be forced to crash-land the plane. The men put through the controversial — and by today's standards unethical — fear-provoking situations in these Human Resources Research Office tests were then given "long psychiatric interviews before and after and again weeks later to see whether there were any hidden effects. None were found."

The Israeli military psychologist Ben Shalit asked Israeli soldiers immediately after combat what most frightened them. The answer that he expected was "loss of life" or "injury and abandonment in the field." He was therefore surprised to discover the low emphasis on fear of bodily harm and death, and the great emphasis on "letting others down."

Shalit conducted a similar survey of Swedish peacekeeping forces who had not had combat experience. In this instance he received the expected answer of "death and injury" as the "most frightening factor in battle. His conclusion was that combat experience decreases fear of death or injury.

In both the Berkun and Shalit studies we see indications that fear of death and injury is not the primary cause of psychiatric casualties on the battlefield. Indeed, Shalit found that even in the face of a society and culture that tell the soldiers that selfish fear of death and injury should be their primary concern, it is instead the fear of not being able to meet the terrible obligations of combat that weighs most heavily on the minds of combat soldiers.

One of the reasons that fear may have been generally accepted as the major explanation for combat stress is that it has become socially acceptable. How many times have we heard in movies and on television that only fools are not afraid? Such acceptance of fear is a part of modern culture. But we still tend to carefully avoid any examination of what kind of fear — fear of death, injury, failure, and so on.

During World War II the U.S. Army intentionally built a permissive attitude toward fear, and Stouffer's landmark World War II studies of 1949 show that men who exhibited controlled fear were not generally poorly regarded by their peers. Indeed, during World War II, in a widely distributed pamphlet entitled *Army Life,* the U.S. Army told its soldiers: "YOU'LL BE SCARED. Sure you'll be scared. Before you go into battle you'll be frightened at the uncertainty, at the thought of being killed." A statistician would call that biasing the sample.

Research in this field has been that of blind men groping at the elephant — one grasps what he thinks is a tree, another finds a wall, and still another discovers a snake. All have a piece of the puzzle, a piece of the truth, but none is completely correct.

There is within us the need to say what is socially acceptable, and like blind men groping at some vast beast, we tend to report that aspect of its anatomy that we already expect to find, and we reject those manifestations with which we feel uncomfortable. The supplied, accepted, comfortable name for this beast is "fear."

And few people are comfortable when dealing with such powerful alternative explanations as guilt. Fear is a specific yet brief and fleeting emotion that lies within the individual, but guilt is often long term and can belong to the society as a whole. When we are faced with hard questions and the difficult task of introspection,

it is very easy to avoid the truth and give the socially acceptable
answers that war literature, Hollywood films, and scientific literature tell us we should give.

Fear's Place in the Soldier's Dilemma

Fear of death and injury is *not* the only, or even the major, cause
of psychiatric casualties in combat. That is not to say that there is
not some wisdom in this common understanding of battle, but
the whole truth is far more complex and horrible. This is also not
to suggest that the carnage and death of battle are not horrible
and that the fear of violent death and injury is not a traumatic
thing. These factors by themselves, however, are not sufficient
to cause the mass exodus of psychiatric casualties found on the
modern battlefield.

There are deeper underlying causes for the psychiatric casualties
suffered by soldiers in combat. Resistance to overt aggressive confrontation, in addition to the fear of death and injury, is responsible
for much of the trauma and stress on the battlefield. Thus, the
Reign of Fear is represented as only one contributing factor in
the soldier's dilemma. Fear, combined with exhaustion, hate, horror, and the irreconcilable task of balancing these with the need
to kill, eventually drives the soldier so deeply into a mire of guilt
and horror that he tips over the brink into that region that we
call insanity. Indeed, fear may be one of the least important of
these factors.

Ending the Reign of Fear

Nonkillers are frequently exposed to the same brutal conditions
as killers, conditions that cause fear, but they do not become
psychiatric casualties. In most circumstances in which nonkillers
are faced with the threat of death and injury in war, the instances
of psychiatric casualties are notably absent. These circumstances
include civilian victims of strategic bombing attacks, civilians and
prisoners of war under artillery fire and bombings, sailors on board

ship during combat, soldiers on reconnaissance missions behind
enemy lines, medical personnel, and officers in combat.

Fear and Civilian Victims of Bombing Attacks

The Italian infantry officer Giulio Douhet became the world's first
recognized airpower theoretician with the publication of his book
Command of the Air in 1921. Douhet declared, "The disintegration
of nations [which] in the last war was brought about by [attrition]
will be accomplished directly by . . . aerial forces."

Prior to World War II, psychologists and military theoreticians
such as Douhet predicted that mass bombing of cities would create
the same degree of psychological trauma seen on the battlefield in
World War I. During World War I the probability of a soldier
becoming a psychiatric casualty was greater than that of his being
killed by enemy fire. As a result of this, authorities envisioned vast
numbers of "gibbering lunatics" being driven from their cities by
a rain of bombs. Among civilians the impact was projected to be
even worse than that seen in combat. When the horror of war
touched women, children, and the elderly, rather than trained and
carefully selected soldiers, the psychological impact was sure to be
too great, and even more civilians than soldiers were expected
to snap.

This body of theory, established by Douhet and later echoed
by many other authorities, played a key role in establishing the
theoretical foundation for the German attempt to bomb Britain
into submission at the beginning of World War II and the subsequent Allied attempt to do the same to Germany. This strategic
bombing of population centers was motivated by quite reasonable
expectations of mass psychiatric casualties resulting from the strategic bombing of civilian populations.

But they were wrong.

The carnage and destruction, and the fear of death and injury
caused by the months of continuous blitz in England during World
War II were as bad as anything faced by any frontline soldier.
Relatives and friends were mutilated and killed, but in a strange
sort of way, that was not the worst of it. These civilians suffered

one indignity that most soldiers need never face. In 1942, Lord Cherwell wrote: "Investigation seems to show that having one's house demolished is most damaging to morale. People seem to mind it more than having their friends or even relatives killed."

For the Germans it was worse. The might of the vast British Empire was brought to bear on the German population via Britain's nighttime area bombing. At the same time, the United States devoted its efforts to "precision" daylight bombing. Day and night for months, even years, the German people suffered horribly.

During the months of firebombings and carpet bombings the German population experienced the distilled essence of the death and injury suffered in combat. They endured fear and horror on a magnitude such as few will ever live to see. This Reign of Fear and horror unleashed among civilians is exactly what most experts hold responsible for the tremendous percentages of psychiatric casualties suffered by soldiers in battle.

And yet, incredibly, the incidence of psychiatric casualties among these individuals was very similar to that of peacetime. There were no incidents of mass psychiatric casualties. The Rand Corporation study of the psychological impact of air raids, published in 1949, found that there was only a very slight increase in the "more or less long-term" psychological disorders as compared with peacetime rates. And those that did appear seemed to "occur primarily among already predisposed persons." Indeed, bombing seemed to have served primarily to harden the hearts and empower the killing ability of those who endured it.

When faced with the failure of their predictions, postwar psychologists and psychiatrists scrambled to find a reason for the obstinate failure of the populations of Germany and England to become mass psychiatric casualties in response to strategic bombing. They finally used the theory of gain through illness as a model to explain what had occurred. This held that these individuals failed to become "ill" because they simply had nothing to gain by doing so.

The theory of gain through illness, however, fails for two reasons: soldiers in combat will become psychiatric casualties even when they have nothing to gain by doing so — such is the nature of insanity — and second, these individuals did have much to gain by "letting slip the bonds of reality" and escaping into the countryside, or better yet escaping to the psychiatric clinics that were usually located far from the targets of strategic bombing.

Fear and Prisoners of War as Artillery and Bombing Victims

Gabriel notes that studies from both the First and Second World Wars show that prisoners of war did not suffer psychiatric reactions when they were subjected to artillery attack or aerial bombardment, *but their guards did.* Here we see a situation in which noncombatants (prisoners) were not traumatized by death and destruction, while the combatants (guards) with them were. The theory of gain through illness has been applied to explain this disparity; that is, the guards could gain by becoming psychiatric casualties and departing to the nearest psychiatric clearing station, while the prisoners had nothing to gain and nowhere to go, so they elected not to become psychiatric casualties. But this theory does not bear up under careful scrutiny.

Soldiers who are surrounded and without cover will flee from battle, even when they have nothing to gain by doing so. An excellent example of this can be seen in one of Custer's cavalry units, which was cut off and surrounded by the Indians for two days before being rescued. (Yes, some of Custer's 7th Cavalry, at a different location under the command of Major Reno, did survive the Little Big Horn. Only the ones with Custer were all killed.) According to Gabriel many of these soldiers, pretending to be ill or wounded, left their defensive positions for the medical station, *even though it offered no protection.* Indeed, the medical station was exposed to hostile fire and was very possibly less safe than positions on the perimeter. This example makes an important point about gain through illness: combatants will try to get out of the battle (a situation where they are required to kill) even when it puts them at risk.

Gabriel discards the gain-through-illness explanation in the case of prisoners of war (POWs) and guards receiving artillery fire or bombardment. He comes much closer to a more plausible explanation when he states that the prisoners "had shifted responsibility for their survival to the guards." The prisoners had indeed relinquished responsibility to their guards: responsibility for survival *and* responsibility for killing.

The prisoners were unarmed, impotent, and strangely at peace with their lot in life. They had no personal capacity or responsibility to kill, and they had no reason to believe that the incoming artillery or bombs were a personal matter. The guards, on the other hand, took the matter as a personal affront. They still had a capacity and a responsibility to fight, and they were faced with the irrefutable evidence that someone was intent on killing them and that they had a responsibility to do likewise. The psychiatric casualties among the guards — as among most other soldiers in the same circumstances — represented an accepted method of escape from the unbearable responsibility inherent in their roles as soldiers.

Fear and Sailors in Naval Combat

For thousands of years naval battles involved missile combat (bow and arrows, ballista, cannons, and so on) at extremely close range, followed by grappling, boarding, and vicious life-or-death, close-in battle with no way to escape. The history of such naval warfare — like that of ground combat — provides many examples of psychiatric casualties resulting from this kind of combat. In its emotional demands naval warfare was very much like its land-based equivalent.

But in the twentieth century, psychiatric casualties during naval warfare have been nearly nonexistent. The great military physician Lord Moran noted the remarkable absence of psychological illness among the men he ministered to aboard ships in World War II. Discussing his experience in two ships, he said, "One was sunk after surviving more than two hundred raids and the whole of the first Libyan campaign. The other was in four major actions in addition to many raids at sea and in harbour, and twice sustained actual damage." Yet the incidence of psychiatric casualties was almost nonexistent. "There were more than five hundred men in the two ships and of these only two came to me about their nerves."

After World War II the fields of psychiatry and psychology attempted to find out why, and again they suggested gain through illness. The sailor obviously had nothing to gain by becoming a psychiatric casualty and therefore did not elect to do so.

The idea that modern sailors had nothing to gain through becoming a psychiatric casualty is simply absurd. The sick bay of a warship is traditionally placed in the safest and most secure heart of the ship. A sailor standing in the open, firing a deck gun at an attacking aircraft, has *much* to gain by making for the relative safety of sick bay. And even if his psychiatric symptoms can't get him completely away from this battle, they can most assuredly get him away from future ones.

So why don't these sailors suffer from the same psychiatric ailments that their brothers on land do? Modern sailors suffer and burn and die just as horribly as their land-bound equivalents. Death and destruction fall all about them. Yet they do not crack. Why?

The answer is that most of them don't have to kill anyone directly, and no one is trying to specifically, personally, kill them.

Dyer observes that there has never been a similar resistance to killing among artillerymen or bomber crews or naval personnel. "Partly," he says, this is due to "the same pressure that keeps machine-gun crews firing, but even more important is the intervention of distance and machinery between them and the enemy." They can simply "pretend they are not killing human beings."

Instead of killing people up close and personal, modern navies kill ships and airplanes. Of course there are people in these ships and airplanes, but psychological and mechanical distances protect the modern sailor. World War I and World War II ships often fired their weapons at enemy ships that could not be seen with the naked eye, and the aircraft they fired at were seldom more than specks in the sky. Intellectually these naval warriors understood that they were killing humans just like themselves and that someone wanted to kill them, but emotionally they could deny it.

A similar phenomenon has occurred in aerial combat. As previously noted, World War I and World War II pilots, in relatively slow-moving aircraft, could see enemy pilots, and thus large

numbers of them failed to fight aggressively. Desert Storm pilots, fighting an enemy seen only on a radar scope, had no
such problems.

Fear and Patrols Behind Enemy Lines

Another circumstance that is free of the usual psychiatric casualties
associated with the battlefield involves patrols behind enemy lines.
Although highly dangerous, such patrols are by their very nature
a different kind of combat, and in wars throughout this century
they have had some common characteristics.

As an infantry company commander and an army Ranger, I
have been trained by the U.S. Army to plan and conduct such
patrols and have done so in training on many occasions. The majority
of patrols are usually reconnaissance patrols. On a recon patrol a
small, lightly armed body of men is sent into enemy territory with
specific orders *not* to engage the enemy. Their mission is to spy
on the enemy, and if a recon patrol runs into an enemy force it
will *immediately* break contact with the enemy. The essence of a
recon patrol is *not* to be found or seen, and there is not enough
firepower with such a patrol to support any kind of offensive operation.

Thus, although recon patrols are dangerous, and the information
produced may result in many enemy soldiers being killed, the
mission itself is a very benign operation. It is an operation completely free of any obligation or intention to directly confront or
kill the enemy. Sometimes there is a requirement to capture a
prisoner, but even this is a relatively limited engagement with the
enemy. What could be psychologically less traumatic than being
ordered to run from enemy aggression?

If a patrol is not a recon patrol, it is usually on an ambush or
a raid, in which a select group of men will attack the enemy at a
planned point. Just as in a recon patrol, a combat patrol will
immediately break contact with the enemy if it is spotted while
moving to or from its objective. The killing actions of a raid or
ambush are focused on one particular spot for one brief period of
time; at all other times the patrol, which depends on surprise for
its success, will run from the enemy.

A raid or ambush patrol is carefully and thoroughly planned and rehearsed prior to leaving friendly lines, and the time in which killing takes place will be extremely brief, and very much like that practiced in rehearsal. The psychologically protective power of (1) hitting a precise, known objective and of (2) conducting such exact rehearsals and visualizations prior to combat (a form of conditioning) is tremendous. Thus, by their very nature, such combat patrols involve far less random killing and are therefore less conducive to psychiatric casualties.

An additional factor to consider here is — as Dyer points out — that the extremely rare "natural soldiers" who are most capable of killing (those identified by Swank and Marchand as the 2 percent predisposed toward aggressive psychopathic tendencies) can be found "mostly congregating in the commando-type special forces [units]." And it is just such units as these that are usually given the mission of conducting combat patrols behind enemy lines.

Here too gain through illness has been used to explain the absence of psychiatric casualties during patrols behind enemy lines, and again it is demonstrably wrong. Aside from the fact that men in combat go mad regardless of whether or not it will do them any good, such soldiers have *much* to gain by becoming psychiatric casualties.

Patrols behind enemy lines are extraordinarily dangerous, and only one or two casualties (psychiatric or otherwise) en route can result in aborting the mission completely. Even if the mission is not aborted, the wounded and incapacitated can be spared much of the danger involved in a patrol by remaining at a secure location where rucksacks, rations, and equipment are kept under the guard of a few men while the mission is completed. Above all else, indications of psychiatric stress by a soldier on patrol would ensure that the soldier would not go on subsequent missions.

Soldiers on patrols behind enemy lines — like civilians suffering from strategic bombing, prisoners of war receiving artillery or bombs, and sailors in modern naval combat — generally do not suffer psychiatric stress because, for the most part, the element that is most responsible for causing combat stress is not present: they are not obligated to engage in face-to-face aggressive activities

against the enemy. Even though these missions are highly dangerous, danger and the fear of death and injury are quite obviously
not the predominant cause of psychiatric casualties in battle.

Fear among Medical Personnel:
"They Take Not Their Courage from Anger."

In a vision of the night I saw them,
    In the battles of the night.
'Mid the roar and the reeling shadows of blood
    They were moving like light . . .

With scrutiny calm, and with fingers
    Patient as swift
They bind up the hurts and the pain-writhen
    Bodies uplift . . .

But they take not their courage from anger
    That blinds the hot being;
They take not their pity from weakness;
    Tender, yet seeing . . .

They endure to have eyes of the watcher
    In hell and not swerve
For an hour from the faith that they follow,
    The light that they serve.

Man true to man, to his kindness
    That overflows all,
To his spirit erect in the thunder
    When all his forts fall, —

This light, in the tiger-mad welter,
    They serve and they save.
What song shall be worthy to sing them —
    Braver than the brave?

— Laurence Binyon, World War I veteran
   "The Healers"

There is a significant body of evidence that indicates that nonkilling military personnel on the battlefield suffer significantly fewer

psychiatric casualties than those whose job it is to kill. Medical
personnel in particular have traditionally been bulwarks of depend-
ability and stability in combat.

Lord Moran, writing about his military experiences in *Anatomy
of Courage,* is one of many such nonkillers who have recorded that
they had never experienced the physical symptoms of fear. He
experienced great emotional trauma and he felt that certifying
his unit as fit, which was his responsibility, was "like signing the
death warrant of two hundred men. And I might be wrong."
He concludes by saying that "even now after twenty years my
conscience is troubled. . . . Was it right that I should hold such
men to the trenches and if they were killed were they or I to
blame?" Yet despite all his experiences, he marvels at his own
ability to "stick" for so very long while the soldiers around him
broke beneath the psychological burdens of combat. In Moran's
case he felt that his lack of psychiatric symptoms during his long
years of continuous combat in the trenches of World War I was
because, as a medical officer, looking after the wounded gave him
something to do. This may be true, but perhaps a large part of
the answer is that he simply was not obliged to kill.

The medic takes not his courage from anger. He runs the same
or greater risks of death and injury, but he, or she, is given over
on the battlefield not to Thanatos and anger, but to kindness and
Eros. And when it comes to the psychological well-being of its
avatar, Thanatos is a far harsher master, and whereas one World
War I veteran-poet understood the nature of Eros on the battlefield
and communicated it to us in "The Healers," another understood
and spoke of the nature of Thanatos on the painful field:

> Efficient, thorough, strong, and brave — his vision is to kill.
> Force is the hearthstone of his might, the pole-star of his will.
> His forges glow malevolent: Their minions never tire
> To deck the goddess of his lust whose twins are blood and fire.
>
> — Robert Grant, World War I veteran
>   "The Superman"

The psychological distinction between being a killer or a helper
on the battlefield was clearly made by one remarkable veteran I

interviewed. He had served as a sergeant in the 101st Airborne Division at Bastogne, was a Veterans of Foreign Wars post commander, and a highly respected member of his community. He seemed to be deeply troubled by his killing experiences, and after World War II he served in Korea and Vietnam as a medic on a U.S. Air Force air-rescue helicopter. His harrowing adventures rescuing and giving medical aid to downed pilots, he quite freely admitted, was a relief from, and a very powerful personal penance for, his relatively brief experience as a killer.

Here, the one-time killer became the archetypal medic, ministering to the wounded soldiers and carrying them off on his back.[3]

Fear among Officers

Very similar to the psychologically protected position of medics is the position of officers. Officers direct the killing but very seldom participate in it. They are buffered from the guilt of killing by the simple fact that they order it, and others carry it out. With the possible exception of rare self-defense situations, most officers in combat never fire a shot at the enemy. Indeed, it is a generally accepted tenet of modern warfare that if an officer is shooting at the enemy, he is not doing his job. And even though line-officer casualties in most wars are consistently much higher than those of their men (in World War I, 27 percent of the British officers who served on the western front were killed, compared with 12 percent of the men), their psychiatric casualties are usually significantly lower (in World War I, the probability of a British officer becoming a psychiatric casualty was half that of the men).

Many observers feel that the lower incidence of psychiatric casualties among officers is due to their greater sense of responsibility or the fact that they are highly visible, with greater social stigma associated with breakdown. Undoubtedly the officer has a greater understanding than his men of what is going on and his place and importance in it. And officers get more recognition and psychological support from military institutions, such as uniforms, awards, and decorations.

These factors are probably all part of the equation, but the officer also has a far smaller burden of individual responsibility for killing on the battlefield. The key difference is that he doesn't have to do it personally.

A Fresh Look at the Reign of Fear

It would appear that, at least in the realm of psychiatric casualty causation, fear does *not* reign supreme on the battlefield. The effect of fear should never be underestimated, but it is clearly not the only, or even the major, factor responsible for psychiatric casualties on the battlefield.

The deaths, destruction, and fear experienced by those who survived months of bombing in England and Germany did not produce anywhere near the psychological breakdown suffered by soldiers in combat. The Rand Corporation studies outlined earlier make it clear that just as the distance involved helped the pilots and bombardiers to partially deny that they were personally killing thousands of innocent civilians, so too did the circumstances and distances involved buffer civilian and POW bombing victims, sailors, and patrols behind enemy lines from the Wind of Hate (which we will examine shortly) and permit them to successfully deny that anyone was personally trying to kill them. They simply didn't take it personally. Indeed, one might think that the civilians' and the POWs' inability to fight back would be a source of stress, but just the opposite appears to be true: most bomber crews and artillery crews would eventually sustain psychiatric casualties, while the noncombatants they attacked generally did not.

During World War II, bomber crews generally had the highest casualty rates of any combatants among the Allied forces. In the British Bomber Command, out of every one hundred men only twenty-four survived. Such figures, faced day after day without respite, appear to have been sufficient to result in the tremendous psychiatric casualty rates suffered by these crews. This fear was intermingled with a comparatively small quantity of horror and some burden of responsibility — one Vietnam-era bomber pilot claimed it was the killing of civilians, even at a distance, that eventually drove him to drink and troubled him the most in subsequent years. But fear may have been the predominant psychological enemy in this particular circumstance. The point is that fear is only one of many factors, and it seldom, if ever, is the sole cause of psychiatric casualties.

The magnitude of the exhaustion and the horror suffered by combat veterans and victims of strategic bombing is generally comparable. The stress factors that soldiers experienced and bombing victims *did not* were the two-edged responsibility of (1) being expected to kill (the irreconcilable balancing of to kill and not to kill) and (2) the stress of looking their potential killers in the face (the Wind of Hate).

Chapter Three

The Weight of Exhaustion

The first quality of a soldier is constancy in enduring fatigue and hardship. Courage is only the second. Poverty, privation and want are the school of the good soldier.

— Napoleon

Exhaustion as Inoculation in Training

The impact of true physical exhaustion is impossible to communicate to those who have not experienced it. I remember sitting in the mud in a state of exhaustion, picking up small frogs from the surrounding swamp, swallowing them one by one, and rinsing them down with water from my canteen. I had not eaten or slept for five days. We were beginning week eight of the eight-week U.S. Army Ranger school, and my peers and I had endured this kind of physical deprivation for seven weeks. At this point swallowing live frogs seemed a very reasonable course of action. And although we were handpicked officers and sergeants in the finest possible condition upon beginning the course, by this time most of us had lost well over twenty pounds of body tissue.

Sunken cheeked and hollow eyed, we were in a state of total starvation-enhanced exhaustion that caused many of us to have repeated hallucinations. These were incredibly vivid dreams that we would experience while wide-awake. To those who experienced them, these hallucinations (which were usually about food) seemed to be real. We carried forty-pound rucksacks over the mountains of Georgia and Tennessee and through the swamps of Florida on endless tactical operations while constantly being assessed on our leadership ability. The mind teetered on the brink of madness, and anyone could drop out at any time simply by failing to perform or asking to quit. Only pride and determination kept us going. For weeks after graduation many of us awoke in panic and disorientation in the middle of the night.

Elite soldiers from all over the world participate in this remarkably effective initiation rite, and fewer than half pass. It is probably the only school in the U.S. Army about which there is no stigma for having failed. "At least," they say, "you had the guts to try." And the graduates of this school — and, to varying degrees, the U.S. Navy SEAL and Underwater Demolitions School, the U.S. Army Special Forces (Green Berets) and Airborne (paratrooper) courses, and U.S. Marine boot camp — are respected by soldiers around the world as individuals who can be trusted to maintain their cool in stressful situations.

The point of such remarkable exercises in self-flagellation is to introduce the combat leader to an intense degree of stress and thereby inoculate him against psychological trauma. United States Army lieutenant colonel Bob Harris explained how Ranger school had done this for him before going to Vietnam:

> It is worth noting that my experiences as a platoon leader convinced me absolutely of the value of Ranger training. While I didn't have occasion to use all of the techniques and skills I was taught, I did use many. More important was the knowledge I had gained of myself in Fort Benning, and in the north Georgia mountains and in the Florida swamps; the understanding that limits are mostly in the mind and can be overcome; the knowledge that I could keep going and be an effective leader in spite of fear, fatigue, and hunger.

Exhaustion in Combat

Even as we consider the sunken-eyed, frog-eating, emaciated, and exhausted soldier of Ranger school, we must understand that the combat exhaustion associated with *months* of *continuous* combat is something even worse, something that few soldiers have experienced outside of World War I, World War II, Korea, and some circumstances in Vietnam. Douglas MacArthur said of the soldier that "he plods and groans, sweats and toils, he growls and curses, and at the end he dies." The American soldier-cartoonist Bill Mauldin understood the mind-numbing fatigue of World War II combat and communicated it in his famous Willie and Joe cartoons. "There are millions," wrote Mauldin, "who have done a great and hard job, but there are only a few hundred thousand who have lived through misery, suffering and death for endless 168-hour weeks."

Psychologist F. C. Bartlett emphasized the psychological impact of physical exhaustion in combat. "In war," he wrote, "there is perhaps no general condition which is more likely to produce a large crop of nervous and mental disorders than a state of prolonged and great fatigue." The four factors of (1) physiological arousal caused by the stress of existing in what is commonly understood as a continual fight-or-flight-arousal condition, (2) cumulative loss of sleep, (3) the reduction in caloric intake, and (4) the toll of the elements — such as rain, cold, heat, and dark of night — assaulting the soldier all combine to form the "state of prolonged and great fatigue" that is the Weight of Exhaustion. Let us briefly review these factors.

Physiological Exhaustion

And then a shell lands behind us, and another over to the side, and by this time we're scurrying and the sarge and I and another guy wind up behind a wall. The sergeant said it was an .88 and then he said, "S—— and s—— some more."

I asked him if he was hit and he sort of smiled and said no, he had just pissed his pants. He always pissed them, he said, just when things started and then he was okay. He wasn't making any apologies either, and then I realized something wasn't quite right with me, either. There was something warm down there and it seemed to be running down my leg. I felt, and it wasn't blood. It was piss.

I told the sarge, I said, "Sarge, I've pissed too," or something
like that and he grinned and said, "Welcome to the war."

— World War II veteran
   quoted in Barry Broadfoot, *Six Year War, 1939–1945*

To understand the intensity of the body's physiological response
to the stress of combat we must understand the mobilization of
resources caused by the body's sympathetic nervous system, and
then we must understand the impact of the body's parasympathetic
backlash response.

The sympathetic nervous system mobilizes and directs the body's
energy resources for action. The parasympathetic system is responsible for the body's digestive and recuperative processes.

Usually these two systems sustain a general balance between
their demands upon the body's resources, but during extremely
stressful circumstances the fight-or-flight response kicks in and
the sympathetic nervous system mobilizes *all* available energy for
survival. In combat this very often results in nonessential activities
such as digestion, bladder control, and sphincter control being
completely shut down. This process is so intense that soldiers very
often suffer stress diarrhea, and it is not at all uncommon for them
to urinate and defecate in their pants as the body literally "blows
its ballast" in an attempt to provide all the energy resources required
to ensure its survival.

A soldier must pay a physiological price for an energizing process
this intense. The price that the body pays is an equally powerful
backlash when the neglected demands of the parasympathetic system return. This parasympathetic backlash occurs as soon as the
danger and the excitement is over, and it takes the form of an
incredibly powerful weariness and sleepiness on the part of the
soldier.

Napoleon stated that the moment of greatest danger was the
instant immediately after victory, and in saying so he demonstrated
a remarkable understanding of how soldiers become physiologically
and psychologically incapacitated by the parasympathetic backlash
that occurs as soon as the momentum of the attack has halted and
the soldier briefly believes himself to be safe. During this period
of vulnerability a counterattack by fresh troops can have an effect

completely out of proportion to the number of troops attacking.

It is basically for this reason that the maintenance of fresh reserves has always been essential in combat, with battles often revolving around which side can hold out and deploy their reserves last. Clausewitz cautioned that these reserves should always be maintained out of sight of the battle. These same basic psychophysiological principles explain why successful military leaders have historically maintained the momentum of a successful attack. Pursuing and maintaining contact with a defeated enemy are vital in order to completely destroy the enemy (the vast majority of the killing in historical battles occurred during the pursuit when the enemy had turned his back), but it is also valuable to maintain contact with the enemy as long as possible in order to delay that inevitable pause in the battle that will result in the culmination point during which pursuing forces will slip into parasympathetic backlash and become vulnerable to a counterattack. Again, an unblown reserve ready to complete this pursuit is of great value in ensuring that this most destructive phase of the battle is effectively executed.

In continuous combat the soldier roller-coasters through seemingly endless surges of adrenaline and subsequent backlashes, and the body's natural, useful, and appropriate response to danger ultimately becomes extremely counterproductive. Unable to flee, and unable to overcome the danger through a brief burst of fighting, posturing, or submission, the bodies of modern soldiers quickly exhaust their capacity to energize and they slide into a state of profound physical and emotional exhaustion of such a magnitude and dimension that it appears to be almost impossible to communicate it to those who have not experienced it. A soldier in this state will inevitably collapse from nervous exhaustion — the body simply will burn out.

Lack of Sleep

I have already mentioned the hallucinations and zombielike states commonly experienced due to lack of sleep in intensive training, such as in the U.S. Army Ranger school. In combat it is often far worse. Holmes's research indicates that tremendous periods of sleep loss are the norm in combat. In one study it was determined that of American soldiers in Italy in 1944, 31 percent averaged

fewer than four hours' sleep a night, and another 54 percent
averaged fewer than six. Those individuals with the lower amounts
of sleep were most likely to have come from the frontline units,
which is also where the highest incidence of psychological casualties
occurred.

Lack of Food

Lack of nourishment resulting from bad, cold food, and a loss of
appetite caused by fatigue, can have a singularly devastating impact
on combat effectiveness. "I would say without hesitation," wrote
the British general Bernard Fergusson, "that lack of food constitutes
the single biggest assault upon morale. . . . Apart from its purely
chemical effects upon the body, it has woeful effects upon the
mind."

In numerous historical incidents lack of food was believed to
have been the single most important military factor. The Army
Historical Series volume on logistics affirms that "lack of food
probably more than any other factor forced the end of resistance
on Bataan" early in World War II, and the Germans at Stalingrad
were "literally starving at the time of their capitulation."

Impact of the Elements

Soldiering, by its very nature, involves facing the forces of nature
as well as the forces of the foe. Limited to those few amenities
that they can carry on their backs *after* room has been made for
the equipment of their profession, most soldiers are more or less
at the mercy of the elements. Thus endless cold, rain, heat, and
suffering become the soldier's lot.

Lord Moran believed that "armies wilt when exposed to the
elements." For him the worst was "the harsh violence of winter,"
which can "find a flaw even in picked men." And the constant
torment of the rain led Henri Barbusse to write that "dampness
rusts men like rifles, more slowly but more deeply."

Another potential enemy of the soldier is the sensory deprivation
of darkness, which can conspire with the cold and the rain to
produce a degree of misery such as the protected shall never
know. For Simon Murry, a French veteran of Algeria, coldness
was "enemy number one." For him, "the misery of crawling into

a sleeping-bag which is wet and sodden in total blackness on top of a mountain with the rain pissing down" was misery "without parallel."

Heat, too, can exhaust and kill; and rats, lice, mosquitoes, and other living elements of nature take their turns at exacting both a physical and a psychological toll upon the soldier, but the most deadly of all these natural enemies that the soldier must face is probably disease. In every American war up until World War II more soldiers died from disease than from enemy action.

And so we see that lack of sleep, lack of food, the impact of the elements, and emotional exhaustion caused by constant fight-or-flight-response activation all conspire to contribute to the soldier's exhaustion. This is a burden that, if not capable of causing psychiatric casualties in and of itself, needs to be taken into consideration as being capable of predisposing the soldier's psyche toward seeking escape from the deprivations that surround him.

Chapter Four

The Mud of Guilt and Horror

I am sick and tired of war. It's glory is all moonshine. It is only those who have neither fired a shot nor heard the shrieks and groans of the wounded who cry aloud for blood, for vengeance, for desolation. War is hell.

— William Tecumseh Sherman

The Impact of the Senses

Beyond fear and exhaustion is a sea of horror that surrounds the soldier and assails his every sense.

Hear the pitiful screams of the wounded and dying. *Smell* the butcher-house smells of feces, blood, burned flesh, and rotting decay, which combine into the awful stench of death. *Feel* the shudder of the ground as the very earth groans at the abuse of artillery and explosives, and *feel* the last shiver of life and the flow of warm blood as friends die in your arms. *Taste* the salt of blood and tears as you hold a dear friend in mutual grieving, and you do not know or care if it is the salt of your tears or his. And *see* what hath been wrought:

You tripped over strings of viscera fifteen feet long, over bodies which had been cut in half at the waist. Legs and arms, and heads bearing only necks, lay fifty feet from the closest torsos. As night fell the beachhead reeked with the stench of burning flesh.

— William Manchester,
  Goodbye, Darkness

The Impact of Memory and the Role of Guilt

Strangely, such horrifying memories seem to have a much more profound effect on the combatant — the participant in battle — than the noncombatant, the correspondent, civilian, POW, or other passive observer of the battle zone. The combat soldier appears to feel a deep sense of responsibility and accountability for what he sees around him. It is as though every enemy dead is a human being he has killed, and every friendly dead is a comrade for whom he was responsible. With every effort to reconcile these two responsibilities, more guilt is added to the horror that surrounds the soldier.

Richard Holmes speaks of "a brave and distinguished" old veteran who, after nearly seventy years, "wept softly . . . as he described a popular officer who had been literally disemboweled by a shell fragment." Often you can keep these things out of your mind when you are young and active, but they come back to haunt your nights in your old age. "We thought we had managed all right," he told Holmes, "kept the awful things out of our minds, but now I'm an old man and they come out from where I hid them. Every night."

And yet, all of this, this horror, is just *one* of the many factors among those that conspire to drive the soldier from the painful field.

Chapter Five

The Wind of Hate

Hate and Trauma in Our Daily Lives

When we consider the matter, are we truly surprised to discover that it is *not* danger that causes psychiatric stress? And is the existence of an intense resistance to participating in aggressive situations really so unexpected?

To a large extent our society — particularly our young men — actively and vicariously pursues physical danger. Through roller coasters, action and horror movies, drugs, rock climbing, white-water rafting, scuba diving, parachuting, hunting, contact sports, and a hundred other methods, our society enjoys danger. To be sure, danger in excess grows old fast, particularly when we feel that we have lost control of it. And the potential for death and injury is an important ingredient in the complex mixture that makes combat so stressful, but it is *not* the major cause of stress in either our daily lives or in combat.

But facing aggression and hatred in our fellow citizens is an experience of an entirely different magnitude. All of us have had to face hostile aggression. On the playground as children, in the impoliteness of strangers, in the malicious gossip and comments of acquaintances, and in the animosity of peers and superiors in the workplace. In all of these instances everyone has known hostility and the stress it can cause. Most avoid confrontations at all costs, and to work ourselves up to an aggressive verbal action — let alone a physical confrontation — is extremely difficult.

Simply confronting the boss about a promotion or a raise is one of the most stressful and upsetting things most people can ever bring themselves to do, and many never even get that far. Facing down the school bully or confronting a hostile acquaintance is something that most will avoid at all costs. Many medical authorities believe that it is the constant hostility and lack of acceptance that they must face — and the resulting stress — that are responsible for the dramatic rate of high blood pressure in African Americans.

The *Diagnostic and Statistical Manual of Mental Disorders* (*DSM-III-R*), the bible of psychology, states that in post-traumatic stress disorders "the disorder is apparently more severe and longer lasting when the stressor is of human design." We want desperately to be liked, loved, and in control of our lives; and intentional, overt, *human* hostility and aggression — more than anything else in life — assaults our self-image, our sense of control, our sense of the world as a meaningful and comprehensible place, and, ultimately, our mental and physical health.

The ultimate fear and horror in most modern lives is to be raped or beaten, to be physically degraded in front of our loved ones, to have our family harmed and the sanctity of our homes invaded by aggressive and hateful intruders. Death and debilitation by disease or accident are statistically far more likely to occur than death and debilitation by malicious action, but the statistics do not calm our basically irrational fears. It is not fear of death and injury from disease or accident but rather acts of personal depredation and domination by our fellow human beings that strike terror and loathing in our hearts.

In rape the psychological harm usually far exceeds the physical injury. The trauma of rape, like that of combat, involves minimal fear of death or injury; far more damaging is the impotence, shock, and horror in being so hated and despised as to be debased and abused by a fellow human being.

The average citizen resists engaging in aggressive and assertive activities and dreads facing the irrational aggression and hatred of others. The soldier in combat is no different: he resists the powerful obligation and coercion to engage in aggressive and assertive actions on the battlefield, and he dreads facing the irrational aggression and hostility embodied in the enemy.

Indeed, history is full of tales of soldiers who have committed suicide or inflicted terrible wounds upon themselves to avoid combat. It isn't fear of death that motivates these men to kill themselves. Like many of their civilian counterparts who commit suicide, these men would rather die or mutilate themselves than face the aggression and hostility of a very hostile world.

The Impact of Hate in Nazi Death Camps

An abnormal reaction to an abnormal situation is normal behavior.

— Victor Frankl, Nazi concentration-camp survivor

Perhaps a deeper understanding of the power of the buffeting of hate can be obtained from a study of survivors of Nazi concentration camps. Even the briefest review of available literature reveals that these individuals did suffer from great, lifelong, psychological damage as a result of their experiences in concentration camps, even though they did not have any obligation or ability to kill their tormentors.[4] Among bombing victims, POWs under artillery fire, sailors in naval combat, and soldiers on patrols behind enemy lines we do not find any large-scale incidence of psychiatric casualties, but in such places as Dachau and Auschwitz they were the rule rather than the exception.

This is one historical circumstance in which noncombatants *did* suffer a horrifyingly high incidence of psychiatric casualties and post-traumatic stress. Physical exhaustion is not the only or even the primary factor involved here. And neither is the horror of the death and destruction around them principally responsible for the psychic shock of this situation. The distinguishing characteristic here, as opposed to numerous other noncombatant circumstances marked by an absence of psychiatric casualties, is that those in concentration camps had to face aggression and death on a highly personal, face-to-face basis. Nazi Germany placed a remarkable concentration of aggressive psychopaths in charge of these camps, and the lives of victims of these camps were completely dominated by the personalities of these terrifyingly brutal individuals.

Dyer tells us that concentration camps were staffed, whenever possible, with "both male and female thugs and sadists." Unlike the victims of aerial bombing, the victims of these camps had to look their sadistic killers in the face and know that another human being denied their humanity and hated them enough to personally slaughter them, their families, and their race as though they were nothing more than animals.

During strategic bombing the pilots and bombardiers were protected by distance and could deny to themselves that they were attempting to kill any specific individual. In the same way, civilian bombing victims were protected by distance, and they could deny that anyone was personally trying to kill them. And among the POWs who were subject to bombing (as we saw earlier) the bombs were not personal, and the guards were no threat to the POWs as long as they played by the rules. But in the death camps it was starkly, horribly personal. Victims of this horror had to look the darkest, most loathsome depths of human hatred in the eye. There was no room for denial, and the only escape was more madness.

It is here, in this sordid account of man's inhumanity to man, that we see the flip side of the aversion to killing in combat. Not only does the average soldier's psyche resist killing and the obligation to kill, but he is equally horrified by the inescapable fact that someone hates him and denies his humanity enough to kill him.

The soldier's response to the overtly hostile actions of the enemy is usually one of profound shock, surprise, and outrage. Countless veterans echo novelist and Vietnam veteran Phillip Caputo's first reaction to enemy fire in Vietnam. "Why does he want to kill *me?*" thought Caputo. "What did I ever do to *him?*"

One Vietnam-era pilot told me that he was largely undisturbed by the impersonal flak around him, but he was memorably disturbed when he once focused on one lone enemy soldier "standing casually next to his hooch [hut], carefully firing up at me." It was one of the rare times he had ever been able to distinguish an individual enemy soldier, and his immediate response was an indignant "What did I ever do to him?" Then came a hurt and angry "I do not like you Sam I Am, I do not like you one damned bit." And he then directed all the resources and assets of his aircraft to kill this one individual and "blow up his little hooch."

An Application: Attrition Versus Maneuver Warfare

In the field of strategy and tactics the impact and influence of the Wind of Hate have been widely overlooked. Numerous tacticians and strategists advocate attrition warfare theories, in which the will of enemy forces is destroyed through the application of long-range artillery and bombing. The advocates of such theories persist in such beliefs even in the face of evidence, such as the post–World War II U.S. Strategic Bombing Survey, which, in the words of Paul Fussell, ascertained that "German military and industrial production seemed to increase — just like civilian determination not to surrender — the more bombs were dropped." Psychologically, aerial and artillery bombardments are effective, but only in the front lines when they are combined with the Wind of Hate, as manifested in the threat of the personal infantry attack that usually follows such bombardments.

This is why there were mass psychiatric casualties following World War I artillery bombardments, but World War II's mass bombings of cities were surprisingly counterproductive in breaking the enemy's will. Such bombardments without an accompanying close-range assault, or at least the threat of such an assault, are ineffective and may even serve no other purpose than to stiffen the will and resolve of the enemy!

Today a few pioneering authors such as William Lind and Robert Leonhard have focused their research and writings on the field of maneuver warfare, in which they attempt to refute the advocates of attrition warfare and understand the process of destroying the enemy's *will* to fight rather than his *ability* to fight. What maneuver warfare advocates have discovered is that over and over in history, civilians and soldiers have withstood the *actuality* of fear, horror, death, and destruction during artillery bombardments and aerial bombardments without losing their will to fight, while the mere *threat* of invasion and close-up interpersonal aggression has consistently turned whole populations into refugees fleeing in panic.

This is why putting unfriendly troop units in the enemy's rear is infinitely more important and effective than even the most comprehensive bombardments in his rear or attrition along his front. We saw this in the Korean War, in which, during the early years of the war, the rate of psychiatric casualties was almost seven times higher than the average rate for World War II. Only after the war settled down, lines stabilized, and the threat of having enemy in the rear areas decreased, did the average rate go down to slightly less than that of World War II. The *potential* of close-up, inescapable, *inter*personal hatred and aggression is more effective and has greater impact on the morale of the soldier than the *presence* of inescapable, *im*personal death and destruction.

Hate and Psychological Inoculation

Martin Seligman developed the concept of inoculation from stress from his famous studies of learning in dogs. He put dogs in a cage that had an electric shock pass through the floor at random intervals. Initially the dogs would jump, yelp, and scratch pitifully in their attempts to escape the shocks, but after a time they would fall into a depressed, hopeless state of apathy and inactivity that Seligman termed "learned helplessness." After falling into a state of learned helplessness the dogs would not avoid the shocks even when provided with an obvious escape route.

Other dogs were given a means of escape after receiving some shocks but before falling into learned helplessness. These dogs learned that they could and would eventually escape from the shocks, and after only one such escape they became inoculated against learned helplessness. Even after long periods of random, inescapable shocks these inoculated dogs would escape when finally provided with a means to do so.

This is all a very interesting theoretical concept, but what is important to us is to understand that this process of inoculation is exactly what occurs in boot camps and in every other military school worthy of its name. When raw recruits are faced with seemingly sadistic abuse and hardship (which they "escape" through weekend passes and, ultimately, graduation) they are — among many other things — being inoculated against the stresses of combat.

Combining an understanding of (a) those factors that cause combat trauma with (b) an understanding of the inoculation process permits us to understand that in most of these military schools the inoculation is specifically oriented toward hate.

The drill sergeant who screams into the face of a recruit is manifesting overt interpersonal hostility. Another effective means of inoculating a trainee against the Wind of Hate can be seen in U.S. Army and USMC pugil-stick training during boot camp or at the U.S. Military Academy and the British Airborne Brigade, where boxing matches are a traditional part of the training and initiation process. When in the face of all of this manufactured contempt and overt physical hostility the recruit overcomes the situation to graduate with honor and pride, he realizes at both conscious and unconscious levels that he can overcome such overt interpersonal hostility. *He has become partially inoculated against hate.*

I do not believe that military organizations have truly understood the nature of the Wind of Hate, or of the resultant need for this kind of inoculation. It is only since Seligman's research that we have really had the foundation for a clinical understanding of these processes. However, through thousands of years of institutional memory and the harshest kind of survival-of-the-fittest evolution, this kind of inoculation has manifested itself in the traditions of the finest and most aggressive fighting units of many nations. By understanding the role of hate on the battlefield, we now can finally and truly understand the military value of what armies have done for so long and some of the processes by which they have enabled the soldier to physically and psychically survive on the battlefield.

Chapter Six

The Well of Fortitude

Stay with me, God. The night is dark.
The night is cold: my little spark
of courage dies. The night is long;
be with me, God, and make me strong.

— Junius, Vietnam veteran

Many authorities speak and write of emotional stamina on the battlefield as a finite resource. I have termed this the Well of Fortitude. Faced with the soldier's encounters with horror, guilt, fear, exhaustion, and hate, each man draws steadily from his own private reservoir of inner strength and fortitude until finally the well runs dry. And then he becomes just another statistic. I believe that this metaphor of the well is an excellent one for understanding why at least 98 percent of all soldiers in close combat will ultimately become psychiatric casualties.

Fortitude and Individuals

George Keenan tells us that "heroism, the Caucasian mountaineers say, is endurance for one moment more." In the trenches of World War I Lord Moran learned that courage "is not a chance gift of nature like aptitude . . . it is willpower that can be spent — and when it is used up — men are finished. 'Natural courage' does exist; but it is really fearlessness . . . as opposed to the courage of control."

In sustained combat this process of emotional bankruptcy is seen in 98 percent of all soldiers who survive physically. Lord Moran presented the case of Sergeant Taylor, who "was wounded and came back unchanged; he seemed proof against the accidents of his life, he stood in the Company like a rock; men were swept up to him and eddied round him for a little time and ebbed away again, but he remained." He finally suffered a near miss from an artillery shell. When Sergeant Taylor went to the well he found it to be empty, and this indomitable rock shattered: completely and catastrophically.

Fortitude and Depression

Holmes has gathered a list of the symptoms of men suffering from combat exhaustion. For these individuals the demands of combat have caused too great a drain on their own personal stocks of fortitude, resulting in conditions such as

> a general slowing down of mental processes and apathy, as far as they were concerned the situation was one of absolute hopeless-ness. . . . The influence and reassurance of understanding officers and NCOs failed to arouse these soldiers from their hopeless-ness. . . . The soldier was slow-witted. . . . Memory defects became so extreme that he could not be counted on to relay a verbal order. . . . He could then best be described as one leading a vegeta-tive existence. . . . He remained almost constantly in or near his slit trench, and during acute actions took no part, trembling constantly.

This is a vivid description of severe depression. Exhaustion, mem-ory defects, apathy, hopelessness, and all the rest of these are precise descriptions of clinical depression that can be taken straight from the *DSM-III-R*. This is why "fortitude," rather than "courage," is the proper word to describe what is occurring here. It is not just a reaction to fear, but rather a reaction to a host of stressors that suck the will and life out of a man and leave him clinically depressed. The opposite of courage is cowardice, but the opposite of fortitude is exhaustion. When the soldier's well is dry, his very soul is dry, and, in Lord Moran's words, "he had gazed upon the face of death too long until exhaustion had dried him up making him so much tinder, which a chance spark of fear might set alight."

Fortitude from Other Men's Wells, and Replenishment Through Victory

> A brave captain is as a root, out of which, as branches, the courage of his soldiers doth spring.
>
> — Sir Philip Sidney

One key characteristic of a great military leader is an ability to draw from the tremendous depths of fortitude within his own well, and in doing so he is fortifying his own men by permitting them to draw from his well. Many writers have recorded this process as being at work in the combat situations they observed. Lord Moran noted that "a few men had the stuff of leadership in them, they were like rafts to which all the rest of humanity clung for support and hope."

Victory and success in battle also replenish individual and collective wells. Moran tells us that if a soldier is always using up his capital he may from time to time add to it. "There is," says Moran, "a paying in as well as a paying out." He gives as an example General Alexander, who took command of the British forces in North Africa in World War II. When Alexander took command, the men often did not bother to salute an officer, but after their victory of El Alamein all that came to an end, and their self-respect came back. Moran concluded that "achievement is a sharp tonic to morale. . . . But in the main, time is against the soldier."

Fortitude and Units

Depletion of the finite resource of fortitude can be seen in entire units as well as individuals. The fortitude of a unit is no more than the aggregate of the fortitude of its members. And when the individuals are drained to a dry husk, the whole is nothing more than an aggregate of exhausted men.

In Normandy during World War II Field Marshal Montgomery had two classes of divisions. Some were veterans of North Africa, and others were green units, without previous combat experience. Montgomery initially tended to rely on his veteran units (particularly during the disastrous Operation Goodwood), but these units performed poorly, while his green units performed well. In this instance, failing to understand the influence of emotional exhaustion and the Well of Fortitude had a significant negative impact on the Allied effort in World War II.

In the same way, *all* of the aspects of combat trauma impact profoundly upon the individual's contribution to the battlefield and upon the contribution of that aggregate of individuals that we call military units. If we understand these concepts we begin to master the full spectrum of the responses of men in combat. If we ignore them we do so to the detriment of the individual, and to the detriment of that aggregate of individuals that we call our society, our nation, our way of life, and our world. Lord Moran concluded that such ignorance of the ultimate cost of depleting the Well of Fortitude of England's youth in World War I caused that nation "to dissipate like a spend thrift not only the lives but the moral heritage of the youth of England."

Chapter Seven

The Burden of Killing

Alfred de Vigny went to the heart of the military experience when he observed that the soldier is both victim and executioner. Not only does he run the risk of being killed and wounded himself, but he also kills and wounds others.

— John Keegan and Richard Holmes
  Soldiers

The resistance to the close-range killing of one's own species is so great that it is often sufficient to overcome the cumulative influences of the instinct for self-protection, the coercive forces of leadership, the expectancy of peers, and the obligation to preserve the lives of comrades.

The soldier in combat is trapped within this tragic Catch-22. If he overcomes his resistance to killing and kills an enemy soldier in close combat, he will be forever burdened with blood guilt, and if he elects not to kill, then the blood guilt of his fallen comrades and the shame of his profession, nation, and cause lie upon him. He is damned if he does, and damned if he doesn't.

To Kill, and the Guilt Thereof

William Manchester, author and U.S. Marine veteran of World War II, felt remorse and shame after his close-range personal killing of a Japanese soldier. "I can remember," he wrote, "whispering foolishly, 'I'm sorry' and then just throwing up . . . I threw up all over myself. It was a betrayal of what I'd been taught since a child." Other combat veterans tell of the emotional responses associated with a close-range kill that echo Manchester's horror.

The media's depiction of violence tries to tell us that men can easily throw off the moral inhibitions of a lifetime — and whatever other instinctive restraint exists — and kill casually and guiltlessly in combat. The men who have killed, and who will talk about it, tell a different tale. A few of these quotes, which are drawn from Keegan and Holmes, can be found elsewhere in this study, but here they represent the distilled essence of the soldier's emotional response to killing:

Killing is the worst thing that one man can do to another man . . . it's the last thing that should happen anywhere.

— Israeli lieutenant

I reproached myself as a destroyer. An indescribable uneasiness came over me, I felt almost like a criminal.

— Napoleonic-era British soldier

This was the first time I had killed anybody and when things quieted down I went and looked at a German I knew I had shot. I remember thinking that he looked old enough to have a family and I felt very sorry.

— British World War I veteran after his first kill

It didn't hit me all that much then, but when I think of it now — I slaughtered those people. I murdered them.

— German World War II veteran

And I froze, 'cos it was a boy, I would say between the ages of twelve and fourteen. When he turned at me and looked, all of a sudden he turned his whole body and pointed his automatic weapon at me, I just opened up, fired the whole twenty rounds right at the kid, and he just laid there. I dropped my weapon and cried.

— U.S. Special Forces officer and Vietnam veteran

I fired again and somehow got him in the head. There was so much blood . . . I vomited, until the rest of the boys came up.

— Israeli Six-Day War veteran

So this new Peugeot comes towards us, and we shoot. And there was a family there — three children. And I cried, but I couldn't take the chance. . . . Children, father, mother. All the family was killed, but we couldn't take the chance.

— Israeli Lebanon Incursion veteran

The magnitude of the trauma associated with killing became particularly apparent to me in an interview with Paul, a VFW post commander and sergeant of the 101st Airborne at Bastogne in World War II. He talked freely about his experiences and about comrades who had been killed, but when I asked him about his own kills he stated that usually you couldn't be sure who it was that did the killing. Then tears welled up in Paul's eyes, and after a long pause he said, "But the one time I was sure . . ." and then his sentence was stopped by a little sob, and pain racked the face of this old gentleman. "It still hurts, after all these years?" I asked in wonder. "Yes," he said, "after all these years." And he would not speak of it again.

The next day he told me, "You know, Captain, the questions you're asking, you must be very careful not to hurt anyone with these questions. Not me, you know, I can take it, but some of these young guys are still hurting very badly. These guys don't need to be hurt anymore." These memories were the scabs of terrible, hidden wounds in the minds of these kind and gentle men.

Not to Kill, and the Guilt Thereof

With very few exceptions, everyone associated with killing in combat reaps a bitter harvest of guilt.

The Soldier's Guilt . . .

Numerous studies have concluded that men in combat are usually motivated to fight *not* by ideology or hate or fear, but by group pressures and processes involving (1) regard for their comrades,

(2) respect for their leaders, (3) concern for their own reputation with both, and (4) an urge to contribute to the success of the group.[5]

Repeatedly we see combat veterans describe the powerful bonds that men forge in combat as stronger than those of husband and wife. John Early, a Vietnam veteran and an ex–Rhodesian mercenary, described it to Dyer this way:

> This is going to sound really strange, but there's a love relationship that is nurtured in combat because the man next to you — you're depending on him for the most important thing you have, your life, and if he lets you down you're either maimed or killed. If you make a mistake the same thing happens to him, so the bond of trust has to be extremely close, and I'd say this bond is stronger than almost anything, with the exception of parent and child. It's a hell of a lot stronger than man and wife — your life is in his hands, you trust that person with the most valuable thing you have.

This bonding is so intense that it is fear of failing these comrades that preoccupies most combatants. Countless sociological and psychological studies, the personal narratives of numerous veterans, and the interviews I have conducted clearly indicate the strength of the soldier's concern for failing his buddies. The guilt and trauma associated with failing to fully support men who are bonded with friendship and camaraderie on this magnitude is profoundly intense. Yet every soldier and every leader feels this guilt to one degree or another. For those who know that they have not fired while their friends died around them, the guilt is traumatic.

. . . And the Leader's Guilt

The responsibilities of a combat leader represent a remarkable paradox. To be truly good at what he does, he must love his men and be bonded to them with powerful links of mutual responsibility and affection. And then he must ultimately be willing to give the orders that may kill them.

To a significant degree, the social barrier between officer and enlisted man, and between sergeant and private, exists to enable the superior to send his men into mortal danger and to shield him

from the inevitable guilt associated with their deaths. For even the
best leaders make some mistakes that will weigh forever upon their
consciences. Just as any good coach can analyze his conduct of
even a winning game and see where he could have done better,
so does every good combat leader think, at some level, that if he
had just done something different these men — these men he
loved like sons and brothers — might not have died.

It is extraordinarily difficult to get these leaders to reminisce
along these lines:

> Now tactically I had done everything the way it was supposed to
> be done, but we lost some soldiers. There was no other way. We
> could not go around that field; we had to go across it. So did I
> make a mistake? I don't know. Would I have done it differently
> [another time]? I don't think I would have, because that's the way
> I was trained. Did we lose less soldiers by my doing it that way?
> That's a question that'll never be answered.
>
> — Major Robert Ooley, Vietnam veteran
>   quoted in Gwynne Dyer, *War*

This is a deadly, dangerous line of thought for leaders, and the
honors and decorations that are traditionally heaped upon military
leaders at all levels are vitally important for their mental health
in the years that follow. These decorations, medals, mentions in
dispatches, and other forms of recognition represent a powerful
affirmation from the leader's society, telling him that he did well,
he did the right thing, and no one blames him for the lives lost
in doing his duty.

Denial and the Burden of Killing

Balancing the obligation to kill with the resulting toll of guilt
forms a significant cause of psychiatric casualties on the battlefield.
Philosopher-psychologist Peter Marin speaks of the soldier's lesson
in responsibility and guilt. What the soldier knows as a result of
war is that "the dead remain dead, the maimed are forever maimed,
and there is no way to deny one's responsibility or culpability, for
those mistakes are written, forever and as if in fire, in others' flesh."

Ultimately there may be no way to deny one's responsibility or culpability for mistakes written "forever and as if in fire, in others' flesh," but combat is a great furnace fed by the small flickering flames of attempts at denial. The burden of killing is so great that most men try not to admit that they have killed. They deny it to others, and they try to deny it to themselves. Dinter quotes a hardened veteran who, upon being asked about killing, stated emphatically that

> Most of the killing you do in modern war is impersonal. A thing few people realize is that you hardly ever see a German. Very few men — even in the infantry — actually have the experience of aiming a weapon at a German and seeing the man fall.

Even the language of men at war is full of denial of the enormity of what they have done. Most soldiers do not "kill," instead the enemy was knocked over, wasted, greased, taken out, and mopped up. The enemy is hosed, zapped, probed, and fired on. The enemy's humanity is denied, and he becomes a strange beast called a Kraut, Jap, Reb, Yank, dink, slant, or slope. Even the weapons of war receive benign names — Puff the Magic Dragon, Walleye, TOW, Fat Boy, and Thin Man — and the killing weapon of the individual soldier becomes a piece or a hog, and a bullet becomes a round.

Our enemies do the same thing. Matt Brennan tells of Con, a Vietnamese scout assigned to his platoon. This individual had

> been a loyal Viet Cong until a North Vietnamese squad made a mistake and killed his wife and children. Now he loved to run ahead of the Americans, hunting for [North Vietnamese soldiers]. . . . He called the Communists gooks, just as we did, and one night I asked him why.
>
> "Con, do you think it's right to call the VC gooks and dinks?"
>
> He shrugged. "It makes no difference to me. Everything has a name. Do you think the Americans are the only ones who do that? . . . My company in the jungle . . . called you Big Hairy Monkeys. We kill monkeys, and" — he hesitated for an instant — "we eat them."

The dead soldier takes his misery with him, but the man who killed him must forever live and die with him. The lesson becomes increasingly clear: Killing is what war is all about, and killing in combat, by its very nature, causes deep wounds of pain and guilt. The language of war helps us to deny what war is really about, and in doing so it makes war more palatable.

Chapter Eight

The Blind Men and the Elephant

The man who ranges in No Man's Land
Is dogged by shadows on either hand[6]

— James H. Knight-Adkin
  "No Man's Land"

A Host of Observers and a Multitude of Answers

As we have examined each of the components and subcomponents of psychiatric casualty causation, we have consistently found authorities who would claim that their perspective of the problem represents the major or primary cause of stress in battle. Many have held that fear of death and injury was the primary cause of psychiatric casualties. Bartlett feels that "there is perhaps no general condition which is more likely to produce a large crop of nervous and mental disorders than a state of prolonged and great fatigue." General Fergusson states that "lack of food constitutes the single biggest assault upon morale." And Murry holds that "coldness is enemy number one," while Gabriel makes a powerful argument for emotional exhaustion caused by extended periods of autonomic fight-or-flight activation. Holmes, on the other hand, spends a chapter of his book convincing us of the horror of battle, and he claims that "seeing friends killed, or, almost worse, being unable to help them when wounded, leaves enduring scars." In addition to these more obvious factors of fear, exhaustion, and horror, I have added the less obvious but vitally important factors represented by the Wind of Hate and the Burden of Killing.

Like the blind men of the proverb, each individual feels a piece of the elephant, and the enormity of what he has found is overwhelming enough to convince each blindly groping observer that he has found the essence of the beast. But the whole beast is far more enormous and vastly more terrifying than society as a whole is prepared to believe.

It is a combination of factors that forms the beast, and it is a combination of stressors that is responsible for psychiatric casualties. For instance, when we see incidents of mass psychiatric casualties caused by the use of gas in World War I, we must ask ourselves what caused the soldiers' trauma. Were they traumatized by fear and horror at the gas and the unknown aspect of death and injury that it represented? Were they traumatized by the realization that someone would hate them enough to do this horrible thing to them? Or were they simply sane men unconsciously selecting insanity in order to escape from an insane situation, sane men taking advantage of a socially and morally acceptable opportunity to cast off the burden of responsibility in combat and escape from the mutual aggression of the battlefield? Obviously, a concise and complete answer would conclude that all of these factors, and more, are responsible for the soldier's dilemma.

Forces That Impede an Understanding of the Beast

A culture raised on Rambo, Indiana Jones, Luke Skywalker, and James Bond wants to believe that combat and killing can be done with impunity — that we can declare someone to be the enemy and that for cause and country the soldiers will cleanly and remorselessly wipe him from the face of the earth. In many ways it is simply too painful for society to address what it does when it sends its young men off to kill other young men in distant lands.

And what is too painful to remember, we simply choose to

forget. Glenn Gray spoke from personal experience in World War II when he wrote:

> Few of us can hold on to our real selves long enough to discover the real truths about ourselves and this whirling earth to which we cling. This is especially true of men in war. The great god Mars tries to blind us when we enter his realm, and when we leave he gives us a generous cup of the waters of Lethe to drink.

Even the field of psychology seems to be ill prepared to address the guilt caused by war and the attendant moral issues. Peter Marin condemns the "inadequacy" of our psychological terminology in describing the magnitude and reality of the "pain of human conscience." As a society, he says, we seem unable to deal with moral pain or guilt. Instead it is treated as a neurosis or a pathology, "something to escape rather than something to learn from, a disease rather than — as it may well be for the vets — an appropriate if painful response to the past." Marin goes on to note the same thing that I have in my studies, and that is that Veterans Administration psychologists are seldom willing to deal with problems of guilt; indeed, they often do not even raise the issue of what the soldier did in war. Instead they simply, as one VA psychologist put it to Marin, "treat the vet's difficulties as problems in adjustment."

Toward a Greater Understanding of the Heart of Darkness

During the American Civil War the soldier's first experience in combat was called "seeing the elephant." Today the existence of our species and of all life on this planet may depend on our not just seeing but knowing and controlling the beast called war — and the beast within each of us. No more important or vital subject for research exists, yet there is that within us that would turn away in disgust. And so the study of war has been largely left to the soldiers. But Clausewitz warned almost two hundred years ago that "it is to no purpose, it is even against one's better interest, to turn away from the consideration of the affair because the horror of its elements excites repugnance."

SECTION III

Killing and Physical Distance:
From a Distance, You Don't Look Anything
Like a Friend

Unless he is caught up in murderous ecstasy, destroying is easier
when done from a little remove. With every foot of distance there
is a corresponding decrease in reality. Imagination flags and fails
altogether when distances become too great. So it is that much of
the mindless cruelty of recent wars has been perpetrated by warriors
at a distance, who could not guess what havoc their powerful
weapons were occasioning.

— Glenn Gray
  The Warriors

The link between distance and ease of aggression is not a new
discovery. It has long been understood that there is a direct relationship between the empathic and physical proximity of the victim,
and the resultant difficulty and trauma of the kill. This concept
has fascinated and concerned soldiers, philosophers, anthropolo-
gists, and psychologists alike.

At the far end of the spectrum are bombing and artillery, which
are often used to illustrate the relative ease of long-range killing.

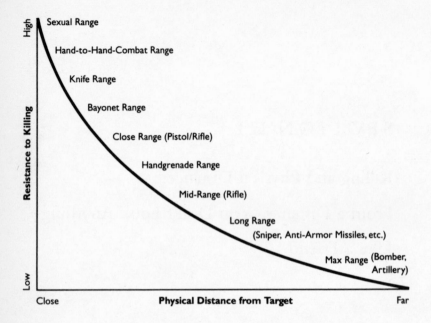

As we draw toward the near end of the spectrum, we begin to realize that the resistance to killing becomes increasingly more intense. This process culminates at the close end of the spectrum, when the resistance to bayoneting or stabbing becomes tremendously intense, and killing with the bare hands (through such common martial arts techniques as crushing the throat with a blow or gouging a thumb through the eye and into the brain) becomes almost unthinkable. Yet even this is not the end, as we will discover when we address the macabre region at the extreme end of the scale, where sex and killing intermingle.

In the same way that the distance relationship has been identified, so too have many observers identified the factor of emotional or empathic distance. But no one has yet attempted to dissect this factor in order to determine its components and the part they play in the killing process.

Chapter One

Distance:

A Qualitative Distinction in Death

The soldier-warrior could kill his collective enemy, which now included women and children, without ever seeing them. The cries of the wounded and dying went unheard by those who inflicted the pain. A man might slay hundreds and never see their blood flow. . . .

Less than a century after the Civil War ended, a single bomb, delivered miles above its target, would take the lives of more than 100,000 people, almost all civilians. The moral distance between this event and the tribal warrior facing a single opponent is far greater than even the thousands of years and transformations of culture that separate them. . . .

The combatants in modern warfare pitch bombs from 20,000 feet in the morning, causing untold suffering to a civilian population, and then eat hamburgers for dinner hundreds of miles away from the drop zone. The prehistoric warrior met his foe in a direct struggle of sinew, muscle, and spirit. If flesh was torn or bone broken he felt it give way under his hand. And though death was more rare than common (perhaps because he felt the pulse of life

and the nearness of death under his fingers), he also had to live his
days remembering the man's eyes whose skull he crushed.

— Richard Heckler
   In Search of the Warrior Spirit

Hamburg and Babylon: Examples at Extreme Ends of the Spectrum

On July 28, 1943, the British Royal Air Force firebombed Hamburg. Gwynne Dyer tells us that they used the standard mixture
of bombs, with

> huge numbers of four-pound incendiaries to start fires on roofs
> and thirty-pound ones to penetrate deeper inside buildings, together
> with four thousand-pound high explosive bombs to blow in doors
> and windows over wide areas and fill the streets with craters and
> rubble to hinder fire-fighting equipment. But on a hot, dry summer
> night with good visibility, the unusually tight concentration of the
> bombs in a densely populated working class district created a new
> phenomenon in history: a firestorm.
>
> Eventually it covered an area of about four square miles, with
> an air temperature at the center of eight hundred degrees Celsius
> and convection winds blowing inward with hurricane force. One
> survivor said the sound of the wind was "like the Devil laughing."
> . . . Practically all the apartment blocks in the firestorm area had
> underground shelters, but nobody who stayed in them survived;
> those who were not cremated died of carbon monoxide poisoning.
> But to venture into the streets was to risk being swept by the wind
> into the very heart of the firestorm.

Seventy thousand people died at Hamburg the night the air caught
fire. They were mostly women, children, and the elderly, since
those of soldiering age were generally at the front. They died
horrible deaths, burning and suffocating. If bomber crew members
had had to turn a flamethrower on each one of these seventy
thousand women and children, or worse yet slit each of their
throats, the awfulness and trauma inherent in the act would have

been of such a magnitude that it simply would not have happened. But when it is done from thousands of feet in the air, where the screams cannot be heard and the burning bodies cannot be seen, it is easy.

It seemed as though the whole of Hamburg was on fire from one end to the other and a huge column of smoke was towering well above us — and we were at 20,000 feet! Set in the darkness was a turbulent dome of bright red fire, lighted and ignited like the glowing heart of a vast brazier. I saw no streets, no outlines of buildings, only brighter fires which flared like yellow torches against a background of bright red ash. Above the city was a misty red haze. I looked down, fascinated but aghast, satisfied yet horrified.

— RAF aircrew over Hamburg, July 28, 1943
  quoted in Gwynne Dyer, *War*

From twenty thousand feet the killer could feel fascinated and satisfied with his work, but this is what the people on the ground were experiencing:

Mother wrapped me in wet sheets, kissed me, and said, "Run!" I hesitated at the door. In front of me I could see only fire — everything red, like the door to a furnace. An intense heat struck me. A burning beam fell in front of my feet. I shied back but then, when I was ready to jump over it, it was whirled away by a ghostly hand. The sheets around me acted as sails and I had the feeling that I was being carried away by the storm. I reached the front of a five-story building . . . which . . . had been bombed and burned out in a previous raid and there was not much in it for the fire to get hold of. Someone came out, grabbed me in their arms, and pulled me into the doorway.

— Traute Koch, age fifteen in 1943
  quoted in Gwynne Dyer, *War*

Seventy thousand died at Hamburg. Eighty thousand or so died in 1945 during a similar firebombing in Dresden. Two hundred and twenty-five thousand died in firestorms over Tokyo as a result of only two firebomb raids. When the atomic bomb was dropped over Hiroshima, seventy thousand died. Throughout World War II bomber crews on both sides killed millions of women, children, and elderly people, no different from their own wives, children, and parents. The pilots, navigators, bombardiers, and gunners in these aircraft were able to bring themselves to kill these civilians primarily through application of the mental leverage provided to them by the distance factor. Intellectually, they understood the horror of what they were doing. Emotionally, the distance involved permitted them to deny it. Despite what a recent popular song might tell us, from a distance you don't look anything like a friend. From a distance, I can deny your humanity; and from a distance, I cannot hear your screams.

Babylon

In 689 B.C. King Sennacherib of Assyria destroyed the city of Babylon:

> I leveled the city and its houses from the foundations to the top, I destroyed them and consumed them with fire. I tore down and removed the outer and inner walls, the temples and the ziggurats built of brick, and dumped the rubble in the Arahtu canal. And after I had destroyed Babylon, smashed its gods and massacred its population, I tore up its soil and threw it into the Euphrates so that it was carried by the river down to the sea.

Gwynne Dyer uses this quote to point out that although more labor intensive than nuclear weapons, the physical effect on Babylon was little different from the effect of nuclear weapons at Hiroshima or firebombs at Dresden. Physically the effect is the same, but *psychologically* the difference is tremendous.

No personal accounts of this horror have lasted through the ages, but we can see an echo of murder on such a scale in the accounts of survivors of Nazi atrocities. In *This Way for the Gas, Ladies and Gentlemen,* Tadeusz Borowski's memoir of his experiences in a Nazi death camp, he gives us a brief glimpse of the sheer horror of such mass killing:

We climb inside [a railroad car]. In the corners amid human ex-
crement and abandoned wrist-watches lie squashed, trampled in-
fants, naked little monsters with enormous heads and bloated
bellies. We carry them out like chickens, holding several in each
hand.

. . . I see four . . . men lugging a corpse: a huge swollen female corpse. Cursing, dripping wet from the strain, they kick out
of their way some stray children who have been running all over
the ramp, howling like dogs. The men pick them up by the collars,
heads, arms, and toss them inside the trucks, on top of the heaps.
The four men have trouble lifting the fat corpse onto the car, they
call others for help, and all together they hoist up the mound of
meat. Big swollen, puffed-up corpses are being collected from
all over the ramp; on top of them are piled the invalids, the
smothered, the sick, the unconscious. The heap seethes, howls,
groans.

In Babylon someone had to personally hold down tens of thousands
of men, women, and children, while someone else stabbed and
hacked at these horrified Babylonians. One by one. Grandfathers
struggled and wept as screaming grandchildren and daughters and
sons were raped and slaughtered. Mothers and fathers writhed in
their dying agony as they watched their children being raped and
butchered. Again, Borowski captures a faint timeless echo of this
mass murder of the innocent in a terse paragraph telling of the
murder of a single lost, confused, frightened little Jewish girl:

This time a little girl pushes herself halfway through the small
window [of the cattle car] and, losing her balance, falls out on the
gravel. Stunned, she lies still for a moment, then stands up and
begins walking around in a circle, faster and faster, waving her
rigid arms in the air, breathing loudly and spasmodically, whining
in a faint voice. Her mind has given way . . . an S.S. man approaches
calmly, his heavy boot strikes between her shoulders. She falls.
Holding her down with his foot, he draws his revolver, fires once,
then again. She remains face down, kicking the gravel with her
feet, until she stiffens.

Exchange the revolver for a sword, and then multiply this scene by tens of thousands, and you have the horror that was the sack of Babylon and a thousand other forgotten cities and nations.

Borowski knew that with these Jewish victims of a later-day Babylon "experienced professionals will probe into every recess of their flesh, will pull the gold from under the tongue and the diamonds from the uterus and the colon." History tells us that in Babylon and other such situations the victims were held down while their bodies were slit open to determine if they had swallowed or secreted valuables, and then they were often left to die slowly as they crawled off with their torn intestines and stomach dragging after them.

Even the Nazis usually segregated sexes and families and could seldom bring themselves to individually bayonet their victims. They preferred machine guns upon occasion, and gas chamber showers for the really big work. The horror of Babylon staggers the imagination.[1]

The Difference

I could not visualize the horrible deaths my bombs . . . had caused here. I had no feeling of guilt. I had no feeling of accomplishment.

— J. Douglas Harvey, World War II bomber pilot, visiting rebuilt Berlin in the 1960s
quoted in Paul Fussell, *Wartime*

What is the difference between what happened in Hamburg and in Babylon? There was no distinction in the results — in both, the innocent populations involved died horribly and their cities were destroyed. So what is the difference?

The difference is the difference between what the Nazi executioners did to the Jews and what the Allied bombardiers did to Germany and Japan. The difference is the difference between what Lieutenant Calley did to a village full of Vietnamese, and what many pilots and artillerymen did to similar Vietnamese villages.

The difference is that, emotionally, when we dwell on the butchers of Babylon or Auschwitz or My Lai, we feel revulsion at the psychotic and alien state that permitted these individuals to perform their awful deeds. We cannot understand how anyone could perform such inhuman atrocities on their fellow man. We call it murder, and we hunt down and prosecute the criminals responsible, be they Nazi war criminals or American war criminals. And by prosecuting these individuals we gain peace of mind by affirming to ourselves that this is an aberration that civilized societies do not tolerate.

But when most people think of those who bombed Hamburg or Hiroshima, there is no feeling of disgust for the deed, certainly not the intensity of disgust felt for Nazi executioners. When we mentally empathize with the bomber crews, when we put ourselves in their places, most cannot truly see themselves doing any different than they did. Therefore we do not judge them as criminals. We rationalize their actions and most of us have a gut feeling that we could have done what the bomber crews did, but could not ever have done what the executioners did.

When we reach out with empathy in these circumstances, we also empathize with the victims. Oddly enough, very few survivors of strategic bombing in Britain and Germany suffered from long-term emotional trauma resulting from their experiences, while most of the survivors of Nazi concentration camps — and many soldiers in battle — did and continue to do so. Incredibly, yet undeniably, there is a qualitative distinction in the eyes of those who suffered: the survivors of Auschwitz were personally traumatized by criminals and suffered lifelong psychological damage from their experiences, whereas the survivors of Hamburg were incidental victims of an act of war and were able to put it behind them.

Glenn Gray, a trained philosopher, served in an intelligence unit in World War II that was responsible for dealing with civilians ranging from spies to Nazi collaborators to survivors of concentration camps. He understood this qualitative distinction in the manner of death:

> Not the frequency of death but the manner of dying makes a qualitative difference. Death in war is commonly caused by members of my own species actively seeking my end, despite the fact that they may never have seen me and have no personal reason for enmity. It is death brought about by hostile intent rather than

by accident or natural causes that separates war from peace so completely.

Even our legal system is established around a determination of intent. Emotionally and intellectually we can readily grasp the difference between premeditated murder and manslaughter. The distinction based on intent represents an institutionalization of our emotional responses to these situations.

The issue of relative trauma in killing situations (for both the victim and the killer) was addressed earlier. It is sufficient to say here that at some instinctive, empathic level both survivors and historical observers understand the qualitative distinction between dying in a bombing attack and dying in a concentration camp. Bombing deaths are buffered by the all-important factor of distance. They represent an impersonal act of war in which specific deaths are unintended and almost accidental in nature. ("Collateral damage" is the military euphemism for such killing of civilians while bombing military targets.) Execution of innocent civilians, a subject to be addressed later in this study, is on the other hand a highly personal act of psychotic irrationality that openly refutes the humanity of the victims.

So what is the difference? Ultimately, the difference is distance.

Chapter Two

Killing at Maximum and Long Range: Never a Need for Repentance or Regret

To fight from a distance is instinctive in man. From the first day he has worked to this end, and he continues to do so.

— Ardant du Picq
  Battle Studies

Maximum Range: "They Can Pretend They Are Not Killing Human Beings"

Our examination of the killing process at different points along the distance spectrum begins at maximum range. For our purposes "maximum range" is defined as a range at which the killer is unable to perceive his individual victims without using some form of mechanical assistance — binoculars, radar, periscope, remote TV camera, and so on.

Gray states the matter clearly: "Many a pilot or artilleryman who has destroyed untold numbers of terrified noncombatants has never felt any need for repentance or regret." And Dyer echoes and reinforces Gray when he notes that there has never been any difficulty in getting artillerymen, bomber crews, or naval personnel to kill:

Partly it is the same pressure that keeps machine gun crews firing — they are being observed by their fellows — but even more
important is the intervention of distance and machinery between
them and the enemy; they can pretend they are not killing human beings.

On the whole, however, distance is a sufficient buffer: gunners
fire at grid references they cannot see; submarine crews fire torpedoes at "ships" (and not, somehow, at the people in the ships);
pilots launch their missiles at "targets."

Dyer covers most of the maximum-range types of killing here.
Artillery crews, bomber crews, naval gunners, and missile crews —
at sea and on the ground — are all protected by the same powerful
combination of group absolution, mechanical distance, and, most
pertinent to our current discussion, physical distance.

In years of research and reading on the subject of killing in
combat I have not found one single instance of individuals who
have refused to kill the enemy under these circumstances, nor
have I found a single instance of psychiatric trauma associated with
this type of killing. Even in the case of the individuals who dropped
the atomic bombs on Hiroshima and Nagasaki, contrary to popular
myth, there are no indications of psychological problems. Historical
accounts indicate that the pilot of the aircraft that made the weather
reconnaissance for the *Enola Gay* had a series of disciplinary and
criminal problems before the bombing, and it was his continued
problems after leaving the service that formed the sole basis of the
popular myth of suicide and mental problems among these crews.

Long Range: "Not Eyeball to Eyeball with the Sweat and the Emotions of Combat"

"Long range" is defined here as the range at which the average
soldier may be able to see the enemy, but is unable to kill him
without some form of special weaponry — sniper weapons, anti-
armor missiles, or tank fire.

Holmes tells of a World War I Australian sniper recalling how,
after shooting a German observer, "a queer thrill shot through
me, it was a different feeling to that which I had when I shot my

first kangaroo when I was a boy. For an instant I felt sick and faint; but the feeling soon passed."

Here we begin to see some disturbance at the act of killing, but snipers doctrinally operate as teams, and like maximum-range killers they are protected by the same potent combination of group absolution, mechanical distance (the rifle scope), and physical distance. Their observations and the accounts of their kills are strangely depersonalized and different from those that we will see at closer ranges:

> At 2109 [on February 3, 1969] five Viet Cong moved from the woodline to the edge of the rice paddy and the first Viet Cong in the group was taken under fire . . . resulting in one Viet Cong killed. Immediately the other Viet Cong formed a huddle around the fallen body, apparently not quite sure of what had taken place. Sergeant Waldron continued engaging the Viet Cong one by one until a total of [all] five Viet Cong were killed.[2]

Even given the buffer of the tremendous distance at which snipers work, some snipers can rationalize their actions by killing only enemy leaders. One marine sniper told D. J. Truby "you don't like to hit ordinary troops, because they're usually scared draftees or worse. . . . The guys to shoot are big brass." And just as a remarkably small percentage of World War II fighter pilots were capable of doing the majority of the air-to-air killing, so too have a few carefully selected and trained snipers made a tremendous and disproportionate contribution to their nation's war effort by remorselessly and mercilessly killing large numbers of the enemy.

From January 7 to July 24, 1969, U.S. Army snipers in Vietnam accounted for 1,245 confirmed kills, with an average of 1.39 bullets expended per kill. (Compare this with the average fifty thousand rounds of ammunition required for every enemy soldier killed in Vietnam.)[3] In the course of calculating confirmed sniper kills, no enemy was counted as a kill unless an American soldier actually was able to physically "place his foot" on the body.

Yet for all its effectiveness, there is a strange revulsion and resistance toward this very personal, one-on-one killing by snipers. Peter Staff, in his book on snipers, notes that after every war "the

United States military rushes to distance itself from its snipers. The same men called upon to perform impossible missions during combat quickly find themselves to be peacetime pariahs. World War I, World War II, Korea. It was the same."

World War II–era fighter pilots, firing their battery of heavy machine guns at the enemy, would probably fit into the long-range category, but they are hampered by lack of group absolution and their powerful identification with an enemy who is so remarkably similar to them. Colonel Barry Bridger of the U.S. Air Force described to Dyer the difference between air combat (long range) and ground battle (medium and close range):

> I would draw one distinction between being a combat aviator and being someone who is fighting the enemy face-to-face on the ground. In the air environment, it's very clinical, very clean, and it's not so personalized. You see an aircraft; you see a target on the ground — you're not eyeball to eyeball with the sweat and the emotions of combat, and so it doesn't become so emotional for you and so personalized. And I think it is easier to do in that sense — you're not so affected.

Yet even with this advantage, only 1 percent of U.S. fighter pilots accounted for nearly 40 percent of all enemy pilots shot down in World War II; the majority apparently did not shoot anyone down or even try to.

Chapter Three

Killing at Mid- and Hand-Grenade Range:
"You Can Never Be Sure It Was You"

Midrange: Denial Based "on the Thinnest of Evidence"

We will call midrange that range at which the soldier can see and engage the enemy with rifle fire while still unable to perceive the extent of the wounds inflicted or the sounds and facial expressions of the victim when he is hit. In fact, at this range, the soldier can still deny that it was he who killed the enemy. When asked about his experiences, one World War II veteran told me that "there were so many other guys firing, you can never be sure it was you. You shoot, you see a guy fall, and anyone could have been the one that hit him."

This is a fairly typical response by veterans to those who ask about their personal kills. Holmes states, "Most of the veterans I interviewed were infantrymen with front-line service, yet fewer than half of them believed that they had actually killed an enemy, and often this belief was based on the thinnest of evidence."

When soldiers do kill the enemy they appear to go through a series of emotional stages. The actual kill is usually described as being reflexive or automatic. Immediately after the kill the soldier goes through a period of euphoria and elation, which is usually followed by a period of guilt and remorse.[4] The intensity and duration of these periods are closely related to distance. At midrange we see much of the euphoria stage. The future field marshal Slim wrote of experiencing this euphoria upon shooting a Turk in Mesopotamia in 1917. "I suppose it is brutal," wrote Slim, "but I had a feeling of the most intense satisfaction as the wretched Turk went spinning down."

After this euphoria stage, even at midrange, the remorse stage can hit hard. One Napoleonic-era British soldier quoted by Holmes described how he was overcome with horror when he first shot a Frenchman. "I reproached myself as a destroyer," he wrote. "An indescribable uneasiness came over me, I felt almost like a criminal."

If a soldier goes up and looks at his kill — a common occurrence when the tactical situation permits — the trauma grows even worse, since some of the psychological buffer created by a midrange kill disappears upon seeing the victim at close range. Holmes tells of a World War I British veteran who was a seventeen-year-old private when he viewed his handiwork: "This was the first time I had killed anybody and when things quieted down I went and looked at a German I knew I had shot. I remember thinking that he looked old enough to have a family and I felt very sorry."

Hand-Grenade Range: "We Heard the Shrieks and Were Nauseated"

Hand-grenade range can be anywhere from a few yards to as many as thirty-five or forty yards. For the purposes of the physical range spectrum, when we use the term "hand-grenade range" we are referring to a specific kill in which a hand grenade is used. A hand-grenade kill is distinguished from a close kill in that the killer does not have to see his victims as they die. In fact, at close range to midrange, if a soldier is in direct line of sight when his grenade explodes, he will become a victim of his own instrument.

Holmes tells how in the trenches of World War I one soldier threw a grenade at a group of Germans, and terrible cries followed its explosion. "Although we had been terribly hardened," said the soldier, "my blood froze." Not having to look at one's victim should make this a killing method that is largely free of trauma, *if* the soldier does not have to look at his handiwork, and *if* it were not for these screams.

The particular effectiveness of these psychologically and physically powerful weapons in the trenches of World War I is told of in detail by Holmes:

> Both sides habitually bombed [hand-grenaded] dugouts containing men who might have surrendered had they been given a chance to do so. A British soldier, newly captured in March 1918, told his captor that there were some wounded in one of the dugouts: "He took a stick grenade out, pulled the pin out and threw it down the dug-out. We heard the shrieks and were nauseated, but we were completely powerless. But it was all in a melee and we might have done the same in the circumstances."

In the close-in trench battles of World War I hand grenades were psychologically and physically easier to use, so much so that Keegan and Holmes tell us that "the infantryman had forgotten how to deliver accurate fire with his rifle; his main weapon had become the grenade." And we can begin to understand that this is because the emotional trauma associated with a grenade kill can be less than that of a close-range kill, especially if the killer does not have to look at his victims or hear them die.

Chapter Four

Killing at Close Range: "I Knew That It Was up to Me, Personally, to Kill Him"

An Israeli paratrooper came face to face with a huge Jordanian during the capture of the Old City of Jerusalem in 1967. "We looked at each other for half a second and I knew that it was up to me, personally, to kill him, there was no one else there. The whole thing must have lasted less than a second, but it's printed on my mind like a slow motion movie. I fired from the hip and I can still see the bullets splashed against the wall about a meter to his left. I moved the Uzi, slowly, slowly it seemed, until I hit him in the body. He slipped to his knees, then he raised his head, with his face terrible, twisted in pain and hate, yes such hate. I fired again and somehow got him in the head. There was so much blood . . . I vomited, until the rest of the boys came up."

— John Keegan and Richard Holmes
  Soldiers

Close range involves any kill with a projectile weapon from point-blank range, extending to midrange. The key factor in close range is the undeniable certainty of responsibility on the part of the killer. In Vietnam the term "personal kill" was used to distinguish the act of killing a specific individual with a direct-fire weapon and being absolutely sure of having done it oneself. The vast majority of personal kills and the resultant trauma occur at this range.

For analysis purposes I have divided examples of close-range encounters into those in which the narrator elects to kill, and those in which he does not kill.

To Kill . . .

At close range the euphoria stage, although brief, fleeting, and not often mentioned, still appears to be experienced in some form by most soldiers. Upon being asked, most of the combat veterans whom I have interviewed will admit to having experienced a brief feeling of elation upon succeeding in killing the enemy. Usually this euphoria stage is almost instantly overwhelmed by the guilt stage as the soldier is faced with the undeniable evidence of what he has done, and the guilt stage is often so strong as to result in physical revulsion and vomiting.

When the soldier kills at close range, it is by its very nature an intensely vivid and personal matter. A U.S. Special Forces (Green Beret) officer described his revulsion during a personal kill while reacting to an ambush in Vietnam:

> I took two of the men and went around the flank . . . to outflank them and take them out. Well, I got around to the side and pointed my M16 at them and this person turned around and just stared, and I froze, 'cos it was a boy, I would say between the ages of twelve and fourteen. When he turned at me and looked, all of a sudden he turned his whole body and pointed his automatic weapon at me, I just opened up, fired the whole twenty rounds right at the kid, and he just laid there. I dropped my weapon and cried.

— John Keegan and Richard Holmes
  Soldiers

Author and World War II marine veteran William Manchester vividly described the same psychological responses to his own close-range kill:

> I was utterly terrified — petrified — but I knew there had to be a Japanese sniper in a small fishing shack near the shore. He was

firing in the other direction at Marines in another battalion, but I knew as soon as he picked off the people there — there was a window on our side — that he would start picking us off. And there was nobody else to go . . . and so I ran towards the shack and broke in and found myself in an empty room.

There was a door which meant there was another room and the sniper was in that — and I just broke that down. I was just absolutely gripped by the fear that this man would expect me and would shoot me. But as it turned out he was in a sniper harness and he couldn't turn around fast enough. He was entangled in the harness so I shot him with a .45 and I felt remorse and shame. I can remember whispering foolishly, "I'm sorry" and then just throwing up . . . I threw up all over myself. It was a betrayal of what I'd been taught since a child.

At this range the screams and cries of the enemy can be heard, adding greatly to the extent of the trauma experienced by the killer. Major General Frank Richardson told Holmes that "it is a touching fact that men, dying in battle, often call upon their mothers. I have heard them do so in five languages."

Oftentimes the death inflicted on the enemy during a close-range kill is not instant, and the killer finds himself in the position of comforting his victim in his last moments. Here we see Harry Stewart, a Ranger and U.S. Army master sergeant — the epitome of toughness and professionalism — telling of a remarkable incident that occurred during the Tet offensive in 1968:

All of a sudden there was a guy firing a pistol right at us. It looked as big as a 175 [mm howitzer] just then. The first round hit the fireman on my left in the chest. The second round hit me in the right arm, although I didn't know it. The third round hit the fireman on my right in the gut. By this time I had bounced off the wall to my left. . . .

I charged the VC [Viet Cong], firing my M-16. He fell at my feet. He was still alive but would soon die. I reached down and took the pistol from his hand. I can still see those eyes, looking at me in hate. . . .

Later I walked over to take another look at the VC I had shot. He was still alive and looking at me with those eyes. The flies were beginning to get all over him. I put a blanket over him and rubbed water from my canteen onto his lips. That hard stare started to leave his eyes. He wanted to talk but was too far gone. I lit a cigarette, took a few puffs, and put it to his lips. He could barely puff. We each had had a few drags and that hard look had left his eyes before he died.[5]

Even when the killer has every motivation to hate and despise his victim, and every reason to quickly depart his close-range kill, he is often riveted, frozen by the magnitude of what he has done. Here Lieutenant Dieter Dengler — recipient of the Navy Cross, America's second-highest decoration for heroism, and the only U.S. flier to escape from a Southeast Asian prison camp after being shot down and captured — found himself in just such a situation. Upon securing a weapon and breaking out of prison, Dieter was confronted by one of the sadistic guards who had tormented him:

Only three feet away, Moron [their nickname for this particular guard] was coming at me full gallop, his machete cocked high over his head. I fired from the hip point-blank into him. The force of the blast hung him in the air, his machete still raised, and then spun him backwards to the ground. There was blood gushing from a huge hole in his back. I stood over him with my mouth open wide, amazed that a single slug could do such damage and mindful of nothing but the horrible-looking back.

In all of these narratives it is this emotional reaction that the writer wanted to tell us about. Of all the things that occurred in the months and years of war experienced by these men, the close-range kills quoted here, and all the many throughout this study, appear to be something these veterans wanted to get off their chests. A first sergeant who was a Vietnam Special Forces veteran once put it this way when describing combat to me: "When you get up close and personal," he drawled with a cud of chewing tobacco in his cheek, "where you can hear 'em scream and see 'em die," and here he spit tobacco for emphasis, "it's a bitch."

. . . And Not to Kill

At close range the resistance to killing an opponent is tremendous. When one looks an opponent in the eye, and knows that he is young or old, scared or angry, it is not possible to deny that the individual about to be killed is much like oneself. It is here that many personal narratives of nonkilling situations occur. Marshall, Keegan, Holmes, Griffith, virtually all who have studied the matter in depth, agree that such nonparticipation is apparently very common in midrange conflict, but in close-range situations it becomes so remarkable — and undeniable — that we can find numerous first-person narratives.

Keegan and Holmes tell of a group of Americans who jumped into a ditch while under artillery fire in Sicily during World War II:

> And lo and behold there were about five Germans, and maybe four or five of us, and we didn't give any thought whatsoever to fighting at first. . . . Then I realized that they had their rifles, we had ours and then shells were landing and we were cowering against the side of the ditch, the Germans were doing the same thing. And then the next thing you know, there was a lull, we took cigarettes out and we passed 'em around, we were smoking and it's a feeling I cannot describe, but it was a feeling that this was not the time to be shooting at one another. . . . They were human beings, like us, they were just as scared.

Marshall describes a similar situation when Captain Willis, an American company commander leading his unit along a streambed in Vietnam, was suddenly confronted with a North Vietnamese soldier:

> Willis came abreast of him, his M–16 pointed at the man's chest. They stood not five feet apart. The soldier's AK 47 was pointed straight at Willis.
> The captain vigorously shook his head.
> The NVA soldier shook his head just as vigorously.
> It was a truce, cease-fire, gentleman's agreement or a deal. . . .
> The soldier sank back into the darkness and Willis stumbled on.

As men draw this near it becomes extremely difficult to deny their humanity. Looking in a man's face, seeing his eyes and his fear, eliminate denial. At this range the interpersonal nature of the killing has shifted. Instead of shooting at a uniform and killing a generalized enemy, now the killer must shoot at a person and kill a specific individual. Most simply cannot or will not do it.

Chapter Five

Killing at Edged-Weapons Range:
An "Intimate Brutality"

At the physical distance in which a soldier has to use a nonprojectile weapon, such as a bayonet or spear, two important corollaries of the physical relationship come into play.

First we must recognize that it is psychologically easier to kill with an edged weapon that permits a long stand-off range, and increasingly more difficult as the stand-off range decreases. Thus it is considerably easier to impale a man with a twenty-foot pike than it is to stab him with a six-inch knife.

The physical range provided by the spears of the Greek and Macedonian phalanx provided much of the psychological leverage that permitted Alexander the Great to conquer the known world.[6] The psychological leverage provided by the hedge of pikes was so powerful that the phalanx was resurrected in the Middle Ages and used successfully in the era of mounted knights. Ultimately the phalanx was only replaced by the advent of the superior posturing and psychological leverage provided by gunpowder projectile weapons.

The second corollary to the distance relationship is that it is far easier to deliver a slashing or hacking blow than a piercing blow.

To pierce is to penetrate, while to slash is to sidestep or deny the objective of piercing into the enemy's essence.

For a bayonet-, spear-, or sword-armed soldier his weapon becomes a natural extension of his body — an appendage. And the piercing of the enemy's body with this appendage is an act with some of the sexual connotations we will see in hand-to-hand combat range. To reach out and penetrate the enemy's flesh and thrust a portion of ourselves into his vitals is deeply akin to the sexual act, yet deadly, and is therefore strongly repulsive to us.

The Romans apparently had a serious problem with their soldiers not wanting to use piercing blows, for the ancient Roman tactician and historian Vegetius emphasized this point at length in a section entitled "Not to Cut, but to Thrust with the Sword." He says:

> They were likewise taught not to cut but to thrust with their swords. For the Romans not only made jest of those who fought with the edge of that weapon, but always found them an easy conquest. A stroke with the edges, though made with ever so much force, seldom kills, as the vital parts of the body are defended by the bones and armor. On the contrary, a stab, though it penetrates but two inches, is generally fatal.[7]

Bayonet Range

Bob McKenna, a professional soldier and magazine columnist, draws upon more than sixteen years of active military service in Africa, Central America, and Southeast Asia in order to understand what he calls the "intimate brutality" of bayonet kills. "The thought of cold steel sliding into your guts," says McKenna, "is more horrific and real than the thought of a bullet doing the same — perhaps because you can see the steel coming." This powerful revulsion to being killed with cold steel can also be observed in mutinous Indian soldiers captured during the 1857 Sepoy Mutiny who "begged for the bullet" by pleading to be executed with a rifle shot rather than the bayonet. More recently, according to AP news articles, we have seen this in Rwanda, where the Hutu tribesmen made their Tutsi victims purchase the bullets they would be killed with in order to avoid being hacked to death.

It is not just the killer who feels this profound revulsion toward the intimate brutality of a bayonet kill. John Keegan's landmark book *The Face of Battle* makes a comparative study of Agincourt (1415), Waterloo (1815), and the Somme (1916). In his analysis of these three battles spanning more than five hundred years, Keegan repeatedly notes the amazing absence of bayonet wounds incurred during the massed bayonet attacks at Waterloo and the Somme. At Waterloo Keegan notes that "there were numbers of sword and lance wounds to be treated and some bayonet wounds, though these had usually been inflicted after the man had already been disabled, there being no evidence of the armies having crossed bayonets at Waterloo." By World War I edged-weapon combat had almost disappeared, and Keegan notes that in the Battle of the Somme, "edged-weapon wounds were a fraction of one per cent of all wounds inflicted."

Three major psychological factors come into play in bayonet combat. First, the vast majority of soldiers who do approach bayonet range with the enemy use the butt of the weapon or any other available means to incapacitate or injure the enemy rather than skewer him. Second, when the bayonet is used, the close range at which the work is done results in a situation with enormous potential for psychological trauma. And, finally, the resistance to killing with the bayonet is equal only to the enemy's horror at having this done to him. Thus in bayonet charges one side or the other invariably flees before the actual crossing of bayonets occurs.

Actual bayonet combat is extremely rare in military history. General Trochu saw only one bayonet fight in a lifetime of soldiering with the French army in the nineteenth century, and that was when French units collided by accident with a Russian regiment in the heavy fog of the Crimean War's Battle of Inkerman in 1854. And in these rare bayonet engagements actual bayonet wounds were even rarer yet.

When this uncommon event does occur, and one bayonet-armed man stands face-to-face with another, what happens most commonly is anything but a thrust with the bayonet. Just as Roman legionnaires had to fight the tendency to slash with their swords rather than thrust, so too do modern soldiers tend to use their weapons in a manner that will not necessitate thrusting into their enemy's bodies.

Holmes says that despite all the bayonet training soldiers receive, "in combat they very often reversed their weapons and used them as clubs. . . . The Germans seem to have a positive penchant for using the butt rather than the bayonet. . . . In close-in fighting the Germans preferred clubs, coshes, and sharpened spades." Note that all of these are bludgeoning or hacking weapons.

He goes on to give a superb example of the subtle and unconscious nature of this resistance to bayoneting: "Prince Frederick Charles asked a [World War I] German infantryman why he did this. 'I don't know,' replied the soldier. 'When you get your dander up the thing turns round in your hand of itself.'"

Numerous accounts of American Civil War battles indicate the same resistance to use of the bayonet on the part of the vast majority of soldiers on both sides. In melees both Yank and Reb preferred to use the butt of the weapon, or to swing their muskets by the barrel like a club, rather than gut the enemy with their bayonets. Some writers have concluded that a specific characteristic of this brother-against-brother civil war must have been the cause of the soldier's reluctance to bayonet his enemy, but wound statistics from nearly two centuries of battles indicate that what is revealed here is a basic, profound, and universal insight into human nature. First, the closer the soldier draws to his enemy the harder it is to kill him, until at bayonet range it becomes extremely difficult, and, second, the average human being has a strong resistance to piercing the body of another of his own kind with a handheld edged weapon, preferring to club or slash at the enemy.

Since personal kills with a bayonet are so extraordinarily rare on the battlefield, it is much to Richard Holmes's credit that his lifetime of study in this field has gleaned the following personal narratives from individuals who contributed to this "fraction of one per cent of all wounds inflicted" in modern war.

In one such narrative, a lance corporal in the German infantry in 1915 describes a bayonet kill:

> We got the order to storm a French position, strongly held by the
> enemy, and during the ensuing melee a French corporal suddenly
> stood before me, both our bayonets at the ready, he to kill me, I
> to kill him. Saber duels in Freiburg had taught me to be quicker
> than he and pushing his weapon aside I stabbed him through the
> chest. He dropped his rifle and fell, and the blood shot out of his
> mouth. I stood over him for a few seconds and then I gave him
> the coup de grace. After we had taken the enemy position, I felt
> giddy, my knees shook, and I was actually sick.

He goes on to state that this bayoneted Frenchman, apparently
above all other incidents in combat, haunted his dreams for many
nights thereafter. Indeed, the "intimate brutality" of bayonet killing gives every indication of being a circumstance with tremendous potential for psychological trauma.

An Australian soldier in World War I, writing in a letter to his
father, puts a distinctly different light on bayoneting Germans:

> Strike me pink the square heads are dead mongrels. They will keep
> firing until you are two yds. off them & then drop their rifles &
> ask for mercy. They get it too right where the chicken gets the
> axe. . . . I . . . will fix a few more before I have finished. Its good
> sport father when the bayonet goes in there eyes bulge out like
> prawns. [*Sic.*]

If we can believe what is said here, and if both the killing and the
lack of remorse were not just idle bragging to his father, then this
soldier represents one of those rare soldiers who have the internal
makeup to participate in such an act. Later in this book we will
address predisposition as a factor in killing, with particular emphasis
on the 2 percent who are predisposed toward what has been termed
"aggressive psychopathic" tendencies. And in the section "Killing
and Atrocities" we will more closely consider the process in which
soldiers who fight at close range and attempt to surrender stand a
good chance of being killed on the spot by the soldiers they had
most recently been trying to kill. The objective here is to gain
insight into the nature of killing with edged weapons, and into
the nature of those who are able to kill in this manner. And from

what we can observe, it must be a rare and unusual individual who can find such activity to be "good sport."

Another Australian, a World War I veteran of the first Battle of Gaza, who apparently did not participate in any bayonet kills, described bayonet fighting as "just berserk slaughter . . . the grunting breaths, the gritting teeth and the staring eyes of the lunging Turk, the sobbing scream as the bayonet ripped home." Here we see combat at its most personal. When a man bayonets a person who is facing him, the "sobbing scream," the blood shooting out of his mouth, and his eyes bulging out "like prawns" are all part of the memory the killer must carry forever. This is killing with edged weapons, and it is no wonder that it is so extraordinarily rare in modern warfare.

We can understand then that the average soldier has an intense resistance toward bayoneting his fellow man, and that this act is surpassed only by the resistance to *being* bayoneted. The horror of being bayoneted is intense. Lord Moran said that during his long years of experience in the trenches of World War I, the one time "when I had a bayonet a few inches from my belly I was more frightened than by any shell." And Remarque, in *All Quiet on the Western Front,* tells of a German soldier who was caught while in possession of one of the saw-backed pioneer bayonets and was subsequently brutally killed and left as an example to his peers. Holmes tells us that Germans in both wars who were found with such weapons were so treated by captors who were horrified by the weapon and thought that it was deliberately designed to cause added suffering.[8]

Soldiers who would bravely face a hail of bullets will consistently flee before a determined individual with cold steel in his hands. Du Picq noted, "Each nation in Europe says: 'No one stands his ground before a bayonet charge made by us.' And all are right." A human wave of cold steel — be it pikes, spears, or bayonets — coming at one's position would be cause for understandable concern on anyone's part, and as Holmes puts it "one side or the other usually recalls an urgent appointment elsewhere before bayonets cross." Very often neither side can bring itself to

close with the enemy's bayonets, the advance falters, and the two
parties begin to fire at one another from ridiculously short ranges.
World War II veteran Fred Majdalany wrote that there was

> a lot of loose talk about the use of the bayonet. But relatively few
> soldiers could truthfully say that they had stuck a bayonet into a
> German. It is the threat of the bayonet and the sight of the point
> that usually does the work. The man almost invariably surrenders
> *before* the point is stuck into him.

In the modern bayonet charge one side or the other usually breaks
and runs before they meet, and then the psychological balance tips
significantly. But this does not mean that bayonets and bayonet
charges are ineffective. As Paddy Griffith points out:

> A great deal of misunderstanding has arisen from the fact that a
> "bayonet charge" could be highly effective even without any bayo-
> net actually touching an enemy soldier, let alone killing him. One
> hundred per cent of the casualties might be caused by musketry,
> yet the bayonet could still be the instrument of victory. This was
> because its purpose was not to kill soldiers but to disorganize
> regiments and win ground. It was the flourish of the bayonet and
> the determination in the eyes of its owner that on some occasions
> produced shock.

Units with a history and tradition of close-combat, hand-to-hand
killing inspire special dread and fear in an enemy by capitalizing
upon this natural aversion to the "hate" manifested in this determination to engage in close-range interpersonal aggression. The British Gurkha battalions have been historically effective at this (as can
be seen in the Argentinean's dread of them during the Falklands
War), but any unit that puts a measure of faith in the bayonet has
grasped a little of the natural dread with which an enemy responds
to the possibility of facing an opponent who is determined to
come within "skewering range."

What these units (or at least their leaders) must understand is
that actual skewering almost *never* happens; but the powerful human
revulsion to the threat of such activity, when a soldier is confronted
with superior posturing represented by a willingness or at least a

reputation for participation in close-range killing, has a devastating effect upon the enemy's morale.

Back Stabbing and the Chase Instinct

Combat at close quarters does not exist. At close quarters occurs the ancient carnage when one force strikes the other in the back.

— Ardant du Picq
  Battle Studies

It is when the bayonet charge has forced one side's soldiers to turn their backs and flee that the killing truly begins, and at some visceral level the soldier intuitively understands this and is very, very frightened when he has to turn his back to the enemy. Griffith dwells on this fear of retreating: "Perhaps this fear of retreat [in the face of the enemy] was linked to a horror of turning one's back on the threat. . . . A type of reverse ostrich syndrome may have applied, whereby the danger was bearable only while the men continued to watch it." And in his superb study of the American Civil War, Griffith also notes many instances in which the most effective firing and killing occurred when the enemy had begun to flee the field.

I believe that there are two factors in play in this increased killing of an enemy whose back is turned, and of the resultant fear of turning one's back to the enemy. The first factor is the concept of a chase instinct. A lifetime of working with and training dogs has taught me that the worst thing you can ever do is run from an animal. I have never yet met a dog I could not face down or at least incapacitate with a kick as it charged, but I have always known both instinctively and rationally that if I were to turn and run I should be in great danger. There is a chase instinct in most animals that will cause even a well-trained and nonaggressive dog to instinctively chase and pull down anything that runs. As long as your back is turned you are in danger. In the same way, there appears to be a chase instinct in man that permits him to kill a fleeing enemy.

The second factor that enables killing from behind is a process in which close proximity on the physical distance spectrum can be negated when the face cannot be seen. The essence of the whole physical distance spectrum may simply revolve around the degree to which the killer can see the face of the victim. There appears to be a kind of intuitive understanding of this process in our cultural image of back shooting and back stabbing as cowardly acts, and it seems that soldiers intuitively understand that when they turn their backs, they are more apt to be killed by the enemy.

This same enabling process explains why Nazi, Communist, and gangland executions are traditionally conducted with a bullet in the back of the head, and why individuals being executed by hanging or firing squad are blindfolded or hooded. And we know from Miron and Goldstein's 1979 research that the risk of death for a kidnap victim is much greater if the victim is hooded. In each of these instances the presence of the hood or blindfold ensures that the execution is completed and serves to protect the mental health of the executioners. Not having to look at the face of the victim provides a form of psychological distance that enables the execution party and assists in their subsequent denial and the rationalization and acceptance of having killed a fellow human being.

The eyes are the window of the soul, and if one does not have to look into the eyes when killing, it is much easier to deny the humanity of the victim. The eyes bulging out "like prawns" and blood shooting out of the mouth are not seen. The victim remains faceless, and one never needs to know one's victim as a person. And the price most killers have to pay for a close-range kill — the memory of the "face terrible, twisted in pain and hate, yes such hate" — this price need never be paid if we can simply avoid looking at our victim's face.

In combat the impact of back stabbing and the chase instinct can be observed in casualty rates, which increase significantly after the enemy forces have turned their backs and begun to flee. Clausewitz and du Picq both expound at length on the fact that the vast majority of casualties in historical battles were inflicted upon the losing side during the pursuit that followed the victory. In this vein Ardant du Picq holds out the example of Alexander the Great, whose forces, during all his years of warfare, lost fewer than seven hundred men "to the sword." They suffered so few casualties simply because they never lost a battle and therefore only had to endure the very, very minor casualties inflicted by reluctant combatants in close combat and never had to suffer the very significant losses associated with being pursued by a victorious enemy.

Knife Range

As we bring the physical distance spectrum down to its culmination point we must recognize that killing with a knife is significantly more difficult than killing with the bayonet affixed to the end of a rifle. Many knife kills appear to be of the commando nature, in which someone slips up on a victim and kills him from behind. These kills, like all kills from behind, are less traumatic than a kill from the front, since the face and all its messages and contortions are not seen. But what is felt are the bucking and shuddering of the victim's body and the warm sticky blood gushing out, and what is heard is the the final breath hissing out.

The U.S. Army, along with armies in many other nations, trains its Rangers and Green Berets to execute a knife kill from the rear by plunging the knife through the lower back and into the kidney. Such a blow is so remarkably painful that its effect is to completely paralyze the victim as he quickly dies, resulting in an extremely silent kill.

This kidney strike is contrary to the natural inclination of most soldiers, who — if they have thought about the matter at all — would prefer to slit the throat while holding a hand over the victim's mouth. This option, though psychologically and culturally more desirable (it is a slashing rather than a thrusting blow), has far less potential for silence, since an improperly slit throat is capable of making considerable noise and holding a hand over someone's mouth is not always an easy thing to do. The victim also has a capacity to bite, and a marine gunnery sergeant who is the USMC's proponent agent for hand-to-hand-combat tells me that several individuals have told him of cutting their own hand while trying to cut the enemy's throat in the dark. But here again we see the natural preference for a slashing blow over a more effective thrusting or penetrating blow.

Holmes tells us that the French in World War II preferred knives and daggers for close-in work, but Keegan's findings of the singular absence of such wounds would indicate that few of these knives were ever used. Indeed, narratives of incidents in which individuals used a knife in modern combat are extremely rare, and knife kills other than the silencing of sentries from behind are almost unheard of.

The one personal narrative of a knife kill that I have been able to obtain as a result of my interviews is from a man who had been an infantryman in the Pacific during World War II. He had many personal kills that he was willing to discuss, but it was his one kill with a knife that caused him to have nightmares long after the war was over. An enemy soldier had slipped into his foxhole one night, and during the process of a hand-to-hand struggle he pinned down the smaller Japanese soldier and slit his throat. The horror associated with pinning the man down and feeling him struggle and watching him bleed to death is something that he can barely tolerate to this very day.

Chapter Six

Killing at Hand-to-Hand-Combat Range

In modern battle, which is delivered with combatants so far apart,
man has come to have a horror of man. He comes to hand-to-
hand fighting only to defend his body or if forced to it.

— Ardant du Picq
  Battle Studies

Hand-to-Hand-Combat Range

At hand-to-hand-combat range the instinctive resistance to killing
becomes strongest. While some who have studied the subject claim
that man is the only higher-order species that does not have an
instinctive resistance to killing his own species, its existence is
recognized by almost any high-level karate practitioner.

An obvious method of killing an opponent involves a crushing
blow to the throat. In movie combat we often see one individual
grab another by the throat and attempt to choke him. And Hollywood heroes give the enemy a good old punch in the jaw. In
both instances a blow to the throat (with the hand held in various
prescribed shapes) would be a vastly superior form of disabling or
killing the foe, yet it is not a natural act; it is a repellent one.

The single most effective and mechanically easiest way to inflict
significant damage on a human being with one's hand is to punch
a thumb through his eye and on into the brain, subsequently

stirring the intruding digit around inside the skull, cocking it off toward the side, and forcefully pulling the eye and other matter out with the thumb.

One karate instructor trains his high-level students in this killing technique by having them practice punching their thumbs into oranges held or taped over the eye socket of an opponent. As we will observe when we study the process by which the U.S. Army raised its firing rates from 15 to 20 percent in World War II to 90 to 95 percent in Vietnam, this procedure of precisely rehearsing and mimicking a killing action is an excellent way of ensuring that the individual is capable of performing the act in combat.

In the case of the orange held over the victim's eye, the process is made even more realistic by having the victim scream, twitch, and jerk as the killer punches his thumb to the hilt into the orange and then rips it back out. Few individuals can walk away from their first such rehearsal without being badly shaken and disturbed by the action they have just mimicked. The fact that they are overcoming some form of natural resistance is obvious.

Tracy Arnold, an actress in the X-rated (for violence) movie *Henry: Portrait of a Serial Killer,* passed out twice during the filming of a scene in which her character was portrayed stabbing a man in the eye with a rat-tailed comb. This is a professional actress. She can portray killing, lying, and sex on the screen with relative ease, but even the pretense of stabbing someone in the eye seems to have touched a resistance so powerful and deep-seated that her body and emotions — the tools of the professional actress — literally refused to cooperate. In fact, I cannot find any references to anyone in the history of human combat having ever used this simple technique. Indeed, it is almost too painful to think of it.

Man has a tremendous resistance to killing effectively with his bare hands. When man first picked up a club or a rock and killed his fellow man, he gained more than mechanical energy and mechanical leverage. He also gained psychological energy and psychological leverage that was every bit as necessary in the killing process. In some distant part of man's past he acquired this ability. Two major religious works, the Bible and the Torah, both speak of partaking of the fruit of the Tree of Knowledge of Good and Evil, and one of its first uses was Cain's overcoming his instinctive resistance in order to kill his brother, Abel. He probably did so not with his bare hands, but with an application of mechanical and psychological leverage not available to any other creature on the face of the earth.[9]

Chapter Seven

Killing at Sexual Range: "The Primal Aggression, the Release, and the Orgasmic Discharge"

One night as a young lieutenant on a long deployment to the Arctic, I sat in our little Officer/Senior NCO Club nursing a beer, while several old sergeants became quite drunk. One old Vietnam vet hit on a popular theme during the discussion and said, "F—— Jane Fonda."

Another old sergeant vet who was sitting next to me was roused to respond by saying, "F—— Jane Fonda? Huh! Skull-f—— Jane Fonda! Pop an eyeball out and skull-f—— the bitch."

This macabre concept of combining sex with death was so offensive that even the hardened veterans around the speaker were momentarily shocked. Yet the procreative act and the destructive act are inextricably interlinked. Much of the attraction to the killing process, and much of the resistance to close-in killing, revolves around the vicious side of ourselves that would pervert sex in such a manner that we *can* conceive of such things.

At a surface level, the link between sex and aggression is obvious and not so blatantly offensive. The most powerful stag, stallion, ram, male lion, or gorilla wins the harem; lesser or younger males remain only if they are subservient. Much has been made of the relationship between male sexuality and the power of motorcycles

(1,200 cc of power throbbing between your legs) and muscle cars. The continuing popularity of magazines in which motorcycles and cars are displayed along with scantily clad women in provocative positions make this relationship clear.

This kind of sex–power linkage also exists in the gun world. A video recently advertised in gun magazines, *Sexy Girls and Sexy Guns,* taps this same vein. "You've got to see this tape to believe it," says the ad. "14 outrageous sexy girls in string bikinis and high heels blasting away with the sexiest full auto machine guns ever produced."

The psychological state that is satisfied by *Sexy Girls and Sexy Guns* is not widely shared among gun aficionados and is often viewed with considerable scorn. One editorial comment from a magazine that advertised these movies reveals a perceptive under-standing of the nature of this kind of "full autoeroticism and 'Debbie Does the Paris Arms Show' pap":

> You may have seen the rash of mindless "machine-gun videos" that dish out a bilgy froth of bikinis, boobs and burp guns — neither instruction nor entertainment, evidently marketed to exploit a rather narrow spectrum of psychoses which hopes to see pendulous mammillae caught in a closing breach. While these video bikinis might have satisfied the Freudian hostilities of a disturbed few, there has been a need for legitimate orientation-instruction machine gun videos for those who properly regard these weapons as indis-pensable tools of respectable trades.
>
> — D. McLean
>   "Firestorm"

Yet, in reality, our *Sexy Girls and Sexy Guns* video is only a little removed from the not-so-subliminal message of virility implied in the familiar image of a barely clad woman clinging to James Bond as he coolly brandishes a pistol.[10]

Killing as Sex . . .

The linkage between sex and killing becomes unpleasantly apparent when we enter the realm of warfare. Many societies have long recognized the existence of this twisted region in which battle, like sex, is a milestone in adolescent masculinity. Yet the sexual aspects of killing continue beyond the region in which both are thought to be rites of manhood and into the area in which killing becomes like sex and sex like killing.

A British paratrooper who served in the Falklands told Holmes that one particular attack was "the most exciting thing since getting my leg across." One American soldier compared the killings at My Lai to the closely linked guilt and satisfaction that accompany masturbation.

The Israeli military psychologist Ben Shalit touched on this relationship when he described some of his observations of combat:

> On my right was mounted a heavy machine gun. The gunner (normally the cook) was firing away with what I can only describe as a beatific smile on his face. He was exhilarated by the squeezing of the trigger, the hammering of the gun, and the flight of his tracers rushing out into the dark shore. It struck me then (and was confirmed by him and many others later) that squeezing the trigger — releasing a hail of bullets — gives enormous pleasure and satisfaction. These are the pleasures of combat, not in terms of the intellectual planning — of the tactical and strategic chess game — but of the primal aggression, the release, and the orgasmic discharge.

Shalit addresses this subject through symbolic language, but one Vietnam veteran was not nearly so subtle when he told Mark Baker that "a gun is power. To some people carrying a gun was like having a permanent hard-on. It was a pure sexual trip every time you got to pull the trigger." Many men who have carried and fired a gun — especially a full automatic weapon — must confess in their hearts that the power and pleasure of explosively spewing a stream of bullets is akin to the emotions felt when explosively spewing a stream of semen.

One of the veterans I interviewed had six tours in Vietnam. He stated that ultimately he "had to get out of there" because he was becoming consumed by what was happening to him. "Killing can be like sex," he told me, "and you can get carried away with it; it can consume you just like sex can."

. . . And Sex as Killing

And just as the highly personal, close-up, one-on-one, intense experience of killing can be like sex, so can sex be like killing. Glenn Gray speaks of this relationship. "To be sure," he says,

> the sexual partner is not actually destroyed in the encounter, merely overthrown. And the psychological aftereffects of sexual lust are different from those of battle lusts. These differences, however, do not alter the fact that the passions have a common source and affect their victims in the same way while they are in their grip.

The concept of sex as a process of domination and defeat is closely related to the lust for rape and the trauma associated with the rape victim. Thrusting the sexual appendage (the penis) deep into the body of the victim can be perversely linked to thrusting the killing appendage (a bayonet or knife) deep into the body of the victim.

This process can be seen in pornographic movies in which the sexual act is twisted, such that the male ejaculates — or "shoots his wad" — into a female's face. The grip of a firer on the pistol grip of a gun is much like the grip on an erect penis, and holding the penis in this fashion while ejaculating into the victim's face is at some level an act of domination and symbolic destruction. The culmination of this intertwining of sex and death can be seen in snuff films, in which a victim is raped and then murdered on film.

The force of darkness and destruction within us is balanced with a force of light and love for our fellow man. These forces struggle and strive within the heart of each of us. To ignore one is to ignore the other. We cannot know the light if we do not acknowledge the dark. We cannot know life if we do not acknowledge death. The link between sex and war and the process of denial in both fields are well represented by Richard Heckler's observation that "it is in the mythological marriage of Ares [the god of war] and Aphrodite [the god of sex] that Harmonia is born."

SECTION IV

An Anatomy of Killing:
All Factors Considered

The starting point for the understanding of war is the understanding of human nature.

— S. L. A. Marshall
  Men Against Fire

Chapter One

The Demands of Authority:
Milgram and the Military

Riflemen miss if orders sound unsure;
They only are secure who seem secure . . .

— Kingsley Amis
"The Masters"

Dr. Stanley Milgram's famous studies at Yale University on obedience and aggression found that in a controlled laboratory environment more than 65 percent of his subjects could be readily manipulated into inflicting a (seemingly) lethal electrical charge on a total stranger. The subjects sincerely believed that they were causing great physical pain, but despite their victim's pitiful pleas for them to stop, 65 percent continued to obey orders, increase the voltage, and inflict the shocks until long after the screams stopped and there could be little doubt that their victim was dead.

Prior to beginning his experiments Milgram asked a group of psychiatrists and psychologists to predict how many of his subjects would use the maximum voltage on their victims. They estimated that a fraction of 1 percent of the subjects would do so. They, like most people, really didn't have a clue — until Milgram taught us this lesson about ourselves.

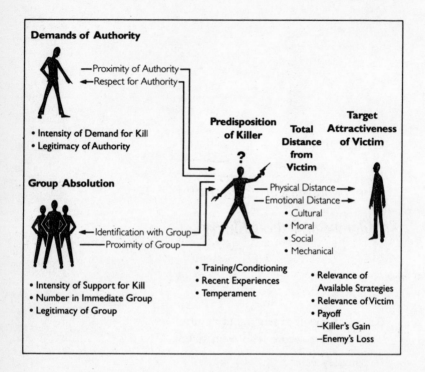

Freud warned us to "never underestimate the power of the need to obey," and this research by Milgram (which has since been replicated many times in half a dozen different countries) validates Freud's intuitive understanding of human nature. Even when the trappings of authority are no more than a white lab coat and a clipboard, this is the kind of response that Milgram was able to elicit:

> I observed a mature and initially poised businessman enter the laboratory smiling and confident. Within 20 minutes he was reduced to a twitching, stuttering wreck, who was rapidly approaching a point of nervous collapse. . . . At one point he pushed his fist into his forehead and muttered: "Oh God, let's stop it." And yet he continued to respond to every word of the experimenter and obeyed to the end.

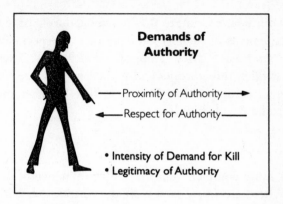

If this kind of obedience could be obtained with a lab coat and a clipboard by an authority figure who has been known for only a few minutes, how much more would the trappings of military authority and months of bonding accomplish?

The Demands of Authority

> The mass needs, and we give it, leaders who have the firmness and decision of command proceeding from habit and an entire faith in their unquestionable right to command as established by tradition, law and society.

— Ardant du Picq
  Battle Studies

Someone who has not studied the matter would underestimate the influence of leadership in enabling killing on the battlefield, but those who have been there know better. A 1973 study by Kranss, Kaplan, and Kranss investigated the factors that make a soldier fire. They found that the individuals who had no combat experience assumed that "being fired upon" would be the critical factor in making them fire. However, veterans listed "being told to fire" as the most critical factor.

More than a century ago, Ardant du Picq found the same thing in his study based on a survey of military officers. He noted one incident during the Crimean War in which, during heavy fighting, two detachments of soldiers suddenly met unexpectedly face-to-face, at "ten paces." They "stopped thunderstruck. Then, forgetting their rifles, threw stones and withdrew." The reason for this behavior, according to du Picq, was that "neither of the two groups had a decided leader."

Authority Factors

But it is more complex than the simple influence of orders by a leader. There are many factors in the relationship between the potential killer and the authority that influence the decision to kill.

In Milgram's experiments the demands of authority were represented by an individual with a clipboard and a white lab coat. This authority figure stood immediately behind the individual who was inflicting shocks and directed that he increase the voltage each time the victim answered a question incorrectly. When the authority figure was not personally present but called over a phone, the number of subjects who were willing to inflict the maximum shock dropped sharply. This process can be generalized to combat circumstances and "operationalized" into a number of subfactors: proximity of the authority figure, respect for the authority figure, intensity of the authority figure's demands, and the authority figure's legitimacy.

- *Proximity of the authority figure to the subject.* Marshall noted many specific World War II incidents in which almost all soldiers would fire their weapons while their leaders observed and encouraged them in a combat situation, but when the leaders left, the firing rate immediately dropped to 15 to 20 percent.

- *Killer's subjective respect for the authority figure.* To be truly effective, soldiers must bond to their leader just as they must bond to their group. Shalit notes a 1973 Israeli study that shows that the primary factor in ensuring the will to fight is identification with the direct commanding officer. Compared with an established and respected leader, an unknown or discredited leader has much less chance of gaining compliance from soldiers in combat.

• *Intensity of the authority figure's demands for killing behavior.* The leader's mere presence is not always sufficient to ensure killing activity. The leader must also communicate a clear expectancy of killing behavior. When he does, the influence can be enormous. When Lieutenant Calley first ordered his men to kill a group of women and children in the village of My Lai, he said, "You know what to do with them," and left. When he came back he asked, "Why haven't you killed them?" The soldier he confronted said, "I didn't think you wanted us to kill them." "No," Calley responded, "I want them dead," and proceeded to fire at them himself. Only then was he able to get his soldiers to start shooting in this extraordinary circumstance in which the soldiers' resistance to killing was, understandably, very high.

• *Legitimacy of the authority figure's authority and demands.* Leaders with legitimate, societally sanctioned authority have greater influence on their soldiers; and legitimate, lawful demands are more likely to be obeyed than illegal or unanticipated demands. Gang leaders and mercenary commanders have to carefully work around their shortcomings in this area, but military officers (with their trappings of power and the legitimate authority of their nation behind them) have tremendous potential to cause their soldiers to overcome individual resistance and reluctance in combat.

The Centurion Factor: The Role of Obedience in Military History

Many factors are at play on the battlefield, but one of the most powerful is the influence of leaders. This influence can be seen throughout history. In particular, the success of the Roman military machine can be seen in light of its mastery of leadership processes.

The Romans pioneered the concepts of leadership development and the NCO corps as we know it, and when the professional Roman army went up against the Greek citizen-soldiers, leadership can be seen as a key factor in the Romans' success.

Both sides had the political legitimacy of their nations and city-states behind them, but there was a real difference in the military legitimacy that these leaders probably had in the eyes of their soldiers. The Roman centurion was a professional leader who had the respect of his soldiers because he had come up through the ranks and had previously demonstrated his ability in combat. This kind of legitimacy is completely different from that associated with leadership in civilian life, and the Greek leader was primarily a civilian whose peacetime legitimacy was not easily transferred to the battlefield and was often tainted by the spoils system and the petty politics associated with the local village he had come from.

In the Greek phalanx the leader at squad and platoon level was a spear-carrying member of the masses. The primary function of these leaders (as defined by their equipment and lack of mobility within the formation) was to participate in the killing. The Roman formation, on the other hand, had a series of mobile, highly trained, and carefully selected leaders whose primary job was not to kill but to stand behind their men and demand that they kill.

Many factors led to the military supremacy that permitted the Romans to conquer the world. For example, their volleys of cleverly designed javelins provided physical distance in the killing process, and their training enabled the individual to use the point and overcame the natural resistance to thrusting. But most authorities agree that a key factor was the degree of professionalism in their small-unit leaders, combined with a formation that facilitated the influence of these leaders.

The influence of an obedience-demanding leader can also be observed in many of the killing circumstances seen in this book. It was the command "That's gotta be Charlie, you asshole. . . . Blow their ass up and run" that spurred Steve Banko into killing a Vietcong soldier. For John Barry Freeman it was a pointed machine gun and the order "Shoot the man" that caused him to shoot one of his fellow mercenaries who had been condemned to death. And for Alan Stuart-Smyth the screamed order "KILL HIM, GODDAMMIT, KILL HIM, NOW!" was necessary to bring him to kill a man who was in the process of swinging the muzzle of a weapon toward him.

In these and many other killing circumstances we can see that it was the demand for killing actions from a leader that was the decisive factor. Never underestimate the power of the need to obey.

"Our Blood and His Guts": The Price the Leader Pays

In many combat situations the ultimate mechanism that leads to
defeat is when the leader of a group can no longer bring himself
to demand sacrifice by his men. One of Bill Mauldin's famous
World War II cartoons shows Willie and Joe discussing General
"Old Blood and Guts" Patton. "Yeah," says the weary, disheveled
combat soldier, "our blood and his guts." Although intended as
sarcasm, there is a profound truth in this statement, for often it *is*
the soldiers' blood and the leader's guts that stave off defeat. And
when the leader's guts or will to sacrifice his men gives out, then
the force he is leading is defeated.

This equation becomes particularly apparent in situations in
which soldiers are cut off from higher authority. In these kinds of
situations the leader is trapped with his men. He sees his soldiers
dying, he sees the wounded suffering; there is no buffer of distance
to enable any denial of the results of his actions. He has no contact
with higher authority, and he knows that at any time he can end
the horror by surrendering and that the decision is solely his to
make. As each of his men is wounded or killed, their suffering
hangs on his conscience, and he knows that it is he and he alone
who is making it continue. He and his will to accept the suffering
of his men are all that keep the battle going. At some point he
can no longer bring himself to muster the will to fight, and with
one short sentence the horror is ended.

Some leaders choose to fight to their deaths, taking their men
with them in a blaze of glory. In many ways it is easier for the
leader if he can die quickly and cleanly with his men and need
never live with what he has done. One of the more striking of
such situations is that of Major James Devereux, the commander
of the U.S. Marines defending Wake Island. The small marine
detachment on Wake held out against overwhelming Japanese
forces from December 8 to December 22, 1941. The last message
sent out before Devereux and his men were overwhelmed was
received by radio telegraphy and said simply: S...E...N...D....
M...O...R...E...J...A...P...S...

But the price for the leader who has lived through such a
situation is high. He must answer to the widows and the orphans

of his men, and he must live forevermore with what he has done to those who entrusted their lives to his care. When I interview combatants, many tell of remorse and anguish that they have never told anyone of before. But I have not yet had any success at getting a leader to confront his emotions revolving around the soldiers who have died in combat as a result of his orders. In interviews, such men work around reservoirs of guilt and denial that appear to be buried too deeply to be tapped, and perhaps this is for the best.

The Lost Battalion of World War I is a famous example of a unit that was sustained by its leader's will. This unit, a battalion of the 77th Division, was cut off and surrounded by Germans during an attack. They continued to fight for days. They ran out of food, water, and ammunition. The survivors were surrounded by friends and comrades suffering from horrible wounds that could not receive medical attention until they surrendered. The Germans brought up flamethrowers and tried to burn them out. Still their commander would not surrender.

They were not an elite or specially trained unit. They were only a composite infantry battalion made up of citizen-soldiers in a National Guard Division. Yet they performed a feat that will shine forever in the annals of military glory.

All the survivors gave full credit for their achievement to the incredible fortitude of their battalion commander, Major C. W. Whittlesey, who refused to surrender and constantly encouraged the dwindling survivors of his battalion to fight on. After five days their battalion was rescued. Major Whittlesey was given the Congressional Medal of Honor. Many people know this story. What they don't know is that Whittlesey committed suicide shortly after the war.

Chapter Two

Group Absolution: "The Individual Is Not a Killer, but the Group Is"

Disintegration of a combat unit . . . usually occurs at the 50%
casualty point, and is marked by increasing numbers of individuals
refusing to kill in combat. . . . Motivation and will to kill the enemy
has evaporated along with their peers and comrades.

— Peter Watson
War on the Mind

A tremendous volume of research indicates that the primary factor
that motivates a soldier to do the things that no sane man *wants*
to do in combat (that is, killing and dying) is not the force of self-
preservation but a powerful sense of accountability to his comrades
on the battlefield. Richard Gabriel notes that "in military writings
on unit cohesion, one consistently finds the assertion that the bonds
combat soldiers form with one another are stronger than the bonds
most men have with their wives." The defeat of even the most
elite group is usually achieved when so many casualties have been
inflicted (usually somewhere around the 50 percent point) that the
group slips into a form of mass depression and apathy. Dinter
points out that "The integration of the individual in the group is
so strong sometimes that the group's destruction, e.g. by force or

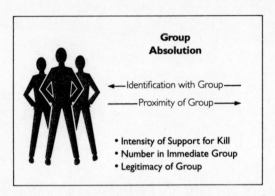

captivity, may lead to depression and subsequent suicide." Among the Japanese in World War II this manifested itself in mass suicide. In most historical groups it results in the group suicide of surrender.

Among men who are bonded together so intensely, there is a powerful process of peer pressure in which the individual cares so deeply about his comrades and what they think about him that he would rather die than let them down. A U.S. Marine Corps Vietnam vet interviewed by Gwynne Dyer communicated this process clearly when he said that "your first instinct, regardless of all your training, is to live. . . . But you can't turn around and run the other way. Peer pressure, you know?" Dyer calls this "a special kind of love that has nothing to do with sex or idealism," and Ardant du Picq referred to it as "mutual surveillance" and considered it to be the predominant psychological factor on the battlefield.

Marshall noted that a single soldier falling back from a broken and retreating unit will be of little value if pressed into service in another unit. But if a pair of soldiers or the remnants of a squad or platoon are put to use, they can generally be counted upon to fight well. The difference in these two situations is the degree to which the soldiers have bonded or developed a sense of accountability to the small number of men they will be fighting with — which is distinctly different from the more generalized cohesion of the army as a whole. *If* the individual is bonded with his comrades, and *if* he is with "his" group, then the probability that the individual will participate in killing is significantly increased. But if those factors are absent, the probability that the individual will be an active participant in combat is quite low.

Du Picq sums this matter up when he says, "Four brave men who do not know each other will not dare to attack a lion. Four less brave, but knowing each other well, sure of their reliability and consequently of mutual aid, will attack resolutely. There," says du Picq, "is the science of the organization of armies in a nutshell."

Anonymity and Group Absolution

In addition to creating a sense of accountability, groups also enable killing through developing in their members a sense of anonymity that contributes further to violence. In some circumstances this process of group anonymity seems to facilitate a kind of atavistic killing hysteria that can also be seen in the animal kingdom. Kruck's 1972 research describes scenes from the animal kingdom that show that senseless and wanton killing does occur. These include the slaughter of gazelles by hyenas, in quantities way beyond their need or capacity to eat, or the destruction of gulls that could not fly on a stormy night and thus were "sitting ducks" for foxes that proceed to kill them beyond any possible need for food. Shalit points out that "such senseless violence in the animal world — as well as most of the violence in the human domain — is shown by groups rather than by individuals."

Konrad Lorenz tells us that "man is not a killer, but the group is." Shalit demonstrates a profound understanding of this process and has researched it extensively:

> All crowding has an intensifying effect. If aggression exists, it will become more so as a result of crowding; if joy exists, it will become intensified by the crowd. It has been shown by some studies . . . that a mirror in front of an aggressor tends to increase his aggression — if he was disposed to be aggressive. However, if this individual were not so disposed, the effect of the mirror would be to further enhance his nonaggressive tendencies. The effect of the

crowd seems to be much like a mirror, reflecting each individual's behavior in those around him and thus intensifying the existing pattern of behavior.

Psychologists have long understood that a diffusion of responsibility can be caused by the anonymity created in a crowd. It has been demonstrated in literally dozens of studies that bystanders will be less likely to interfere in a situation in direct relationship to the numbers who are witnessing the circumstance. Thus, in large crowds, horrendous crimes can occur but the likelihood of a bystander interfering is very low. However, if the bystander is alone and is faced with a circumstance in which there is no one else to diffuse the responsibility to, then the probability of intervention is very high. In the same way groups can provide a diffusion of responsibility that will enable individuals in mobs and soldiers in military units to commit acts that they would never dream of doing as individuals, acts such as lynching someone because of the color of his skin or shooting someone because of the color of his uniform.

Death in the Crowd: Accountability and Anonymity on the Battlefield

The influence of groups on killing occurs through a strange and powerful interaction of accountability and anonymity. Although at first glance the influence of these two factors would seem to be paradoxical, in actuality they interact in such a manner as to magnify and amplify each other in order to enable violence.

Police are aware of these accountability and anonymity processes and are trained to unhinge them by calling individuals within a group by name whenever possible. Doing so causes the people so named to reduce their identification with the group and begin to think of themselves as individuals with personal accountability. This inhibits violence by limiting the individuals' sense of accountability to the group and negating their sense of anonymity.

Among groups in combat, this accountability (to one's friends) and anonymity (to reduce one's sense of personal responsibility for killing) combine to play a significant role in enabling killing.

As we have seen so far in this study, killing another human being is an extraordinarily difficult thing to do. But if a soldier feels he is letting his friends down if he doesn't kill, and if he can get others to share in the killing process (thus diffusing his personal responsibility by giving each individual a slice of the guilt), then killing can be easier. In general, the more members in the group, the more psychologically bonded the group, and the more the group is in close proximity, the more powerful the enabling can be.

Still, just the presence of a group in combat does not guarantee aggression. (It could be a group of pacifists, in which case pacifism might be enabled by the group!) The individual must identify with and be bonded with a group that has a legitimate demand for killing. And he must be with or close to the group for it to influence his behavior.

Chariot, Phalanx, Cannon, and Machine Gun: The Role of Groups in Military History

These processes can be seen throughout military history. For example, military historians have often wondered why the chariot dominated military history for so long. Tactically, economically, and mechanically it was not a cost-effective instrument on the battlefield, yet for many centuries it was the king of battle. But if we examine the psychological leverage provided by the chariot to enable killing on the battlefield, we soon realize that the chariot was successful because it was the first crew-served weapon.

Several factors were at play here — the bow as a distance weapon, the social distance created by the archers' having come from the nobility, and the psychological distance created by using the chariot in pursuit and shooting men in the back — but the key issue is that the chariot crew traditionally consisted of two men: a driver and an archer. And this was all that was needed to provide the same accountability and anonymity in close-proximity groups that in World War II permitted nearly 100 percent of crew-served weapons (such as machine guns) to fire while only 15 to 20 percent of the riflemen fired.

The chariot was defeated by the phalanx, which succeeded by turning the whole formation into a massive crew-served weapon.

Although he did not have the designated leaders of the later Roman formations, each man in the phalanx was under a powerful mutual surveillance system, and in the charge it would be hard to fail to strike home without having others notice that your spear had been raised or dropped at the critical moment. And, of course, in addition to this accountability system the closely packed phalanx provided a high degree of mob anonymity.

For nearly half a millennium the Romans' professional military (with, among other things, their superior application of leadership) eclipsed the phalanx in the Western way of war. But the phalanx's application of group processes was so simple and so effective that during the period of more than a thousand years between the fall of the Roman Empire and the full integration of gunpowder, the phalanx and the pike ruled infantry tactics.

And when gunpowder was introduced, it was the crew-served cannon, later augmented by the machine gun, that did most of the killing. Gustavus Adolphus revolutionized warfare by introducing a small three-pound cannon that was pulled around by each platoon, thus becoming the first platoon crew-served weapon and presaging the platoon machine guns of today. Napoleon, an artilleryman, recognized the role of the artillery (often firing grapeshot at very close ranges), which was the real killer on the battlefield, and throughout his years he consistently ensured that he had greater numbers of artillery than any of his opponents. During World War I the machine gun was introduced and termed the "distilled essence of the infantry," but it really was the continuation of the cannon, as artillery became an indirect-fire weapon (shooting over the soldiers' heads from miles back), and the machine gun replaced the cannon in the direct-fire, mid-range role.

Britain's World War I Machine Gun Corps Monument, next to the Wellington Monument in London, is a statue of a young David, inscribed with a Bible verse that exemplifies the meaning of the machine gun in that terrible war that sucked so much of the marrow from the bones of that great nation:

Sol has slain his thousands
And David has slain his tens of thousands.

"They Were Killing My Friends": Groups on the Modern Battlefield

The influence of groups can be seen clearly when we closely examine the killing case studies outlined throughout this book. Note the absence of group influence in many of the situations in which combatants chose *not* to kill each other. For example, in the section "Killing and Physical Distance," Captain Willis was alone when he was suddenly confronted with a single North Vietnamese soldier. He "vigorously shook his head" and initiated "a truce, cease-fire, gentleman's agreement or a deal," after which the enemy soldier "sank back into the darkness and Willis stumbled on."

Again, at the beginning of the section "Killing and the Existence of Resistance," Michael Kathman, a tunnel rat crawling alone in a Vietcong tunnel, was alone when he switched on the light and suddenly found "not more than 15 feet away . . . a [lone] Viet Cong eating a handful of rice. . . . After a moment, he put his pouch of rice on the floor of the tunnel beside him, turned his back to me and slowly started crawling away." Kathman, in turn, switched off his flashlight and slipped away in the other direction.

And as you read these case studies note also the presence and influence of groups in most situations in which soldiers *do* elect to kill. The classic example is Audie Murphy, the most decorated American soldier of World War II. He won the Medal of Honor by single-handedly taking on a German infantry company. He fought alone, but when asked what motivated him to do this, he responded simply, "They were killing my friends."

Chapter Three

Emotional Distance: "To Me They Were Less than Animals"

Increasing the distance between the [combatants] — whether by emphasizing their differences or by increasing the chain of responsibility between the aggressor and his victim allows for an increase in the degree of aggression.

— Ben Shalit
  The Psychology of Conflict and Combat

Cracks in the Veil of Denial

One evening after giving a presentation on "The Price and Process of Killing" to a group of vets in New York, I was asked by a retired World War II veteran who had been in the audience if I could talk with him privately in the bar. After we were alone he said that there was something he had never told anyone about, something that, after hearing my presentation, he wanted to share with me.

He had been an army officer in the South Pacific, and one night the Japanese launched an infiltration attack on his position. During the attack a Japanese soldier charged him.

"I had my forty-five [-caliber pistol] in my hand," he said, "and the point of his bayonet was no further than you are from me

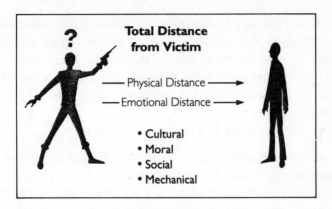

when I shot him. After everything had settled down I helped search his body, you know, for intelligence purposes, and I found a photograph."

Then there was a long pause, and he continued. "It was a picture of his wife, and these two beautiful children. Ever since" — and here tears began to roll down his cheeks, although his voice remained firm and steady — "I've been haunted by the thought of these two beautiful children growing up without their father, because I murdered their daddy. I'm not a young man anymore, and soon I'll have to answer to my Maker for what I have done."[1]

A year later, in a pub in England, I told a Vietnam veteran who is currently a colonel in the U.S. Army about this incident. As I told him about the photographs he said, "Oh, no. Don't tell me. There was an address on the back of the photo."

"No," I replied. "At least he never mentioned it if there was."

Later in the evening I got back around to asking why he would have thought there was an address on the photos, and he told me that he had had a similar experience in Vietnam, but his photos had addresses on the back of them. "And you know," he said, as his eyes lost focus and he slipped into that haunted, thousand-yard stare I've seen in so many vets when their minds and emotions return to the battlefield, "I've always meant to send those photos back."

Each of these men had attained the rank of colonel in the U.S. Army. Both are the distilled essence of all that is good and noble in their generation. And both of them have been haunted by simple photographs. But what those photographs represented was a crack in the veil of denial that makes war possible.

The Social Obstacles to Emotional Distance

The physical distance process has been addressed previously, but distance in war is not merely physical. There is also an emotional distance process that plays a vital part in overcoming the resistance to killing. Factors such as cultural distance, moral distance, social distance, and mechanical distance are just as effective as physical distance in permitting the killer to deny that he is killing a human being.

There was a popular and rather clever saying during the 1960s that asked, "What if they gave a war and nobody came?" This is not quite as ludicrous a concept as it may seem on the surface. There is a constant danger on the battlefield that, in periods of extended close combat, the combatants will get to know and acknowledge one another as individuals and subsequently may refuse to kill each other. This danger and the process by which it can occur is poignantly represented by Henry Metelmann's account of his experiences as a German soldier on the Russian front during World War II.

There was a lull in the battle, during which Metelmann saw two Russians coming out of their foxhole,

and I walked over towards them . . . they introduced themselves . . . [and] offered me a cigarette and, as a non-smoker, I thought if they offer me a cigarette I'll smoke it. But it was horrible stuff. I coughed and later on my mates said "You made a horrible impression, standing there with those two Russians and coughing your head off." . . . I talked to them and said it was all right to come closer to the foxhole, because there were three dead Russian soldiers lying there, and I, to my shame, had killed them. They wanted to get the [dog tags] off them, and the paybooks. . . . I kind of helped them and we were all bending down and we found some photos in one of the paybooks and they showed them to me: we all three stood up and looked at the photos. . . . We shook hands again, and one patted on my back and they walked away.

Metelmann was called away to drive a half-track back to the field hospital. When he returned to the battlefield, over an hour later, he found that the Germans had overrun the Russian position. And although there were some of his friends killed, he found himself to be most concerned about what happened to "those two Russians."

"Oh they got killed," they said.
I said: "How did it happen?"
"Oh, they didn't want to give in. Then we shouted at them to come out with their hands up and they did not, so one of us went over with a tank," he said, "and really got them, and silenced them that way." My feeling was very sad. I had met them on a very human basis, on a comradely basis. They called me comrade and at that moment, strange as it may seem, I was more sad that they had to die in this mad confrontation than my own mates and I still think sadly about it.

This identification with one's victim is also reflected in the Stockholm syndrome. Most people know of the Stockholm syndrome as a process in which the victim of a hostage situation comes to identify with the hostage taker, but it is actually more complex than that and occurs in three stages:

• First the *victim* experiences an increase in association with the hostage taker.
• Then the victim usually experiences a decrease in identification with the authorities who are dealing with the hostage taker.
• Finally the *hostage taker* experiences an increase in identification and bonding with the victim.

One of the more interesting of many such cases was the Moluccan train siege in Holland in 1975. In this instance the terrorists had already shot one hostage and then selected another for execution. This intended victim then asked permission to write a final note to his family, and his request was granted. He was a journalist, and he must have been a very good one, for he wrote such a heart-wrenching letter that, upon reading it, the terrorists took pity on him . . . and shot someone else instead.

Sometimes this process can happen on a vast scale. Many times in World War I there were unofficial suspensions of hostilities that came about through the process of coming to know each other too well. During Christmas of 1914 British and German soldiers in many sectors met peacefully, exchanged presents, took photographs and even played soccer. Holmes notes that "in some areas the truce went on until well into the New Year, despite the High Command's insistence that it should be war as usual."

Erich Fromm states that "there is good clinical evidence for the assumption that destructive aggression occurs, at least to a large degree, in conjunction with a momentary or chronic emotional withdrawal." The situations described above represent a breakdown in the psychological distance that is a key method of removing one's sense of empathy and achieving this "emotional withdrawal." Again, some of the mechanisms that facilitate this process include:

- Cultural distance, such as racial and ethnic differences, which permit the killer to dehumanize the victim
- Moral distance, which takes into consideration the kind of intense belief in moral superiority and vengeful/vigilante actions associated with many civil wars
- Social distance, which considers the impact of a lifetime of practice in thinking of a particular class as less than human in a socially stratified environment
- Mechanical distance, which includes the sterile Nintendo-game unreality of killing through a TV screen, a thermal sight, a sniper sight, or some other kind of mechanical buffer that permits the killer to deny the humanity of his victim

Cultural Distance: "Inferior Forms of Life"

In the section "Killing in America," we will examine the methodology a U.S. Navy psychiatrist developed to psychologically enable assassins for the U.S. Navy. This "formula" primarily involved classical conditioning and systematic desensitization using violent movies, but it also integrated cultural distance processes in order

> to get the men to think of the potential enemies they will have to face as inferior forms of life [with films] biased to present the enemy as less than human: the stupidity of local customs is ridiculed, local personalities are presented as evil demigods.

— quoted in Peter Watson, *War on the Mind*

The Israeli research mentioned earlier indicates that the risk of death for a kidnap victim is much greater if the victim is hooded. Cultural distance is a form of emotional hooding that can work just as effectively. Shalit notes that "the nearer or more similar the victim of aggression is, the more we can identify with him." And the harder it is to kill him.

This process also works the other way around. It is so much easier to kill someone if they look distinctly different from you. If your propaganda machine can convince your soldiers that their opponents are not really human but are "inferior forms of life," then their natural resistance to killing their own species will be reduced. Often the enemy's humanity is denied by referring to him as a "gook," "Kraut," or "Nip." In Vietnam this process was assisted by the "body count" mentality, in which we referred to and thought of the enemy as numbers. One Vietnam vet told me that this permitted him to think that killing the NVA and VC was like "stepping on ants."

The greatest master of this in recent times may have been Adolf Hitler, with his myth of the Aryan master race: the *Ubermensch,* whose duty was to cleanse the world of the *Untermensch.*

The adolescent soldier against whom such propaganda is directed is desperately trying to rationalize what he is being *forced* to do, and he is therefore predisposed to believe this nonsense. Once he begins to herd people like cattle and then to slaughter them like cattle, he very quickly begins to think of them as cattle — or, if you will, *Untermensch.*

According to Trevor Dupuy, the Germans, in all stages of World War II, consistently inflicted 50 percent more casualties on the Americans and British than were inflicted on them. And the Nazi leadership would probably be the first to tell you that it was this carefully nurtured belief in their racial and cultural superiority that enabled the soldiers to be so successful. (But, as we shall see in "Killing and Atrocities," this enabling also contained an entrapment that contributed greatly to the Nazis' ultimate defeat.)

But the Nazis are hardly the only ones to wield the sword of racial and ethnic hatred in war. European imperial defeat and domination of "the darker races" was facilitated by cultural distance factors.

However, this can be a double-edged sword. Once oppressors begin to think of their victims as not being the same species, then these victims can accept and use that cultural distance to kill and oppress their colonial masters when they finally gain the upper hand. This double-edged sword was turned on the oppressors when colonial nations rose up in fierce insurrections such as the Sepoy Mutiny or the Mau Mau Uprising. In the final battles that overthrew imperialism around the world, the backlash of this double-edged sword was a major factor in empowering local populations.

The United States is a comparatively egalitarian nation and therefore has a little more difficulty getting its population to wholeheartedly embrace wartime ethnic and racial hatreds. But in combat against Japan we had an enemy so different and alien that we were able to effectively implement cultural distance (combined with a powerful dose of moral distance, since we were "avenging" Pearl Harbor). Thus, according to Stouffer's research, 44 percent of American soldiers in World War II said they would "really like to kill a Japanese soldier," but only 6 percent expressed that degree of enthusiasm for killing Germans.

In Vietnam cultural distance would have backlashed against us, since our enemy was racially and culturally indistinguishable from our ally. Therefore we tried hard (at a national policy level) not to emphasize any cultural distance from our enemies. The primary psychological distance factor utilized in Vietnam was moral distance, deriving from our moral "crusade" against communism.

But try as we might we were not completely successful at keeping the genie of racial hatred in its bottle.

Most of the Vietnam veterans I have interviewed developed a profound love for the Vietnamese culture and people. Many married Vietnamese women. This egalitarian tendency to mingle with and accept, admire, and even love another culture is an American strong point. Because of it America was able to turn occupied Germany and Japan from defeated enemies to friends and allies. But many U.S. soldiers in Vietnam spent their year in-country isolated from the positive, friendly aspects of Vietnamese culture and people. The only Vietnamese they met were either trying to kill them or were suspected of being or supporting Vietcong. This environment had the capacity to develop profound suspicion and hatred. One Vietnam veteran told me that, to him, "they were less than animals."

Because of this ability to accept other cultures, Americans probably committed fewer atrocities than most other nations would have under the circumstances associated with guerrilla warfare in Vietnam. Certainly fewer than was the track record of most colonial powers. Yet still we had our My Lai, and our efforts in that war were profoundly, perhaps fatally, undermined by that single incident.

It can be easy to unleash this genie of racial and ethnic hatred in order to facilitate killing in time of war. It can be more difficult to keep the cork in the bottle and completely restrain it. Once it *is* out, and the war is over, the genie is not easily put back in the bottle. Such hatred lingers over the decades, even centuries, as can be seen today in Lebanon and what was once Yugoslavia.

It would be easy to feel some smug, self-righteous sense of superiority and convince ourselves that such lingering hatred exists only in distant, insular nations like Lebanon or Yugoslavia. The truth is that we are still trying to suppress racism more than a century after the end of slavery, and our limited use of cultural distance in World War II and Vietnam still tarnishes our dealings with our opponents in those wars.

On some future battlefield we may be tempted to once again manipulate this two-edged sword of cultural distance to our advantage. But before we do, we would be well advised to carefully consider the costs. The costs both during the war and in the peace that we hope to have attained when the war is over.

Moral Distance: "Their Cause Is Holy, So How Can They Sin?"

> We who strike the enemy where his heart beats have been slandered as "baby-killers" and "murders of women." . . . What we do is repugnant to us too, but necessary. Very necessary. Nowadays there is no such animal as a non-combatant; modern warfare is total warfare. A soldier cannot function at the front without the factory worker, the farmer, and all the other providers behind him. You and I, Mother, have discussed this subject, and I know you understand what I say. My men are brave and honourable. Their cause is holy, so how can they sin while doing their duty? If what we do is frightful, then may frightfulness be Germany's salvation.
>
> — Captain Peter Strasser, head of Germany's World War I airship division, in a letter quoted in Gwynne Dyer, *War*

Moral distance involves legitimizing oneself and one's cause. It can generally be divided into two components. The first component usually is the determination and condemnation of the enemy's guilt, which, of course, must be punished or avenged. The other is an affirmation of the legality and legitimacy of one's own cause.

Moral distance establishes that the enemy's cause is clearly wrong, his leaders are criminal, and his soldiers are either simply misguided or are sharing in their leader's guilt. But the enemy is still a human, and killing him is an act of justice rather than the extermination that is often motivated by cultural distance.[2]

In the same way that this process has traditionally enabled violence in police forces, it can also enable violence on the battlefield. Alfred Vagts recognized this as a process in which

> enemies are to be deemed criminals in advance, guilty of starting the war; the business of locating the aggressor is to begin before or shortly after the outbreak of the war; the methods of conducting the war are to be branded as criminal; and victory is not to be a triumph of honour and bravery over honour and bravery but the

climax of a police hunt for bloodthirsty wretches who have violated law, order, and everything else esteemed good and holy.

Vagts felt that this kind of propaganda has had an increasing influence on modern war, and he may well be right. But this is really nothing new. In the West it dates back at least to those days when the pope, then the undisputed moral leader of Western civilization, established the moral justification for the tragic and bloody wars we call the Crusades.

Punishment Justification: "Remember the Alamo/Maine/ Pearl Harbor"

The establishment of the enemy's guilt and the need to punish or avenge is a fundamental and widely accepted justification for violence. Most nations reserve the right to "administer" capital punishment, and if a state directs a soldier to kill a criminal who is guilty of a sufficiently heinous crime, then the killing can be readily rationalized as nothing more than the administration of justice.

The mechanism of punishment justification is so fundamental that it can sometimes be artificially manipulated. In World War II, some Japanese leaders cultivated an artificial punishment justification. "Colonel Masonobu Tsuji," says Holmes,

> who masterminded Japanese planning for the invasion of Malaya, wrote a tract designed, amongst other things, to screw his soldiers to a pitch of fighting fury. "When you encounter the enemy after landing, think of yourself as an avenger come at last face to face with your father's murderer. Here is the man whose death will lighten your heart of its burden of brooding anger. If you fail to destroy him utterly you can never rest in peace."

Legal Affirmation: "We Hold These Truths to Be Self-Evident"

When in the Course of human events, it becomes necessary for one people to dissolve the political bonds which have connected them with another, and to assume among the powers of the earth, the separate and equal station to which the Laws of Nature and of Nature's God entitle them, a decent respect to the opinions of

mankind requires that they should declare the causes which impel
them to the separation. . . .
    We hold these truths to be self-evident.

— Declaration of Independence

The affirmation of the legality of one's own case is the flip side
of punishment motivation. This process of asserting the legitimacy
of your cause is one of the primary mechanisms enabling violence
in civil wars, since the similarities of the combatants make it difficult
to develop cultural distance. But moral distance is, in varying
degrees, also a violence-enabling factor in all wars, not just civil
wars.

One of the major manifestations of moral distance is what might
be called the home-court advantage. The moral advantage associated with defending one's own den, home, or nation has a long
tradition that can be found in the animal kingdom as well, and it
should not be neglected in assessing the impact of moral distance
in empowering a nation's violence. Winston Churchill said that
"it is the primary right of men to die and kill for the land they
live in, and to punish with exceptional severity all members of their
own race who have warmed their hands at the invader's hearth."

American wars have usually been characterized by a distinctive
tendency toward moral rather than cultural distance. Cultural distance has been a little harder to develop in America's comparatively
egalitarian culture with its ethnically and racially diverse population. In the American Revolution the Boston Massacre provided
a degree of punishment justification, and the Declaration of Independence ("We hold these truths to be self-evident") represented
the legal affirmation that set the tone for American wars for the
next two centuries. The War of 1812 was waged in "self-defense"
with the home-court advantage very much on our side and the
burning of the White House and the bombardment of Fort
McHenry ("Oh! say, can you see, by the dawn's early light")
serving as rallying points for punishment justification. The moral
foundations of our legal affirmation for our nation's concern for
the oppression of others can be seen in the Civil War and the
very sincere motivation on the part of many Northern soldiers to

end slavery ("Mine eyes have seen the glory of the coming of the Lord"), while a degree of punishment motivation can be seen in the bombardment of Fort Sumter.

In the last hundred years we have moved slightly away from moral affirmation as a justification for starting wars and have focused more on the punishment aspect of moral distance. In the Spanish-American War it was the sinking of the *Maine* that provided the punishment justification for war. In World War I it was the *Lusitania,* in World War II it was Pearl Harbor, in Korea it was an unprovoked attack on American troops, in Vietnam it was the Gulf of Tonkin Incident, and in the Gulf War it was the invasion of Kuwait.[3]

It is interesting to note that although punishment was used to justify starting American involvement in these wars, moral affirmation came into play later and lent a very American flavor to some of these conflicts. Once the Allies began to liberate concentration camps, General Eisenhower began to view World War II as a Crusade, and the justification for the Cold War had consistent underpinnings as a moral battle against totalitarianism and oppression.

Moral distance processes tend to provide a foundation upon which other killing-enabling processes can be built. In general they are less likely to produce atrocities than cultural distance processes, and they are more in keeping with the kind of "rules" (deterring aggression and upholding individual human dignity) that organizations such as the United Nations have attempted to uphold. But as with cultural distance, there is a danger associated with moral distance. That danger is, of course, that every nation seems to think that God is on its side.

Social Distance: Death across the Swine Log

While working as a sergeant in the 82d Airborne Division in the 1970s, I once visited a sister battalion's operations office. Most such offices have a large in-out roster as you come in the door. Usually these rosters have a list of all the people in the office, organized by rank; but this one had a different twist. On top of the list were the officers, then there was a divider section labeled

"Swine Log," and then there was a list of all the enlisted personnel in the office. This concept of the "Swine Log" was a fairly common one, and although it was usually used in good humor, and usually more subtly, there is a social distance between officers and enlisted personnel. I have been a private, a sergeant, and an officer. My wife, my children, and I have all experienced this class structure and the social distance that goes with it. Officers, noncommissioned officers (NCOs), and enlisted members (EMs) all have separate clubs on a military base. Their wives go to separate social functions. Their families live in separate housing areas.

To understand the role of the Swine Log in the military we must understand how hard it is to be the one to give the orders that will send your friends to their deaths, and how easy is the alternative of surrendering honorably and ending the horror. The essence of the military is that to be a good leader you must truly love (in a strangely detached fashion) your men, and then you must be willing to kill (or at least give the orders that will result in the deaths of) that which you love. The paradox of war is that those leaders who are most willing to endanger that which they love can be the ones who are most liable to win, and therefore most likely to protect their men. The social class structure that exists in the military provides a denial mechanism that makes it possible for leaders to order their men to their deaths. But it makes military leadership a very lonely thing.

This class structure is even more pronounced in the British army. During my year at the British Army Staff College, the British officers who were my friends felt very strongly (and I agree with them) that their lifetime of experience in the British class system made them better officers. The influence of social distance must have been very powerful in ages past, when all officers came from the nobility and had a lifetime's experience in wielding the power of life and death.

In nearly all historical battles prior to the age of Napoleon, the serf who looked down his spear or musket at the enemy saw another hapless serf very much like himself, and we can understand that he was not particularly inclined to kill his mirror image. And so it is that the great majority of close-combat killing in ancient history was not done by the mobs of serfs and peasants who formed the great mass of combatants. It was the elite, the nobility, who were the real killers in these battles, and they were enabled by, among other things, social distance.

Mechanical Distance: "I Don't See People . . ."

The development of new weapon systems enables the soldier, even on the battlefield, to fire more lethal weapons more accurately to longer ranges: his enemy is, increasingly, an anonymous figure encircled by a gunsight, glowing on a thermal imager, or shrouded in armour plate.

— Richard Holmes
  Acts of War

Social distance is generally fading as a form of killing enabling in Western war. But even as it disappears in this more egalitarian age, it is being replaced by a new, technologically based form of psychological distance. During the Gulf War this was referred to as "Nintendo warfare."

The infantry kills the enemy up close and personal, but in recent decades the nature of this close-in battle has changed significantly. Until recently in the U.S. Army the night sight was a rare and exotic piece of equipment. Now we fight primarily at night, and there is a thermal-imagery device or a night-vision device for almost every combat soldier. Thermal imagery "sees" the heat emitted by a body as if it were light. Thus it works to see through rain, fog, and smoke. It permits you to perceive through camouflage, and it makes it possible to detect enemy soldiers deep in wood lines and vegetation that would once have completely concealed them.

Night-vision devices provide a superb form of psychological distance by converting the target into an inhuman green blob.

The complete integration of thermal-imagery technology into the modern battlefield will extend to daylight hours the mechanical distance process that currently exists during the night. When this happens the battlefield will appear to every soldier as it did to Gad, an Israeli tank gunner who told Holmes that "you see it all as if it were happening on a TV screen. . . . It occurred to me at the time; I see someone running and I shoot at him, and he falls, and it all looks like something on TV. I don't see people, that's one good thing about it."

Chapter Four

The Nature of the Victim:
Relevance and Payoff

The Shalit Factors: Means, Motive, and Opportunity

Given an opportunity to kill and time to think about it, a soldier in combat becomes very much like a killer in a classical murder mystery, assessing his "means, motive, and opportunity." Israeli military psychologist Ben Shalit has developed a model of target attractiveness revolving around the nature of the victim, which has been modified slightly and incorporated into our overall model of the killing-enabling factors.

Shalit takes into consideration:

- The relevance and effectiveness of available strategies for killing the victim (that is, the means and opportunity)
- The relevance of the victim and the payoff of killing in terms of the killer's gain and the enemy's loss (the motive)

Relevance of Available Strategies: Means and Opportunity

> Man taxes his ingenuity to be able to kill without running the risk of being killed.
>
> — Ardant du Picq
> *Battle Studies*

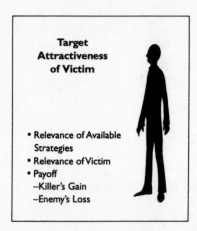

Tactical and technological advantages increase the effectiveness of the combat strategies available to the soldier. Or, as one soldier put it, "You want to make damn sure you don't get your own ass shot off while you are hosing the enemy." This is what has always been achieved by gaining a tactical advantage through ambushes, flank attacks, and rear attacks. In modern warfare this is also achieved by firing through night sights and thermal-imagery devices at a technologically inferior enemy who does not have this capability. This kind of tactical and technological advantage provides the soldier with "means" and "opportunity," thereby increasing the probability that he will kill the enemy.

An example of the influence of this process is outlined in the after-action reports describing the activities of Sergeant First Class Waldron in the section "Killing and Physical Distance." Sergeant Waldron was a sniper, and in this case his killing was made possible by the fact that he was firing at night, at extremely long ranges, with a night-vision scope and a noise suppressor on his rifle. The result was an incredibly sterile kind of killing in which the killer was not at all endangered by his actions:

> The first Viet Cong in the group was taken under fire . . . resulting in one Viet Cong killed. Immediately the other Viet Cong formed

a huddle around the fallen body, *apparently not quite sure of what had taken place* [emphasis added]. Sergeant Waldron continued engaging the Viet Cong one by one until a total of [all] five Viet Cong were killed.

We have seen before that when the enemy is fleeing or has his back turned, he is far more likely to be killed. One reason for this is that in doing so he has provided both means and opportunity for his opponent to kill without endangering himself. Steve Banko achieved both means and opportunity when he was able to sneak up on and shoot a Vietcong soldier. "They didn't know I existed," said Banko, and that made it possible for him to muster his courage, and he "squeezed softly on the trigger."

Relevance of the Victim and Payoff for the Killer: The Motive

After a soldier is confident that he is "able to kill without running the risk of being killed," the next question that comes to mind is, Which enemy soldier should I shoot at? In Shalit's model the question could be phrased: Is killing this individual relevant to the tactical situation, and will there be a payoff for doing so? In our analogy to the classical murder mystery, this is the motive for the killing.

The most obvious motive for killing in combat is the kill-or-be-killed circumstances of self-defense or the defense of one's friends. We have observed this factor many times in the case studies observed thus far:

> [He] was coming at me full gallop, his machete cocked high over his head. . . . All of a sudden there was a guy firing a pistol right at us . . . all of a sudden he turned his whole body and pointed his automatic weapon at me. . . . I knew . . . that he would start picking us off.

It is not very profound to observe that in choosing from a group of enemy targets to kill, a soldier is more likely to kill the one that represents the greatest gain to him and the greatest loss to the enemy. But if no particular soldier poses a specific threat by virtue of his actions, then the process of selecting the most high-value target can take more subtle forms.

One consistent tendency is to elect to shoot leaders and officers. We have already noted the marine sniper who told Truby, "You don't like to hit ordinary troops, because they're usually scared draftees or worse. . . . The guys to shoot are big brass." Throughout military history the leaders and the flag bearers were selected as targets for enemy weapons, since these would represent the highest payoff in terms of the enemy's loss. General James Gavin, the commander of the 82d Airborne Division in World War II, carried an M1 Garand rifle, then the standard American-infantry weapon of World War II. He advised young infantry officers not to carry any equipment that would make them stand out in the eyes of the enemy.

Oftentimes the criteria for deciding whom to kill are dictated by deciding who is manning the most dangerous weapon. In Steve Banko's case he selected the Vietcong soldier who "was sitting closest to the machine gun, and he would die because of it."

Every surrendering soldier instinctively knows that the first thing he should do is drop his weapon, but if he is smart he will also ditch his helmet. Holmes notes that "Brigadier Peter Young, in the second world war, had no more regret about shooting a helmeted German than he would about 'banging a nail on the head.' But somehow he could never bring himself to hit a bareheaded man." It is because of this response to helmets that United Nations peacekeeping forces prefer to wear their traditional beret rather than a helmet, which might very well stop a bullet or save their lives in an artillery barrage.

Killing Without Relevance or Payoff

Being able to identify your victim as a combatant is important to the rationalization that occurs after the kill. If a soldier kills a child, a woman, or anyone who does not represent a potential threat, then he has entered the realm of murder (as opposed to a legitimate, sanctioned combat kill), and the rationalization process becomes quite difficult. Even if he kills in self-defense, there is enormous resistance associated with killing an individual who is not normally associated with relevance or a payoff.

Bruce, a Ranger team leader in Vietnam, had several personal kills, but the one time that he could not bring himself to kill, even when he was directly ordered to do so, was when the target was a Vietcong soldier who was also a woman. Many other narratives and books from Vietnam cover in great detail the shock and horror associated with killing female Vietcong soldiers. And although fighting and killing women in combat is new to Americans and relatively uncommon throughout military history, it is not completely unprecedented. During the French Dahomey expedition in 1892, hardened French foreign legionnaires faced a bizarre army of female warriors, and Holmes notes that many of these tough veterans "experienced a few seconds' hesitation about shooting or bayoneting a half-naked Amazon [and] their delay had fatal results."

The presence of women and children can inhibit aggression in combat, but only if the women and children are not threatened. If they are present, if they become threatened, and if the combatant accepts responsibility for them, then the psychology of battle changes from one of carefully constrained ceremonial combat among males to the unconstrained ferocity of an animal who is defending its den.

Thus the presence of women and children can also increase violence on the battlefield. The Israelis have consistently refused to put women in combat since their experiences in 1948. I have been told by several Israeli officers that this is because in 1948 they experienced recurring incidences of uncontrolled violence among male Israeli soldiers who had had their female combatants killed or injured in combat, and because the Arabs were extremely reluctant to surrender to women.

Holmes has a firm understanding of the inhibiting influences of women and children in combat when he observes:

> When Barbary apes wish to approach a senior male, they borrow a young animal which they carry, in order to inhibit the senior's aggression. Some soldiers do likewise. A British infantryman watched Germans emerging from a dugout to surrender in WWI:

"they were holding up photographs of their families and offering watches and other valuables in an attempt to gain mercy."

However, in some circumstances, even this is not enough. In this instance "as the Germans came up the steps a soldier, not from our battalion, shot each one in the stomach with a burst from his Lewis gun." This soldier, who was willing to kill helpless, surrendering Germans one by one, was probably influenced by yet another factor that enables killing on the battlefield. And that factor is the predisposition of the killer, which we will now examine in detail.

Chapter Five

Aggressive Predisposition of the Killer:
Avengers, Conditioning, and the 2 Percent
Who Like It

World War II–era training was conducted on a grassy firing range (a known-distance, or KD, range), on which the soldier shot at a bull's-eye target. After he fired a series of shots the target was checked, and he was then given feedback that told him where he hit.

Modern training uses what are essentially B. F. Skinner's operant conditioning techniques to develop a firing behavior in the soldier.[4] This training comes as close to simulating actual combat conditions as possible. The soldier stands in a foxhole with full combat equipment, and man-shaped targets pop up briefly in front of him. These are the eliciting stimuli that prompt the target behavior of shooting. If the target is hit, it immediately drops, thus providing immediate feedback. Positive reinforcement is given when these hits are exchanged for marksmanship badges, which usually have some form of privilege or reward (praise, recognition, three-day passes, and so on) associated with them.

Traditional marksmanship training has been transformed into a combat simulator. Watson states that soldiers who have conducted

**Predisposition
of Killer**

• Training
• Recent Experiences
• Temperament

this kind of simulator training "often report, after they have met a real life emergency, that they just carried out the correct drill and completed it before they realized that they were not in the simulator." Vietnam veterans have repeatedly reported similar experiences. Several independent studies indicate that this powerful conditioning process has dramatically increased the firing rate of American soldiers since World War II.

Richard Holmes has noted the ineffectiveness of an army trained in traditional World War II methods as opposed to an army whose soldiers have been conditioned by modern training methods. Holmes interviewed British soldiers returning from the Falklands War and asked them if they had experienced any incidence of nonfiring similar to that observed by Marshall in World War II. The British, who had been trained by modern methods, had not seen any such thing in their soldiers, but they had definitely observed it in the Argentineans, who had received World War II–style training and whose only effective fire had come from machine guns and snipers.[5]

The value of this modern battleproofing can also be seen in the war in Rhodesia in the 1970s. The Rhodesian security force was a highly trained modern army fighting against an ill-trained band of guerrillas. Through superior tactics *and training* the security force maintained an overall kill ratio of about eight-to-one throughout the war. Their commando units actually improved their kill ratio from thirty-five-to-one to fifty-to-one. The Rhodesians achieved this in an environment in which they did not have air and artillery support, nor did they have a significant advantage in weapons over their Soviet-supported opponents. The only thing they had going for them was superior training, and the advantage this gave them added up to nothing less than total tactical superiority.[6]

The effectiveness of modern conditioning techniques that enable killing in combat is irrefutable, and their impact on the modern battlefield is enormous.

Recent Experiences: "That's for My Brother"

Bob Fowler, F Company's popular, tow-headed commander, had bled to death after being hit in the spleen. His orderly, who adored him, snatched up a submachine gun and unforgivably massacred a line of unarmed Japanese soldiers who had just surrendered.

— William Manchester
Goodbye, Darkness

The recent loss of friends and beloved leaders in combat can also enable violence on the battlefield. The deaths of friends and comrades *can* stun, paralyze, and emotionally defeat soldiers. But in many circumstances soldiers react with anger (which is one of the well-known response stages to death and dying), and then the loss of comrades can enable killing.

Our literature is full of examples, and even our law includes concepts such as temporary insanity and extenuating and mitigating circumstances. Revenge killing during a burst of rage has been a recurring theme throughout history, and it needs to be considered in the overall equation of factors that enable killing on the battlefield.

The soldier in combat is a product of his environment, and violence can beget violence. This is the nurture side of the nature-nurture question. But he is also very much influenced by his temperament, or the nature side of the nature-nurture equation, and that is a subject that we will now address in detail.

The Temperament of the "Natural Soldier"

There is such a thing as a "natural soldier": the kind who derives his greatest satisfaction from male companionship, from excitement, and from the conquering of physical obstacles. He doesn't want to kill people as such, but he will have no objections if it occurs within a moral framework that gives him justification — like war — and if it is the price of gaining admission to the kind of environment he craves. Whether such men are born or made, I do not know, but most of them end up in armies (and many move on again to become mercenaries, because regular army life in peacetime is too routine and boring).

But armies are not full of such men. They are so rare that they form only a modest fraction even of small professional armies, mostly congregating in the commando-type special forces. In large conscript armies they virtually disappear beneath the weight of numbers of more ordinary men. And it is these ordinary men, who do not like combat at all, that armies must persuade to kill. Until only a generation ago, they did not even realize how bad a job they were doing.

— Gwynne Dyer
War

Swank and Marchand's World War II study noted the existence of 2 percent of combat soldiers who are predisposed to be "aggressive psychopaths" and apparently do not experience the normal resistance to killing and the resultant psychiatric casualties associated with extended periods of combat. But the negative connotations associated with the term "psychopath," or its modern equivalent "sociopath," are inappropriate here, since this behavior is a generally desirable one for soldiers in combat.

It would be absolutely incorrect to conclude that 2 percent of all veterans are psychopathic killers. Numerous studies indicate that combat veterans are no more inclined to violence than nonvets. A more accurate conclusion would be that there is 2 percent of the male population that, if pushed or if given a legitimate reason, will kill without regret or remorse. What these individuals represent — and this is a terribly important point that I must empha-size — is the capacity for the levelheaded participation in combat that we as a society glorify and that Hollywood would have us believe that all soldiers possess. In the course of interviewing veter-ans as a part of this study I have met several individuals who may fit within this 2 percent, and since returning from combat they have, without fail, proven themselves to be above-average contrib-utors to the prosperity and welfare of our society.

Dyer draws from his own personal experiences as a soldier for understanding:

> Aggression is certainly part of our genetic makeup, and necessarily so, but the normal human being's quota of aggression will not cause him to kill acquaintances, let alone wage war against strangers from a different country. We live among millions of people who have killed fellow human beings with pitiless efficiency — ma-chine-gunning them, using flame throwers on them, dropping explosive bombs on them from twenty thousand feet up — yet we do not fear these people.
>
> The overwhelming majority of those who have killed, now or at any time in the past, have done so as soldiers in war, and we recognize that that has practically nothing to do with the kind of personal aggression that would endanger us as their fellow citizens.

Marshall's World War II figure of a 15 to 20 percent firing rate does not necessarily contradict Swank and Marchand's 2 percent figure, since many of these firers were under extreme empowering circumstances, and many may have been in a posturing mode and merely firing wildly or above the enemy's heads. And later figures of 55 percent (Korea) and 90 to 95 percent (Vietnam) firing rates represent the actions of men empowered by increasingly more effective conditioning processes, but these figures also do not tell us how many were posturing.

Dyer's World War II figure of 1 percent of U.S. Army Air Corps fighter pilots being responsible for 40 percent of all kills is also generally in keeping with the Swank and Marchand estimates. Erich Hartmann, the World War II German ace — unquestionably the greatest fighter pilot of all time, with 351 confirmed victories —

claimed that 80 percent of his victims never knew he was in the same sky with them. This claim, if accurate, provides a remarkable insight into the nature of such a killer. Like the kills of most successful snipers and fighter pilots, the vast majority of the killing done by these men were what some would call simple ambushes and back shootings. No provocation, anger, or emotion empowered *these* killings.

Several senior U.S. Air Force officers have told me that when the U.S. Air Force tried to preselect fighter pilots after World War II, the only common denominator they could find among their World War II aces was that they had been involved in a lot of fights as children. Not bullies — for most true bullies avoid fights with anyone who is reasonably capable of fighting them — but fighters. If you can recapture or imagine the anger and indignity a child feels in a school-yard fight and magnify that into a way of life, then you can begin to understand these individuals and their capacity for violence.

The *Diagnostic and Statistical Manual of Mental Disorders* (*DSM-III-R*) of the American Psychiatric Association (APA) indicates that the incidence of "anti-social personality disorder" (that is, sociopaths) among the general population of American males is approximately 3 percent. These sociopaths are not easily used in armies, since by their very nature they rebel against authority, but over the centuries armies have had considerable success at bending such highly aggressive individuals to their will during wartime. So if two out of three of this 3 percent were able to accept military discipline, a hypothetical 2 percent of soldiers would, by the APA's definition, "have no remorse about the effects of their behavior on others."[7]

There is strong evidence that there exists a genetic predisposition for aggression. In all species the best hunter, the best fighter, the most aggressive male, survives to pass his biological predispositions on to his descendants. There are also environmental processes that can fully develop this predisposition toward aggression; when we combine this genetic predisposition with environmental development we get a killer. But there is another factor: the presence or absence of empathy for others. Again, there may be biological and environmental causes for this empathic process, but, whatever its origin, there is undoubtedly a division in humanity between those who can feel and understand the pain and suffering of others, and those who cannot. The presence of aggression, combined with the absence of empathy, results in sociopathy. The presence of aggression, combined with the presence of empathy, results in a completely different kind of individual from the sociopath.

One veteran I interviewed told me that he thought of most of the world as sheep: gentle, decent, kindly creatures who are essentially incapable of true aggression. In this veteran's mind there is another human subspecies (of which he is a member) that is a kind of dog: faithful, vigilant creatures who are very much capable of aggression when circumstances require. But, according to his model, there are wolves (sociopaths) and packs of wild dogs (gangs and aggressive armies) abroad in the land, and the sheepdogs (the soldiers and policemen of the world) are environmentally and biologically predisposed to be the ones who confront these predators.

Some experts in the psychological and psychiatric community think that these men are simply sociopaths and that the above view of killers is romanticizing. But I believe that there is another category of human beings out there. We know about sociopaths because their condition is, by definition, a pathology or a psychological disorder. But the psychological community does not recognize this other category of human beings, these metaphoric sheepdogs, because their personality type does not represent pathology or disorder. Indeed, they are valuable and contributing members of our society, and it is only in time of war, or on police forces, that these characteristics can be observed.

I have met these men, these "sheepdogs," over and over again as I interviewed veterans. They are men like one U.S. Army lieutenant colonel, a Vietnam veteran, who told me: "I learned early on in life that there are people out there who will hurt you if given the chance, and I have devoted my life to being prepared to face them." These men are quite often armed and always vigilant. They would not misuse or misdirect their aggression any more than a sheepdog would turn on his flock, but in their hearts many of them yearn for a righteous battle, a wolf upon whom to legitimately and lawfully turn their skills.

Richard Heckler speaks of this yearning in his book *In Search of the Warrior Spirit*:

> This urgent calling of nature longs to be tested, seeks to be challenged beyond itself. The warrior within us beseeches Mars, the god of War, to deliver us to that crucial battlefield that will redeem us into the terrifying immediacy of the moment. We want to face our Goliath so we may be reminded that the warrior David is alive, in us. We pray to the war gods to guide us to the walls of Jericho so we may dare the steadfastness and strength of our trumpet call. We aspire to be defeated in battles by powers so much greater than ourself, that the defeat itself will have made us larger than when we arrived. We long for the encounter that will ultimately empower us with dignity and honor. . . . Be not mistaken: the longing is there and it's loving and terrible and beautiful and tragic.

Perhaps there is another analogy. According to Carl Jung, there are deeply ingrained models for behavior called archetypes that exist deep in every human's collective unconscious — an inherited, unconscious reservoir of images derived from our ancestors' universal experiences and shared by the whole human race. These powerful archetypes can drive us by channeling our libidinal energy. They include such Jungian concepts as the mother, the wise old man, the hero, and the warrior. I think that Jung might refer to these individuals, not as "sheepdogs," but as "warriors" and "heroes."[8]

According to Gwynne Dyer, USAF research concerning aggressive killing behavior determined that 1 percent of their fighter pilots in World War II did nearly 40 percent of the air-to-air killing, and the majority of USAF World War II pilots never even tried to shoot anyone down. This 1 percent of World War II fighter pilots, Swank and Marchand's 2 percent, Griffith's low Napoleonic and Civil War killing rates, and Marshall's low World

War II firing rates can all be at least partially explained if only a small percentage of these combatants were actually willing to actively kill the enemy in these combat situations. Whether called sociopaths, sheepdogs, warriors, or heroes, they are there, they are a distinct minority, and in times of danger a nation needs them desperately.

Chapter Six

All Factors Considered:
The Mathematics of Death

A soldier who constantly reflected upon the knee-smashing, widow-making characteristics of his weapon, or who always thought of the enemy as a man exactly as himself, doing much the same task and subjected to exactly the same stresses and strains, would find it difficult to operate effectively in battle. . . . Without the creation of abstract images of the enemy, and without the depersonalization of the enemy during training, battle would become impossible to sustain. But if the abstract image is overdrawn or depersonalization is stretched into hatred, the restraints on human behavior in war are easily swept aside. If, on the other hand, men reflect too deeply upon the enemy's common humanity, then they risk being unable to proceed with the task whose aims may be eminently just and legitimate. This conundrum lies, like a Gordian knot linking the diverse strands of hostility and affection, at the heart of the soldier's relationship with the enemy.

— Richard Holmes
  Acts of War

All of the killing processes examined in this section have the same basic problem. By manipulating variables, modern armies direct the flow of violence, turning killing on and off like a faucet. But this is a delicate and dangerous process. Too much, and you end up with a My Lai, which can undermine your efforts. Too little, and your soldiers will be defeated and killed by someone who is more aggressively disposed.

An understanding of the physical distance factor, addressed in the section "Killing and Physical Distance," combined with a study of all of the other personal-kill-enabling factors identified thus far, permits us to develop an "equation" that can represent the total resistance involved in a specific killing circumstance.

To recap, the variables represented in our equation include the Milgram factors, the Shalit factors, and the predisposition of the killer.

The Milgram Factors

Milgram's famous studies of killing behavior in laboratory conditions (the willingness of subjects to engage in behavior that they believed was killing a fellow subject) identified three primary situational variables that influence or enable killing behavior; in this model I have called these (1) the demands of authority, (2) group absolution (remarkably similar to the concept of diffusion of responsibility), and (3) the distance from the victim. Each of these variables can be further "operationalized" as follows:

Demands of Authority

- Proximity of the obedience-demanding authority figure to the subject
- Subject's subjective respect for the obedience-demanding authority figure
- Intensity of the obedience-demanding authority figure's demands of killing behavior
- Legitimacy of the obedience-demanding authority figure's authority and demands

Group Absolution

- Subject's identification with the group
- Proximity of the group to the subject

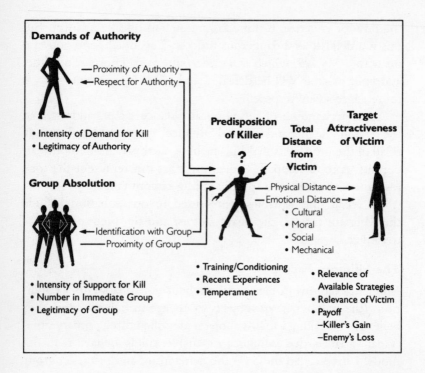

* Intensity of the group's support for the kill
* Number in the immediate group
* Legitimacy of the group

Total Distance from the Victim

* Physical distance between the killer and the victim
* Emotional distance between the killer and the victim, including:

    —Social distance, which considers the impact of a lifetime of
    viewing a particular class as less than human in a socially
    stratified environment
    —Cultural distance, which includes racial and ethnic differences
    that permit the killer to "dehumanize" the victim

—Moral distance, which takes into consideration intense belief in moral superiority and "vengeful" actions

—Mechanical distance, which includes the sterile "video game" unreality of killing through a TV screen, a thermal sight, a sniper sight, or some other kind of mechanical buffer

The Shalit Factors

Israeli military psychology has developed a model revolving around the nature of the victim, which I have incorporated into this model. This model considers the tactical circumstances associated with:

• Relevance and effectiveness of available strategies for killing the victim
• Relevance of the victim as a threat to the killer and his tactical situation
• Payoff of the killer's action in terms of

—Killer's gain
—Enemy's loss

The Predisposition of the Killer

This area considers such factors as:

• Training/conditioning of the soldier (Marshall's contributions to the U.S. Army's training program increased the firing rate of the individual infantryman from 15 to 20 percent in World War II to 55 percent in Korea and nearly 90 to 95 percent in Vietnam.)
• Recent experiences of the soldier (For example, having a friend or relative killed by the enemy has been strongly linked with killing behavior on the battlefield.)

The temperament that predisposes a soldier to killing behavior is one of the most difficult areas to research. However, Swank and Marchand did propose the existence of 2 percent of combat soldiers who are predisposed to be "aggressive psychopaths" and who apparently do not experience the trauma commonly associated with killing behavior. These findings have been tentatively confirmed by other observers and by USAF figures concerning aggressive killing behavior among fighter pilots.[9]

An Application: The Road to My Lai

We can see some of these factors at work in the participation of
Lieutenant Calley and his platoon in the infamous My Lai Massacre.
Tim O'Brien writes that "to understand what happens to the GI
among the mine fields of My Lai, you must know something
about what happens in America. You must understand Fort Lewis,
Washington. You must understand a thing called basic training."
O'Brien perceives both cultural distance and training/conditioning
(although he does not use those terms) in the bayonet training he
received when his drill sergeant bellowed in his ear, "Dinks are
little s——s. If you want their guts, you gotta go low. Crouch
and dig." In the same way, Holmes concludes that "the road to
My Lai was paved, first and foremost, by the dehumanization of
the Vietnamese and the 'mere gook rule' which declared that
killing a Vietnamese civilian did not really count."

Lieutenant Calley's platoon had received a series of casualties
from enemies who were seldom seen and who seemed always to
melt back into the civilian population. The day before the massacre,
the popular Sergeant Cox was killed by a booby trap. (Increasing
the "relevance" of their civilian victims and adding the recent
experience of losing friends to the enemy, while also increasing the
intensity of group support for killing.) According to one witness,
Calley's company commander, Captain Medina, stated in a briefing
to his men that "'our job is to go in rapidly, and to neutralize
everything. To kill everything.' 'Captain Medina? Do you mean
women and children, too?' 'I mean everything.'" (Moderately
intense demands of a legitimate and respected authority figure.)

When we look at photographs of the piles of dead women and
children at My Lai it seems impossible to understand how any
American could participate in such an atrocity, but it also seems
impossible to believe that 65 percent of Milgram's subjects would
shock someone to death in a laboratory experiment, despite the
screams and pleas of the "victim," merely because an unknown
obedience-demanding authority told them to. Although it is *not*
an excuse for such behavior, we can at least understand how My
Lai could have happened (and possibly prevent such occurrences

in the future) by understanding the power of the cumulative factors associated with a soldier ordered to kill by a legitimate, proximate, and respected authority, in the midst of a proximate, respected, legitimate, consenting group, predisposed by desensitization and conditioning during training and recent loss of friends, distanced from his victims by a widely accepted cultural and moral gulf, confronted with an act that would be a relevant loss to an enemy who has denied and frustrated other available strategies.

A veteran quoted by Dyer shows a deep understanding of the tremendous pressures many of these factors place on the "ordinary, basically decent" American soldier:

> You put those same kids in the jungle for a while, get them real scared, deprive them of sleep, and let a few incidents change some of their fears to hate. Give them a sergeant who has seen too many of his men killed by booby traps and by lack of distrust, and who feels that Vietnamese are dumb, dirty, and weak, because they are not like him. Add a little mob pressure, and those nice kids who accompany us today would rape like champions. Kill, rape and steal is the name of the game.

Each Man a Firing Squad

In summary, most of the factors that enable killing on the battlefield can be seen in the diffusion of responsibility that exists in an execution by firing squad. Because, in combat, each man *is* really a member of a huge firing squad. The leader gives the command and provides the demands of authority, but he does not have to actually kill. The firing squad provides conformity and absolution processes. Blindfolding the victim provides psychological distance. And the knowledge of the victim's guilt provides relevance and rationalization.

The killing-enabling factors provide a powerful set of tools to bypass or overcome the soldier's resistance to killing. But as we will see in the section "Killing in Vietnam," the higher the resistance bypassed, the higher the trauma that must be overcome in the subsequent rationalization process. Killing comes with a price, and societies must learn that their soldiers will have to spend the rest

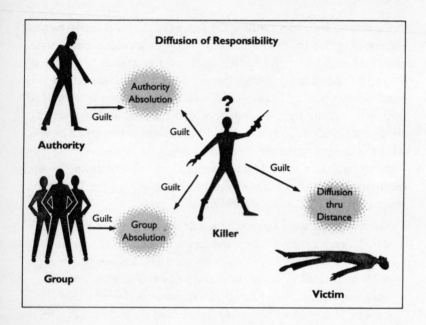

Diffusion of Responsibility

of their lives living with what they have done. The research outlined in this book has permitted us to understand that, although the mechanism of the firing squad ensures killing, the psychological toll on the members of a firing squad is tremendous. In the same way, society must now begin to understand the enormity of the price and process of killing in combat. Once they do, killing will never be the same again.

SECTION V

Killing and Atrocities:
"No Honor Here, No Virtue"

> The basic aim of a nation at war is establishing an image of the
> enemy in order to distinguish as sharply as possible the act of killing
> from the act of murder.
>
> — Glenn Gray
>   *The Warriors*

"Atrocity" can be defined as the killing of a noncombatant, either
an erstwhile combatant who is no longer fighting or has given up
or a civilian. But modern war, and particularly guerrilla warfare,
makes such distinctions blurry.

Atrocity has always been part of war, and in order to understand
war we must understand atrocity. Let us begin to understand it
by examining the full spectrum of atrocity.

Chapter One

The Full Spectrum of Atrocity

We often think of Nazi atrocities in World War II as all having been committed by psychopaths or sadistic killers, but there is a fortuitous shortage of such individuals in society. In reality, the problem of distinguishing murder from killing in combat is extremely complex. If we examine atrocity as a spectrum of occurrences rather than a precisely defined type of occurrence, then perhaps we can better understand the nature of this phenomenon.

This spectrum is intended to address only individual personal kills and will leave out the indiscriminate killing of civilians caused by bombs and artillery.

Slaying the Noble Enemy

Anchoring one end of the spectrum of atrocity is the act of killing an armed enemy who is trying to kill you. This end of the spectrum is not atrocity at all, but serves as a standard against which other kinds of killing can be measured.

The enemy who fights to a "noble" death validates and affirms the killer's belief in his *own* nobility and the glory of his cause. Thus a World War I British officer could speak admiringly to Holmes of German machine gunners who remained faithful unto death: "Topping fellows. Fight until they are killed. They gave us hell." And T. E. Lawrence (Lawrence of Arabia) immortalized in prose the German units who stood firm against his Arab forces during the rout of the Turkish army in World War I:

> I grew proud of the enemy who had killed my brothers. They were two thousand miles from home, without hope and without guides, in conditions bad enough to break the bravest nerves. Yet their sections held together, sheering through the wrack of Turk and Arab like armoured ships, high faced and silent. When attacked they halted, took position, fired to order. There was no haste, no crying, no hesitation. They were glorious.

These are "noble kills," which place the minimum possible burden on the conscience of the killer. And thus the soldier is able to further rationalize his kill by honoring his fallen foes, thereby gaining stature and peace by virtue of the nobility of those he has slain.

Gray Areas: Ambushes and Guerrilla Warfare

Many kills in modern combat are ambushes and surprise attacks in which the enemy represents no immediate threat to the killer, but is killed anyway, without opportunity to surrender. Steve Banko provides an excellent example of such a kill: "They didn't know I existed . . . but I sure as hell saw them. . . . This is one f——ed up way to die, I thought as I squeezed softly on the trigger."

Such a kill is by no means considered an atrocity, but it is also distinctly different from a noble kill and potentially harder for the killer to rationalize and deal with. Until this century such ambush kills were extremely rare in combat, and many civilizations partially protected themselves and their consciences and mental health by declaring such forms of warfare dishonorable.

One of the things that made Vietnam particularly traumatic was that due to the nature of guerrilla warfare, soldiers were often placed in situations in which the line between combatant and noncombatant was blurred:

> For the tense, battle-primed GIs ordered to seal off the village, the often subtle nuances and indicators used by interrogators to identify

VC from civilian, combatant from non-combatant, were a luxury they felt they could not afford. The decision, VC or not VC, often had to be reached in a split second and was compounded by the language barrier. The consequences of any ambiguity sometimes proved fatal to Vietnamese villagers. In Ben Suc, one unit of American soldiers, crouching near a road leading out of the village, were on the lookout for VC. A Vietnamese man approached their position on a bicycle. He wore black pajamas, the peasant outfit adopted by the VC. As he rode 20 yards past the point where he first came into view, a machine gun crackled some 30 yards in front of him. The man tumbled dead into a muddy ditch.

One soldier grimly commented: "That's a VC for you. He's a VC all right. That's what they wear. He was leaving town. He had to have some reason."

Maj Charles Malloy added: "What're you going to do when you spot a guy in black pajamas? Wait for him to get out his automatic weapon and start shooting? I'm telling you I'm not."

The soldiers never found out whether the Vietnamese was VC or not. Such was the perplexity of a war in which the enemy was not a foreign force but lived and fought among the people.

— Edward Doyle
  "Three Battles"

As we read the words of these men, we can place ourselves in their shoes and understand what they are saying. They were men trained to kill in a tense situation; they had no real need to justify their actions. So why did they try so hard? "That's a VC for you. He's a VC all right. That's what they wear. He was leaving town. He had to have some reason." It may be that what we are hearing here is someone trying desperately to justify his actions to himself. He has been placed in a situation in which he has been forced to take these kinds of actions, maybe even make these kinds of mistakes, and he *needs* desperately to have someone tell him that what he did was right and necessary.

Sometimes it was even more difficult. For example, consider the situation that this U.S. Army helicopter pilot found himself in in Vietnam:

Off to our left we could see a couple of downed Hueys [helicopters] inside the paddy. Strangely, just as I reached the center of the hub I noticed an old lady, standing almost dead center of the hub, casually planting rice. Still zigzagging, I looked back over my shoulder at her trying to figure out what she was doing there — was she crazy or just determined not to let the war interfere with her schedule? Glancing again at the burning Hueys it dawned on me what she was doing out there and I turned back.

"Shoot that old woman, Hall," I yelled, but Hall [the door gunner], who had been busy on his own side of the chopper had not seen her before and looked at me as if I had gone crazy, so we passed her without firing and I zigzagged around the paddies, dodging sniper fire, while I filled Hall in.

"She has a 360 degree view over the trees around the villages, Hall," I yelled. "The machine gunners are watching her and when she sees Hueys coming, she faces them and they concentrate their fire over the spot. That's why so many are down around here — she's a goddamned weathervane for them. Shoot her!"

Hall gave me a thumbs up and I turned to make another pass, but Jerry and Paul [in another helicopter] had caught on to her also and had put her down. For some reason, as I again passed our burning Hueys, I could not feel anything but relief at the old woman's death.

— D. Bray
  "Prowling for POWs"

Was the woman being forced to do what she was doing? Was she truly a Vietcong sympathizer, or a victim? Were Vietcong weapons being held on her or her family?

And would anyone have done any differently than these pilots under the circumstances? Possibly. But possibly they would not have lived to tell about it if they had done differently. Certainly no one will ever prosecute these men, and most certainly they will have to live with these kinds of doubts for the rest of their lives.

Sometimes the trauma associated with these gray-area killings in modern combat can be tremendous:

Look, I don't like to kill people, but I've killed Arabs [note the
unconscious dehumanizing of the enemy]. Maybe I'll tell you a
story. A car came towards us, in the middle of the [Lebanese] war,
without a white flag. Five minutes before another car had come,
and there were four Palestinians with RPGs [rocket-propelled gre-
nades] in it — killed three of my friends. So this new Peugeot
comes towards us, and we shoot. And there was a family there —
three children. And I cried, but I couldn't take the chance. It's a
real problem. . . . Children, father, mother. All the family was
killed, but we couldn't take the chance.

— Gaby Bashan, Israeli reservist in Lebanon, 1982
   quoted in Gwynne Dyer, *War*

Once again, we see killing in modern warfare, in an age of guerrillas
and terrorists, as increasingly moving from black and white to
shades of gray. And as we continue down the atrocity spectrum,
we will see a steady fade to black.

Dark Areas: Slaying the Ignoble Enemy

The close-range murder of prisoners and civilians during war is a
demonstrably counterproductive action. Executing enemy prisoners stiffens the will of the enemy and makes him less likely to
surrender. Yet in the heat of battle, it happens quite often.

Several of the Vietnam veterans I interviewed said, without
detailed explanation, that they "never took prisoners." Often in
school and training situations when it is impractical to take prisoners
during operations behind enemy lines, there is an unspoken
agreement that the prisoners have to be "taken care of."

But in the heat of battle it is not really all that simple. In order
to fight at close range one must deny the humanity of one's enemy.
Surrender requires the opposite — that one recognize and take
pity on the humanity of the enemy. A surrender in the heat of
battle requires a complete, and very difficult, emotional turnaround
by both parties. The enemy who opts to posture or fight and then
dies in battle becomes a noble enemy. But if at the last minute he
tries to surrender he runs a great risk of being killed immediately.

Holmes writes at length on this process:

Surrendering during battle is difficult. Charles Carrington suggested, "No soldier can claim a right to 'quarter' if he fights to the extremity." T.P. Marks saw seven German machine-gunners shot. "They were defenseless, but they have chosen to make themselves so. We did not ask them to abandon their guns. They only did so when they saw that those who were not mown down were getting closer to them and the boot was now on the other foot."

Ernst Junger agreed that the defender had no moral right to surrender in these circumstances: "the defending force, after driving their bullets into the attacking one at five paces' distance, must take the consequences. A man cannot change his feelings again during the last rush with a veil of blood before his eyes. He does not want to take prisoners but to kill."

During the cavalry action at Moncel in 1914 Sergeant James Taylor of the 9th Lancers saw how difficult it was to restrain excited men. "Then there was a bit of a melee, horses neighing and a lot of yelling and shouting. . . . I remember seeing Corporal Bolte run his lance right through a dismounted German who had his hands up and thinking that it was a rather bad thing to do."

Harold Dearden, a medical officer on the Western Front, read a letter written by a young soldier to his mother. "When we jumped into their trench, mother, they all held up their hands and shouted 'Camerad, Camerad' and that means 'I give in' in their language. But they had to have it, mother. I think that is all from your loving Albert ."

. . . No soldier who fights until his enemy is at close small-arms range, in any war, has more than perhaps a fifty-fifty chance of being granted quarter. If he stands up to surrender he risks being shot with the time-honoured comment, 'Too late, chum.' If he lies low, he will fall victim to the grenades of the mopping-up party, in no mood to take chances.

Yet Holmes concludes that the consistently remarkable thing in such circumstances is not how many soldiers are killed while trying to surrender, but how few. Even under this kind of provocation, the general resistance to killing runs true.

Surrender-executions are clearly wrong and counterproductive to a force that has dedicated itself to fighting in a fashion that the nation and the soldiers can live with after battle. They are, however, completed in the heat of battle and are rarely prosecuted. It is only the individual soldier who must hold himself accountable for his actions most of the time.

Executions in cold blood are another matter entirely.

Black Areas: Executions

"Execution" is defined here as the close-range killing of a noncombatant (civilian or POW) who represents no significant or immediate military or personal threat to the killer. The effect of such kills on the killer is intensely traumatic, since the killer has limited internal motivation to kill the victim and kills almost entirely out of external motivations. The close range of the kill severely hampers the killer in his attempts to deny the humanity of the victim and severely hampers denial of personal responsibility for the kill.

Jim Morris is an ex–Green Beret and a Vietnam veteran turned writer. Here he interviews an Australian veteran of the Malaysian counterinsurgency who is trying to live with the memory of an execution. His story is entitled "Killers in Retirement: 'No Heroes, No Villains, Just Mates.'"

> This time we leaned against a wall on the opposite side of the room. He leaned forward, speaking softly and earnestly. This time there was no pretense. Here was a man baring his soul.
>
> "We attacked a terrorist prison camp, and took a woman prisoner. She must have been high up in the party. She wore the tabs of a commissar. I'd already told my men we took no prisoners, but I'd never killed a woman. 'She must die quickly. We must leave!' my sergeant said.
>
> "Oh god, I was sweatin'," Harry went on. "She was magnificent. 'What's the matter, Mister Ballentine?' she asked. 'You're sweatin'.'
>
> "'Not for you,' I said. 'It's a malaria recurrence.' I gave my pistol to my sergeant, but he just shook his head. . . . None of them would do it, and if I didn't I'd never be able to control that unit again.

"'You're sweatin', Mr. Ballentine,' she said again.

"'Not for you,' I said."

"Did you kill her?"

"¡Hell, I blew 'er f——in' 'ead off," he replied. . . .

"My platoon all gathered 'round and smiled. 'You are our *tuan* [Malay for "sir" or "leader"],' my sergeant said. 'You are our *tuan*.'"

I'm not a priest. I'm not even an officer any more. . . . I hoped my look told Harry that I liked him, that it was okay with me if he forgave himself. It's hard to do though.

This is the spectrum of atrocity, this is how atrocity happens, but not why. Let us now examine the why of atrocity, the rationale of atrocity, and the dark power that atrocity lends to those who wield it.

Chapter Two

The Dark Power of Atrocity

The Problem: "Righteousness Comes Out of a Gun Barrel [?]"

On a cold, rainy training day at Fort Lewis, Washington, I listened to soldiers talk who had just completed a prisoner of war exercise. One held that the enemy troops should be marched through an area saturated with persistent nerve gas. Another stated that the claymore mine presented the most cost-effective and energy-efficient method of disposing of POWs. His buddy claimed that they were both being wasteful and that POWs could best be used for minefield clearing and reconnaissance for nuclear- and chemical-contaminated areas. The battalion chaplain, who was standing nearby, began to address this obvious moral issue.

The chaplain cited the Geneva conventions and discussed our nation as a force of righteousness and the support of God for our cause. To pragmatic soldiers this moral approach didn't go far. The Geneva convention was dismissed, and our forward observer said that in school they had told him that "the Geneva convention says you can't fire white phosphorus at troops; so you call it in on their equipment." The young artilleryman's logic was "if we're gonna find ways around the Geneva convention, what do you think the enemy is gonna do?" Another said, "If we get captured by the Russians, we might as well kiss it off, so why not give them a dose of the same medicine?" To the chaplain's "righteousness" and "support of God" comments, the cold, wet soldiers' answers were along the lines of "righteousness comes out of a gun barrel" and "the victor writes history."

At Fort Benning I too had heard the "Geneva convention and white phosphorous on equipment" line during the artillery pitch in Officer Candidate School, the Infantry Officer Basic Course, Ranger school, and the Infantry Mortar Platoon Officers Course. The treatment of POWs had been addressed by an instructor at Ranger school, and he clearly communicated his personal belief that in a raid or an ambush, a patrol could not be expected to take POWs. I had noted that most of the outstanding young soldiers coming to us from the Ranger Battalion shared this Ranger-school belief.

A Solution: "I'll Shoot You Myself"

To confront this belief I said basically, "If the enemy finds just one massacre, like our soldiers did at Malmédy in the Battle of the Bulge, then thousands of enemy soldiers will swear never to surrender, and they'll be very tough to fight. Just like our troops were in the Battle of the Bulge when word got around that the Germans were shooting POWs. In addition, that's all the excuse the enemy needs to kill our captured soldiers. So by murdering a few prisoners, who were just poor, tired soldiers like you, you'll make the enemy force a damn-sight tougher, and cause the deaths — murders — of a whole bunch of our boys.

"On the other hand, if you disarm, tie up, and leave a POW out in a clearing somewhere because you can't take him with you, then the word will spread that Americans treat POWs honorably, even when the chips are down, and a whole bunch of scared, tired soldiers will surrender rather than die. In World War II an entire Soviet army corps defected to the Germans. The Germans were treating Soviet POWs like dogs, and yet a whole corps came over to their side. How would they behave if they faced a humane enemy?

"The last thing you ought to know is that if *I* ever catch any of you heroes killing a POW, *I'll* shoot you right on the spot. Because it's illegal, because it's wrong, because it's *dumb*, and it's one of the worst things you could do to help us win a war."

I didn't bother to include the possibility of organizing Soviet POWs and defectors into combat units and the very real importance of capturing POWs for intelligence purposes.

The Lesson and the Greater Problem

The most important point here is that nobody has ever pointed out to me the potential repercussions of improper POW handling. No leader of mine has ever stood up and clearly stated this position to me and defended it. In fact, the opposite has occurred. As a private and a sergeant, I have had enlisted superiors strongly defend the execution of POWs whenever it was inconvenient to take them alive, and at the time I accepted it as reasonable. But they never made me understand the vital importance and the deadly ramifications of POW handling (or mishandling) on the battlefield because I think they themselves did not understand.

On the next battlefield our soldiers may commit war crimes and thereby cause us to lose one of the basic combat multipliers that we have available to us: the tendency of an oppressed people to become disloyal to their nation.

One interviewer of World War II POWs told me that German soldiers repeatedly told him that relatives with World War I combat experience had advised, "Be brave, join the infantry, and surrender to the first American you see." The American reputation for fair play and respect for human life had survived over generations, and the decent actions of American soldiers in World War I had saved the lives of many soldiers in World War II.

This is America's position on the role of atrocity in combat, and this is the logic behind it. But there is another position that many nations have taken on the use of atrocity in warfare, and there is another logic to be considered. This other logic is the twisted logic of atrocity, which we must understand if we are to completely understand killing.

The Empowerment

War . . . has no power to transform, it merely exaggerates the good and evil that are in us.

— Lord Moran
Anatomy of Courage

Empowerment Through Death

The first time I saw a soldier plummet to his death in a parachute jump it took years to sort out my emotions. Part of me was horrified at this soldier's death, but as I watched him fight his tangled reserve chute all the way down another part of me was filled with pride. His death validated and affirmed all that I believe about paratroopers, who stare death in the face daily. That brave, doomed soldier became a living sacrifice to the spirit of the airborne.

After talking to my fellow paratroopers and drinking a toast to the memory of our departed comrade, I began to understand that his death had magnified our own belief in the danger, nobility, and superiority inherent in our elite unit. Instead of being diminished by his loss, we were strangely magnified and empowered by it.[1] This phenomenon is not limited to, although it is always present in, elite fighting groups. Nations celebrate their costliest battles, even losing ones — the Alamo, Pickett's Charge, Dunkerque, Wake Island, and Leningrad are examples — due to the bravery and nobility of the sacrifices involved.

Empowerment Through Atrocity

As churlish as it might be to compare the death of a paratrooper in an airborne action with the sacrifice of the Jews in World War II, I believe that the same process that existed in me when I saw a soldier die exists in a greatly magnified form among those who commit atrocities.

The Holocaust is sometimes misunderstood as the senseless killing of Jews and innocent people. But this killing was not senseless. Vile and evil, but not senseless. Such murders have a very powerful but twisted logic of their own. A logic that we must understand if we are to confront it.

There are many benefits reaped by those who tap the dark power of atrocity. Those who engage in a policy of atrocity usually strike a bargain that exchanges their future for a brief gain in the present. Though brief, that gain is nonetheless real and powerful. In order to understand the attraction of atrocity, we must understand and clearly acknowledge those benefits that cause individuals, groups, and nations to turn to it.

Terrorism

One of the most obvious and blatant benefits of atrocity is that it quite simply scares the hell out of people. The raw horror and savagery of those who murder and abuse cause people to flee, hide, and defend themselves feebly, and often their victims respond with mute passivity. We see this in the newspapers daily when we read of victims who are faced with mass murderers and simply do nothing to protect themselves or others. Hannah Arendt noted this failure to resist the Nazis in her study *The Banality of Evil.*

Jeff Cooper, writing from experience in criminology, comments on this tendency in civilian life:

> Any study of the atrocity list of recent years — Starkweather, Speck, Manson, Richard Hickok and Cary Smith, et al — shows immediately that the victims, by their appalling ineptitude and timidity, virtually assisted in their own murders. . . .
>
> Any man who is a man may not, in honor, submit to threats of violence. But many men who are not cowards are simply unprepared for the fact of human savagery. They have not thought about it (incredible as this may appear to anyone who reads the papers or listens to the news) and they just don't know what to do. When they look right into the face of depravity or violence they are astonished and confounded.

This process that empowers criminals and outcasts in society can work even better when institutionalized as policy by revolutionary organization, armies, and governments. North Vietnam and its Vietcong proxies represent one force that blatantly used atrocity as a policy and was triumphant because of it. In 1959, 250 South Vietnamese officials were assassinated by the Vietcong. The Vietcong found that assassination was easy, it was cheap, and it worked. A year later this toll of murder and horror went up to 1,400, and it continued for twelve more years.

Throughout these years the attrition warfare advocates in the United States visited impotent, futile bombings upon the North. The methodology and targets of these bombings made them very ineffectual compared with the strategic bombing conducted in World War II, yet our own post–World War II studies showed that in England and Germany little was accomplished by such bombings except to steel the resolve of the enemy.

But while the United States was fruitlessly bombing the North, the North was efficiently murdering the infrastructure of the South, one by one in their beds and homes. As we have seen before, death from twenty thousand feet is strangely impersonal and psychologically impotent. But death up close and personal, visiting the manifest intensity of the enemy's Wind of Hate upon its victims, such death can be hideously effective at sapping the will of the enemy and ultimately achieving victory:

> A squad with a death order entered the house of a prominent community leader and shot him, his wife, his married son, and daughter-in-law, a male and female servant and their baby. The family cat was strangled, the family dog was clubbed to death, and the goldfish scooped out of the fishbowl and tossed onto the floor. When the communists left, no life remained in the house — a "family unit" had been eliminated.
>
> — Jim Graves
>   "The Tangled Web"

There is a simple, horrifying, and obvious value resident in atrocity. The Mongols were able to make entire nations submit without a fight just on the basis of their reputation for exterminating whole cities and nations that had resisted them in the past. The term "terrorist" simply means "one who uses terror," and we don't have to look very far — around the world or back in history — to find instances of individuals and nations who have succeeded in achieving power through the ruthless and effective use of terror.

Killing Empowerment

Mass murder and execution can be sources of mass empowerment.

It is as if a pact with the devil had been made, and a host of evil demons had lived and thrived on the victims of the Nazi SS (to select just one example), empowering its nation with an evil strength as a reward for its blood sacrifices. Each killing affirmed and validated in blood the demon of Nazi racial superiority — thereby establishing a powerful pseudospeciation (categorizing a victim as an inferior species) based on moral distance, social distance, and cultural distance.

Dyer's book *War* has a remarkable photograph of Japanese soldiers bayoneting Chinese prisoners. Prisoners in an endless line are in a deep ditch on their knees with their hands bound behind their backs. Along the banks of the ditch stands another endless line of Japanese soldiers with bayonets fixed on their rifles. One by one these soldiers go down into the ditch and inflict the "intimate brutality" of the bayonet on a prisoner. The prisoners hang their heads in dull acceptance and mute horror. Those being bayoneted have their faces contorted in agony. Remarkably, the killers have their faces contorted in a way similar to their victims.

In these execution situations strong forces of moral distance, social distance, cultural distance, group absolution, close proximity, and obedience-demanding authority all join to compel the soldier to execute, overcoming the forlorn forces of his natural and learned decency and his natural resistance to killing.

Each soldier who actively or passively participates in such mass executions is faced with a stark choice. On the one hand, the soldier can resist the incredibly powerful array of forces that call for him to kill, and he will instantly be denied by his nation, his leaders, and his friends and will most likely be executed along with the other victims of this horror. On the other hand, the soldier can bow before the social and psychological forces that demand that he kill, and in doing so he will be strangely empowered.

The soldier who does kill must overcome that part of him that says that he is a murderer of women and children, a foul beast who has done the unforgivable. He *must* deny the guilt within him, and he *must* assure himself that the world is not mad, that his victims are less than animals, that they are evil vermin, and that what his nation and his leaders have told him to do is right.

He *must* believe that not only is this atrocity right, but it is proof that he is morally, socially, and culturally superior to those whom he has killed. It is the ultimate act of denial of their humanity. It is the ultimate act of affirmation of his superiority. And the killer *must* violently suppress any dissonant thought that he has done anything wrong. Further, he *must* violently attack anyone or anything that would threaten his beliefs. His mental health is totally invested in believing that what he has done is good and right.

It is the blood of his victims that binds and empowers him to even greater heights of killing and slaughter. And when we realize that this same basic empowering process is what motivates satanic murders and other such cult killings, the analogy of a satanic pact is not as strange as it seems. This is the strength, the power, and the attraction that have resided in human sacrifices over millennia.

Bonding to Leaders and Peers

Those who command atrocities are powerfully bonded by guilt to those who commit atrocities, and to their cause, since only the success of their cause can ensure that they will not have to answer for their actions. With totalitarian dictators, it is their secret police and other such Praetorian guard–type units who can be counted on to fight for their leader and their cause to the bitter end. Nicolae Ceauşescu's state police in Romania and Hitler's SS units are two examples of units bonded to their leaders by atrocity.

By ensuring that their men participate in atrocities, totalitarian leaders can also ensure that for these minions there is no possibility of reconciliation with the enemy. They are inextricably linked to the fate of their leader. Trapped in their logic and their guilt, those who commit atrocities see no alternatives other than total victory or total defeat in a great Götterdämmerung.

In the absence of a legitimate threat, leaders (be they national leaders or gang leaders) may designate a scapegoat whose defilement and innocent blood empowers the killers and bonds them to their leaders. Traditionally, high-visibility weak groups and minorities — such as Jews and blacks — have filled this role.

Women have also been defiled, debased, and dehumanized for the aggrandizement of others. Throughout history women have been probably the greatest single group of victims of this empowerment process. Rape is a very important part of the process of dominating and dehumanizing an enemy; and this process of mutual empowering and bonding at the expense of others is exactly what occurs during gang rapes. In war, empowerment and bonding through such gang rapes often occur on a national level.

The German-Russian conflict during World War II is an excellent example of a vicious cycle in which both sides became totally invested in atrocity and rape. This reached the point at which, according to Albert Seaton, Soviet soldiers attacking Germany were told that they were not accountable for civil crimes committed in Germany and that personal property and German women were theirs by right.

The incidence of rape as a result of these encouragements appears to have been in the millions. Cornelius Ryan, in *The Last Battle*, estimated that there were one hundred thousand births resulting from rapes in Berlin alone following World War II. In recent years we have seen the use of rape as a political tool by the Serbs in Bosnia. The thing to understand here is that gang rapes and gang or cult killings in times of peace and war are *not* "senseless violence." They are instead powerful acts of group bonding and criminal enabling that, quite often, have a hidden purpose of promoting the wealth, power, or vanity of a specific leader or cause . . . at the expense of the innocent.

Atrocity and Denial

The sheer horror of atrocity serves not only to terrify those who must face it, but also to generate disbelief in distant observers. Whether it is ritual cult killings in our society or mass murders by established governments in the world at large, the common response is often one of total disbelief. And the nearer it hits home, the harder we want to disbelieve it.

Most Americans have been able to accept the millions of murders committed by Nazi Germany because our soldiers were there and were personally exposed to the Nazi death camps. Eyewitness accounts, films, a vocal and powerful Jewish community, and shrines at death camps like Dachau and Auschwitz all combine to make it almost impossible to deny the horror. Yet even in the

face of all this evidence, there is a bizarre minority in our nation
that truly believes that it never happened.

The sheer awfulness of atrocity makes us wish it away, and
when we are faced with events such as genocide in Cambodia we
would rather turn our heads. David Horowitz, a 1960s radical,
writes about how this denial process occurred in him and his friends:

> I and my former comrades in the Left dismissed the anti-Soviet
> "lies" about Stalinist repression. In the society we hailed as a new
> human dawn, 100 million people were put in slave-labor camps,
> in conditions rivaling Auschwitz and Buchenwald. Between 30
> and 40 million people were killed in peacetime in the daily routine
> of socialist rule. While Leftists applauded their progressive policies
> and guarded their frontiers, Soviet Marxists killed more peasants,
> more workers, and even more communists than all the capitalist
> governments combined since the beginning of time.
>
> And for the entire duration of this nightmare, the William Buck-
> leys and Ronald Reagans and other anti-communists went on
> telling the world exactly what was happening. And all that time
> the pro-Soviet Left went on denouncing them as reactionaries and
> liars, using the same contemptuous terms. . . .
>
> The left would *still* be denying the Soviet atrocities if the perpe-
> trators themselves had not finally acknowledged their crime.

Although this is a most remarkable example of näiveté, a significant
and vocal minority in America was trapped in this program of self-
deception. Those who were deceived are mainly good, decent,
highly educated men and women. It is their very goodness and
decency that cause them to be so completely incapable of believing
that someone or something they approve of could be so completely
evil. Perhaps denial of mass atrocity is tied to our innate resistance
to killing. Just as one hesitates to kill in the face of extreme pressure
and despite the threat of violence, one has difficulty imagin-
ing — and believing — the existence of atrocity despite the existence of facts.

But we must not deny it. If we look around the world carefully
we will find somebody somewhere wielding the dark power of
atrocity to support a cause that *we* believe in. It is a simple tenet

of human nature that it is difficult to believe and accept that anyone *we* like and identify with is capable of these acts against our fellow human beings. And this simple, naive tendency to disbelieve or look the other way is, possibly more than any other factor, responsible for the perpetuation of atrocity and horror in our world today.

Chapter Three

The Entrapment of Atrocity

"The Horror! The Horror!"

— Kurtz

  in Joseph Conrad, *Heart of Darkness*[2]

Despite its short-term benefits, atrocity as policy is normally (but not always) self-destructive. Unfortunately this self-destruction usually does not occur in time to save its immediate victims

The process of bonding men by forcing them to commit an atrocity requires a foundation of legitimacy for it to continue for any length of time. The authority of a state (as in Stalinist Russia or Nazi Germany), a state religion (as in the emperor worship of imperial Japan), a heritage of barbarism and cruelty that diminishes the value of individual human life (as existed among the Mongol Hordes, in imperial China, and in many other ancient civilizations), and economic pressures combined with years of prior experience and group bonding (as in the KKK and street gangs) are all examples of varying forms of "legitimizing" factors that, singly or combined, can ensure the continuing commission of atrocities. They also, however, contain the seeds of their own destruction.

Once a group undergoes the process of bonding and empowerment through atrocity, then its members are entrapped in it, as it turns every other force that is aware of their nature against them.

Of course, those who commit atrocities understand that what they are doing will be considered criminal by the rest of the world, and this is why at the level of nation-states they attempt to control their population and press.

Still, controlling people and knowledge is only a stopgap measure, particularly as ubiquitous electronic communication becomes widely available. The existence of the Nazi Holocaust and the Soviet Gulag were debated, and instant worldwide television transmissions of the Tiananmen Square Massacre allowed the Chinese Communist regime no denials.

Burning Bridges and One-Way Streets

Forcing men to commit atrocities is much easier than getting them to accept the atrocity as a bonding and empowering process. But once they have accepted the empowering process and firmly believe that their enemy is less than human and is deserving of what has happened to him, then they are stuck in a profound psychological trap.

Many students of German conduct during World War II are puzzled by the paradox of the Nazis' handling of the war against Russia. On the one hand the Nazis had a remarkably competent war-fighting organization, while on the other hand they failed to capitalize on opportunities to "liberate" the Ukraine and convert defecting Soviet units to their cause. *The problem was that the Nazis were entrapped by the very thing that enabled them.* Their racist, atrocity-based denial of the humanity of their enemies made their forces powerful in battle, while it simultaneously prevented them from treating anyone other than an "Aryan" as a human being. Initially the Ukrainian people greeted the Nazis as liberators, and Soviet forces surrendered en masse, but they soon began to realize that there was something that was even worse than Stalinist Russia.

For now it would appear that atrocity has succeeded as policy in China and in Bosnia. In Vietnam, the North won by using atrocity. And for decades the Soviets stayed in power in Russia and Eastern Europe by wielding the dark power of atrocity. But in most cases those who attempt to wield atrocity as a systematic national policy have been struck down by this two-edged sword.

Those who choose the path of atrocity have burned their bridges behind them. There is no turning back.

Enabling the Enemy

During the Battle of the Bulge in World War II, a German SS unit massacred a group of American POWs at Malmédy. Word of this massacre spread like wildfire through the American forces, and thousands of soldiers resolved never to surrender to the Germans. Conversely, as was mentioned earlier, many Germans who would fight the Russians to their last breath made a point of surrendering to the Americans at the earliest honorable occasion. Those who commit atrocities have burned their bridges behind them and know that they cannot surrender, but even as they have enabled themselves, they have enabled their enemies.

And so we have seen a few of the limitations of atrocity. But all these negative aspects do not really address the most important and difficult manifestation of committing acts of atrocity. The worst part is that when you institute and execute a policy of atrocity, you and your society must live with what you have done. But before we conclude this section by examining the psychological toll taken by atrocity, let us first briefly examine a case study in atrocity.

Chapter Four

A Case Study in Atrocity

This is a firsthand account of the psychological response of a Canadian soldier who was confronted with the vilest possible aspect of atrocity while serving in the UN peacekeeping force sent to the Congo in 1963. It is not pretty. It was written under the nom de plume Alan Stuart-Smyth. Colonel Stuart-Smyth served twenty-three years as a UN peacekeeper, progressing in rank from private to full colonel. Wounded twice, he was awarded the UN medal, a mention in dispatches, the Canadian Decoration, and the Distinguished Service Order. After retirement in 1986 he was offered, and accepted, a professorship at a major American university, where he taught criminology for two years.

Note the two-edged sword of atrocity here. Note the way in which it both enables and entraps the killers in this case, and then note the way that their atrocity enables the soldier who must kill someone caught in the act of atrocity:

> As I approached the building the sound of moaning, punctuated by deep laughs, was clearly audible. The rear of the church contained two small dirty windows at eye level, through which I looked. Although the interior of the church was dark by comparison with the blazing outdoors sunlight, I could pick out the forms of two naked black men torturing a young white woman whom I assumed to be a nun or teacher. She had been stripped naked and

was stretched out in the aisle of the church, arms pulled tightly over her head by one of the rebels, while the other knelt on her stomach and repeatedly touched her nipples with a burning cigarette. She had burn marks on her face and neck as well. Uniforms of the Katangese Gendarmerie were thrown over the back of a pew, and female garments were scattered near the door. A . . . carbine lay in the aisle beside the young woman. Another rifle had been left leaning against the wall near the uniforms. There appeared to be no one else present in the church. . . .

On my signal we burst into the cathedral, our weapons on full auto.

"Stand still," I bellowed. "U.N. troops; you're under arrest." I didn't want to do it that way, but damn it, I was still a soldier, and subject to Queen's Regulations and Orders.

The rebels bounded to their feet to face us, eyes staring wildly. I carried a Sterling 9mm SMG [submachine gun] . . . which I leveled at the two naked men. We were no more than 15 feet apart.

The one who had been holding the nun's arms was visibly shaking with fear, his eyes flying uncontrollably about the room. In a second they rested on the rifle lying in the aisle. The nun had rolled onto her stomach, clutching her breasts and rocking from side to side, moaning in pain.

"Don't be a fool, man," I cautioned. But he did it anyway.

In a burst of panic he emitted a loud, piercing wail and dove for the rifle. Landing on his knees he grabbed the weapon, and turning his terrified face to mine, attempting to bring his weapon to bear. My first burst caught him in the face, the second full in the chest. He was dead before he fell over, a body missing most of its head.

The second terrorist began to wave his arms frantically up and down, like a featherless black bird attempting to take flight. His eyes kept flitting back and forth between the muzzle of the Sterling and his own weapon, which was leaning against the wall a good 10 feet away. . . .

"Don't do it, don't do it," I ordered. But he emitted a loud "Yaaa . . . ," and scrambled for the rifle. I warned him again but he grabbed the weapon, worked the action to place a round in the chamber, and began to swing the muzzle toward me.

"KILL HIM, GODDAMMIT," screamed Cpl Edgerton, who had now entered the church behind us, "KILL HIM, NOW!"

The rebel terrorist was now fully facing me, desperately attempting to swing the long barrel of the bolt-action rifle across his body to align it with my chest. His eyes locked on mine — wild, frantic eyes surrounded by fields of white. They never left mine, not even when the powerful SMG rounds tore into his stomach, walked up his chest, and cut the carotid artery on the left side of his neck. His body hit the floor with a thud, blown apart by the blast of the Sterling, and still the eyes remained riveted to mine. Then his body relaxed and the eyes dilated, blind in death. . . .

Prior to Okonda, I had not killed a human being. That is, I did not know for sure that I had killed. When one is firing at moving, shadowy figures in the confusion of battle one cannot be certain of the results. At Bridge 19 I had killed many men when I detonated the charges, blowing an enemy convoy to kingdom come, but somehow the incident was not psychologically close. They were a long way off, and the cover of night hid their shapes and movement, their very humanity. But here at Okonda it was different. The two men I killed were practically within arm's reach, I could see their facial expressions clearly, even hear their breathing, see their fear, and smell their body odor. And the funny thing was that *I didn't feel a damn thing!* . . . [Stuart-Smyth's emphasis]

There had been two nuns at Okonda: the young one we saved, and the older one we didn't. When I first entered the church I was standing slightly behind the altar, and off to the left side. From that position I couldn't see the front of the altar, a rather large affair made of rough-hewn wood with a cross towering above it. Perhaps it was a good thing I could not, for the rebels had used the altar to butcher the old nun.

They had stripped her naked, but had not assaulted her sexually, probably because she was elderly, and obese. Instead they sat her upright with her back to the altar, and nailed her hands to it in apparent mimicry of the crucifixion. Then they cut off her breasts with a bayonet and, in a final act of savagery, drove the bayonet through her mouth into the altar behind, impaling her in an upright position. Evidence of a struggle showed that she had not died instantly from the bayonet wound, but had probably succumbed to the loss of blood from the wounds on her chest. She had a white man's penis and testicles shoved partially in her vagina. Her severed breasts were not present.

We found the owner of the male genitalia tied spread-eagle in the middle of the village compound, with the nun's breasts attached to his chest with sharpened sticks. . . .

Before we departed Okonda the young nun asked to meet the soldier who had saved her life. She was clothed now, and had cleaned up a little bit with the help of our medic. I was surprised how young she was — early 20s or younger. . . . She required a number of sutures in her vagina, and would need burn treatments as well. I didn't admire her decision to remain in enemy territory when she was given ample opportunity to leave, but I did admire her spunk. When we met she looked me in the eye and said, "Thank God you came." She had been badly beaten, but not defeated.

As for me, I had turned 19 only two days previous, and still suffered from the native upbringing of a good Christian family. I lost a lot of that upbringing at Okonda. There was no honor here, no virtue. The standards of behavior taught in the homes, churches, and schools of America had no place in battle. They were mythical concepts good only for the raising of children, to be cast aside forever from this moment on. No, I didn't feel guilt, shame, or remorse at killing my fellow man — I felt pride!

— Alan Stuart-Smyth
  "Congo Horror"

There are numerous examples of atrocity committed by nearly all national, racial, and ethnic groups, but this example is one of the best, clearest, and most literate representations of the killology aspects of atrocity.

Many of the factors and processes that we have discussed — or will be discussing shortly — can be observed clearly in this case study. We see the rapists' instinctive lashing out and defiling of all that is held dear by those they consider to be their oppressors. We see that the rapists' atrocity has enraged and empowered their opponent. We see the rapists entrapped in atrocity: caught red-handed and knowing that if they surrender they will be executed, they have no option but to try to fight. We see Stuart-Smyth's reluctance to kill these men even in the face of their atrocities. We see the low target attractiveness associated with the ludicrous and harmless sight of a naked man with his arms waving "frantically up and down, like a featherless black bird attempting to take flight." We see the role of obedience-demanding authority in that even in the face of all this provocation Stuart-Smyth must be ordered to kill. We see a diffusion of responsibility in that the individual giving the order to kill did not fire his weapon. We can see the development of Stuart-Smyth's rationalization and acceptance process as he first says, "I didn't feel a damn thing!" and later contradicts this statement by saying, "I didn't feel guilt, shame, or remorse at killing my fellow man — I felt pride!" And we can see that Stuart-Smyth's rationalization and acceptance was greatly assisted by the fact that the men he killed were committing atrocities.

We see all these things. But most of all, as we see them, we see the powerful process of atrocity at work in the lives of the individuals playing out their parts in this tiny microcosm of war.

Chapter Five

The Greatest Trap of All: To Live with That Which Thou Hath Wrought

The Price and Process of Atrocity

The psychological trauma of living with what one has done to one's fellow man may represent the most significant toll taken by atrocity. Those who commit atrocity have made a Faustian bargain with evil. They have sold their conscience, their future, and their peace of mind for a brief, fleeting, self-destructive advantage.

Sections of this study have been devoted to examining the remarkable power of man's resistance to kill, to the psychological leverage and manipulation required to get men to kill, and to the trauma resulting from it. Once we have taken all of these things into consideration, then we can see that the psychological burden of committing atrocities must be tremendous.

But let me make it *absolutely clear* that this examination of the trauma associated with killing is in no way intended to belittle or downplay the horror and trauma of those who have suffered from atrocities. The focus here is to obtain an *understanding* of the processes associated with atrocity, an understanding that is in no way intended to slight the pain and suffering of atrocity's victims.

The Cost of Compliance . . .

The killer can be empowered by his killing, but ultimately, often years later, he may bear the emotional burden of guilt that he has buried with his acts. This guilt becomes virtually unavoidable when the killer's side has lost and must answer for its actions — which, as we have seen, is one of the reasons that forcing participation in atrocities is such a strangely effective way of motivating men in combat.

Here we see a German soldier who, years later, has to face the enormity of his actions:

> [He] retains a stark image of the burning of some peasant huts in Russia, their owners still inside them. "We saw the children and the women with their babies and then I heard the poouff — the flame had broken through the thatched roof and there was a yellow-brown smoke column going up into the air. It didn't hit me all that much then, but when I think of it now — I slaughtered those people. I murdered them."
>
> — John Keegan and Richard Holmes
>   *Soldiers*

The guilt and trauma of an average human being who is forced to murder innocent civilians don't necessarily have to wait years before they well up into revulsion and rebellion. Sometimes, the executioner cannot resist the forces that cause him to kill, but the still, small voice of humanity and guilt wins out shortly thereafter. And if the soldier truly acknowledges the magnitude of his crime, he must rebel violently. As a World War II intelligence officer, Glenn Gray interviewed a German defector who was morally awakened by his participation in an execution:

> I shall always remember the face of a German soldier when he described such a drastic awakening. . . . At the time we picked him up for investigation . . . in 1944, he was fighting with the French Maquis against his own people. To my question concerning his motives for deserting to the French Resistance, he responded by describing his earlier involvement in German reprisal raids against

the French. On one such raid, his unit was ordered to burn a
village and allow none of the villagers to escape.... As he told
how women and children were shot as they fled screaming from
the flames of their burning homes, the soldier's face was contorted
in painful fashion and he was nearly unable to breathe. It was
quite clear that this extreme experience had shocked him into full
awareness of his own guilt, a guilt he feared he would never atone.
At the moment of that awakening he did not have the courage or
resolution to hinder the massacre, but his desertion to the Resistance
soon after was evidence of a radically new course.

On rare occasions those who are commanded to execute human
beings have the remarkable moral fiber necessary to stare directly
into the face of the obedience-demanding authority and refuse to
kill. These situations represent such a degree of moral courage that
they sometimes become legendary. Precise narratives of a soldier's
personal kills are usually very hard to extract in an interview, but
in the case of individuals who refused to participate in acts that
they considered to be wrong, the soldiers are usually extremely
proud of their actions and are pleased to tell their story.

Earlier in this study, we saw the World War I veteran who took
tremendous pride in "outsmarting" the army and intentionally
missing while a member of a firing squad, and we saw the Contra
mercenary who was overjoyed that he and his comrades spontane-
ously decided to intentionally miss a boat full of civilians. A veteran
of the Christian militia in Lebanon had several personal kills that
he was quite willing to tell me about, but he also had a situation
in which he was ordered to fire on a car and refused to do so. He
was unsure of who was in the car, and he was proud to say that
he actually went to the stockade rather than kill in this situation.

All of us would like to believe that we would not participate
in atrocities. That we could deny our friends and leaders and even
turn our weapons on them if need be. But there are profound
processes involved that prevent such confrontation of peers and
leaders in atrocity circumstance. The first involves group absolution
and peer pressure.

In a way, the obedience-demanding authority, the killer, and his peers are all diffusing the responsibility among themselves. The authority is protected from the trauma of, and responsibility for, killing because others do the dirty work. The killer can rationalize that the responsibility really belongs to the authority and that his guilt is diffused among everyone who stands beside him and pulls the trigger with him. This diffusion of responsibility and group absolution of guilt is the basic psychological leverage that makes all firing squads and most atrocity situations function.

Group absolution can work within a group of strangers (as in a firing-squad situation), but if an individual is bonded to the group, then peer pressure interacts with group absolution in such a way as to almost force atrocity participation. Thus it is extraordinarily difficult for a man who is bonded by links of mutual affection and interdependence to break away and openly refuse to participate in what the group is doing, even if it is killing innocent women and children.

Another powerful process that ensures compliance in atrocity situations is the impact of terrorism and self-preservation. The shock and horror of seeing *unprovoked* violent death meted out creates a deep atavistic fear in human beings. Through atrocity the oppressed population can be numbed into a learned helplessness state of submission and compliance. The effect on the atrocity-committing soldiers appears to be very similar. Human life is profoundly cheapened by these acts, and the soldier realizes that one of the lives that has been cheapened is his own.

At some level the soldier says, "There but for the grace of God go I," and he recognizes with a deep gut-level empathy that one of those screaming, twitching, flopping, bleeding, horror-struck human bodies could very easily be his.

. . . And the Cost of Noncompliance

Glenn Gray notes what may have been one of the most remarkable refusals to participate in an atrocity in recorded history:

> In the Netherlands, the Dutch tell of a German soldier who was a member of an execution squad ordered to shoot innocent hostages.

Suddenly he stepped out of rank and refused to participate in the execution. On the spot he was charged with treason by the officer in charge and was placed with the hostages, where he was promptly executed by his comrades. In an act the soldier has abandoned once and for all the security of the group and exposed himself to the ultimate demands of freedom. He responded in the crucial moment to the voice of conscience and was no longer driven by external commands . . . we can only guess what must have been the influence of his deed on slayers and slain. At all events, it was surely not slight, and those who hear of the episode cannot fail to be inspired.

Here, in its finest form, we see the potential for goodness that exists in all human beings. Overcoming group pressure, obedience-demanding authority, and the instinct of self-preservation, this German soldier gives us hope for mankind and makes us just a little proud to be of the same race. This, ultimately, may be the price of noncompliance for those men of conscience trapped in a group or nation that is, itself, trapped in the dead-end horror of the atrocity cycle.

The Greatest Challenge of All: To Pay the Price of Freedom

Let us set for ourselves a standard so high that it will be a glory to live up to it, and then let us live up to it and add a new laurel to the crown of America.

— Woodrow Wilson

In the same way, every soldier who refuses to kill in combat, secretly or openly, represents the latent potential for nobility in mankind. And yet it is a paradoxically dangerous potential if the forces of freedom and humanity must face those whose unrestrained killing is empowered by atrocities.

The "good" that is not willing to overcome its resistance to killing in the face of an undeniable "evil" may be ultimately destined for destruction. Those who cherish liberty, justice, and truth must recognize that there is another force at large in this world. There is a twisted logic and power resident in the forces of oppression, injustice, and deceit, but those who claim this power are trapped in a spiral of destruction and denial that must ultimately destroy them and any victims they can pull with them into the abyss.

Those who value individual human life and dignity must recognize from whence they draw their strength, and if they are forced to make war they must do so with as much concern for innocent lives as humanly possible. They must not be tempted or antagonized into treading the treacherous and counterproductive path of atrocities. For, as Gray put it, "their brutality made fighting the Germans much easier, whereas ours weakened the will and confused the intellect." Unless a group is prepared to totally dedicate itself to the twisted logic of atrocity, it will not gain even the shortsighted advantages of that logic, but will instead be immediately weakened and confused by its own inconsistency and hypocrisy. There are no half measures when one sells one's soul.

Atrocity — this close-range murder of the innocent and helpless — is the most repulsive aspect of war, and that which resides within man and permits him to perform these acts is the most repulsive aspect of mankind. We must not permit ourselves to be attracted to it. Nor can we, in our revulsion, ignore it. Ultimately the purpose of this section, and of this study, has been to look at this ugliest aspect of war, that we might know it, name it, and confront it.

> This let us pray for, this implore:
> That all base dreams thrust out at door,
>   We may in loftier aims excel
>   And, like men waking from a spell,
> Grow stronger, nobler, than before,
>   When there is Peace.
>
> — Austin Dobson, World War I veteran
>   "When There Is Peace"

SECTION VI

The Killing Response Stages:

What Does It Feel Like to Kill?

Chapter One

The Killing Response Stages

What Does It Feel Like to Kill?

In the 1970s Elisabeth Kübler-Ross published her famous research on death which revealed that when people are dying they often go through a series of emotional stages, including denial, anger, bargaining, depression, and acceptance. In the historical narratives I have read, and in my interviews with veterans over the last two decades, I have found a similar series of emotional response stages to killing in combat.

The basic response stages to killing in combat are concern about killing, the actual kill, exhilaration, remorse, and rationalization and acceptance. Like Elisabeth Kübler-Ross's famous stages in response to death and dying, these stages are generally sequential but not necessarily universal. Thus, some individuals may skip certain stages, or blend them, or pass through them so fleetingly that they do not even acknowledge their presence.

Many veterans have told me that this process is similar to — but *much* more powerful than — that experienced by many first-time deer hunters: concern over the possibility of getting buck fever (i.e., failing to fire when an opportunity arises); the actual kill, occurring almost without thinking; the exhilaration and self-praise after a kill; brief remorse and revulsion (many lifelong woodsmen still become ill while gutting and cleaning a deer). And finally

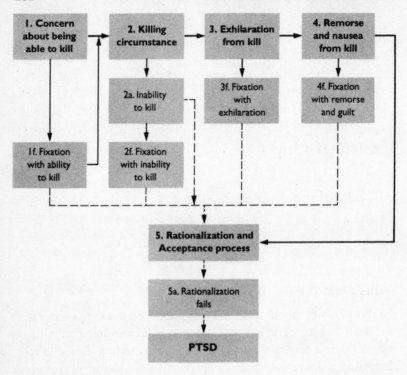

The Killing Response Stages

the acceptance and rationalization process — which in this case is completed by eating the game and honoring its trophy.

The processes may be similar, but the emotional impact of these stages and the magnitude and intensity of the guilt involved in killing human beings are significantly different.[1]

The Concern Stage: "How Am I Going to Do?"

US Marine Sergeant William Rogel summed up the mixture of emotions. "A new man ... has two great fears. One is — it's probably an overriding fear — how am I going to do? — am I going to show the white feather? Am I going to be a coward, or am I going to be able to do my job? And of course the other is the common fear, am I going to survive or get killed or wounded?"

— Richard Holmes
 Acts of War

Holmes's research indicates that one of the soldier's first emotional responses to killing is a concern as to whether, at the moment of truth, he will be able to kill the enemy or will "freeze up" and "let his buddies down." All of my interviews and research verify that these are deep and sincere concerns that exist on the part of most soldiers, and it must be remembered that only 15 to 20 percent of U.S. World War II riflemen went beyond this first stage.

Too much concern and fear can result in fixation, resulting in an obsession with killing on the part of the soldier.[2] This can also be seen in peacetime psychopathologies when individuals become fixated or obsessed with killing. In soldiers — and in individuals fixated with killing in peacetime — this fixation often comes to a conclusion through step two of the process: killing. If a killing circumstance never arises, individuals may continue to feed their fixation by living in a fantasy world of Hollywood-inspired killing, or they may resolve their fixation through the final stage, rationalization and acceptance.

The Killing Stage: "Without Even Thinking"

Two shots. Bam-bam. Just like we had been trained in "quick kill." When I killed, I did it just like that. Just like I'd been trained. Without even thinking.

— Bob, Vietnam veteran

Usually killing in combat is completed in the heat of the moment, and for the modern, properly conditioned soldier, killing in such a circumstance is most often completed reflexively, without conscious thought. It is as though a human being is a weapon. Cocking and taking the safety catch off of this weapon is a complex process, but once it *is* off the actual pulling of the trigger is fast and simple.

Being unable to kill is a very common experience. If on the battlefield the soldier finds himself unable to kill, he can either begin to rationalize what has occurred, or he can become fixated and traumatized by his inability to kill.

The Exhilaration Stage: "I Had a Feeling of the Most Intense Satisfaction"

> Combat Addiction . . . is caused when, during a firefight, the body releases a large amount of adrenaline into your system and you get what is referred to as a "combat high." This combat high is like getting an injection of morphine — you float around, laughing, joking, having a great time, totally oblivious to the dangers around you. The experience is very intense if you live to tell about it.
>
> Problems arise when you begin to want another fix of combat, and another, and another and, before you know it, you're hooked. As with heroin or cocaine addiction, combat addiction will surely get you killed. And like any addict, you get desperate and will do anything to get your fix.
>
> — Jack Thompson
>   "Hidden Enemies"

Jack Thompson, a veteran of close combat in several wars, warned of the dangers of combat addiction. The adrenaline of combat can be greatly increased by another high: the high of killing. What hunter or marksman has not felt a thrill of pleasure and satisfaction upon dropping his target? In combat this thrill can be greatly magnified and can be especially prevalent when the kill is completed at medium to long range.

Fighter pilots, by their nature, and due to the long range of their kills, appear to be particularly susceptible to such killing addiction. Or might it just be more socially acceptable for pilots to speak of it? Whatever the case, many do speak of experiencing such emotions. One fighter pilot told Lord Moran:

> Once you've shot down two or three [planes] the effect is terrific and you'll go on till you're killed. It's love of the sport rather than sense of duty that makes you go on.

And J. A. Kent writes of a World War II fighter pilot's "wildly excited voice on the radio yelling [as he completes an aerial combat kill]: 'Christ! He's coming to pieces, there are bits flying off everywhere. Boy! What a sight!'"

On the ground, too, this exhilaration can take place. In a previous section we noted young Field Marshal Slim's classic response to a World War I personal kill. "I suppose it is brutal," he wrote, "but I had a feeling of the most intense satisfaction as the wretched Turk went spinning down." I have chosen to name this the exhilaration phase because its most intense or extreme form seems to manifest itself as exhilaration, but many veterans echo Slim and call it simply "satisfaction."

The exhilaration felt in this stage can be seen in this narrative by an American tank commander describing to Holmes his intense exhilaration as he first gunned down German soldiers: "The excitement was just fantastic . . . the exhilaration, after all the years of training, the tremendous feeling of lift, of excitement, of exhilaration, it was like the first time you go deer hunting."

For some combatants the lure of exhilaration may become more than a passing occurrence. A few may become fixated in the exhilaration stage and never truly feel remorse. For pilots and snipers, who are assisted by physical distance, this fixation appears to be relatively common. The image of the aggressive pilot who loves what he does (killing) is a part of the twentieth-century heritage. But those who kill completely without remorse at close range are another situation entirely.[3]

Here again we are beginning to explore the region of Swank and Marchand's 2 percent "aggressive psychopaths" (a term that today has evolved into "sociopaths"), who appear to have never developed any sense of responsibility and guilt. As we saw in a previous section, this characteristic, which I prefer to call aggressive personality (a sociopath has the capacity for aggression without any empathy for his fellow human beings; the aggressive personality has the capacity for aggression but may or may not have a capacity for empathy), is probably a matter of degrees rather than a simple categorization.

Those who are truly fixated with the exhilaration of killing either are extremely rare or simply don't talk about it much. A combination of both of these factors is responsible for the lack of individuals (outside of fighter pilots) who like to write about or dwell upon the satisfaction they derived from killing. There is a strong social stigma against saying that one enjoyed killing in combat. Thus it is extraordinary to find an individual expressing emotions like these communicated by R. B. Anderson in "Parting Shot: Vietnam Was Fun(?)":

> Twenty years too late, America has discovered its Vietnam veterans. . . . Well-intentioned souls now offer me their sympathy and tell me how horrible it all must have been.
>
> The fact is, it was fun. Granted, I was lucky enough to come back in one piece. And granted, I was young, dumb, and wilder than a buck Indian. And granted I may be looking back through rose-colored glasses. *But it was great fun* [Anderson's emphasis]. It was so great I even went back for a second helping. Think about it.
>
> . . . Where else could you divide your time between hunting the ultimate big game and partying at "the ville"? Where else could you sit on the side of a hill and watch an air strike destroy a regimental base camp? . . .
>
> Sure there were tough times and there were sad times. But Vietnam is the benchmark of all my experiences. The remainder of my life has been spent hanging around the military trying to recapture some of that old-time feeling. In combat I was a respected man among men. I lived on life's edge and did the most manly thing in the world: I was a warrior in war.
>
> The only person you can discuss these things with is another veteran. Only someone who has seen combat can understand the deep fraternity of the brotherhood of war. Only a veteran can know about the thrill of the kill and the terrible bitterness of losing a friend who is closer to you than your own family.

This narrative gives us a remarkable insight into what there is about combat that can make it addicting to some. Many veterans might disagree strongly with this representation of the war, and some might quietly agree, but few would have this author's courageous openness.[4]

The Remorse Stage: A Collage of Pain and Horror

We have previously observed the tremendous and intense remorse and revulsion associated with a close-range kill:

. . . my experience, was one of revulsion and disgust. . . . I dropped
my weapon and cried. . . . There was so much blood . . . I vomited. . . . And I cried. . . . I felt remorse and shame. I can remember
whispering foolishly, "I'm sorry" and then just throwing up.

We have seen all of these quotes before, and this collage of pain
and horror speaks for itself. Some veterans feel that it is rooted in
a sense of identification or an empathy for the humanity of their
victim. Some are psychologically overwhelmed by these emotions,
and they often become determined never to kill again and thereby
become incapable of further combat. But while most modern
veterans *have* experienced powerful emotions at this stage, they
tend to deny their emotions, becoming cold and hard inside — thus
making subsequent killing much easier.

Whether the killer denies his remorse, deals with it, or is overwhelmed by it, it is nevertheless almost always there. The killer's
remorse is real, it is common, it is intense, and it is something
that he must deal with for the rest of his life.

The Rationalization and Acceptance Stage: "It Took All the Rationalization I Could Muster"

The next personal-kill response stage is a lifelong process in which
the killer attempts to rationalize and accept what he has done.
This process may never truly be completed. The killer never
completely leaves all remorse and guilt behind, but he can usually
come to accept that what he has done was necessary and right.

This narrative by John Foster reveals some of the rationalization
that can take place immediately after the kill:

It was like a volleyball game, he fired, I fired, he fired, I fired. My
serve — I emptied the rest of the magazine into him. The rifle
slipped from his hands and he just fell over. . . .

It sure wasn't like playing army as a kid. We used to shoot each
other for hours. There was always a lot of screaming and yelling.
After getting shot, it was mandatory that you writhe around on
the ground.

. . . I rolled the body over. When the body came to rest, my
eyes riveted on his face. Part of his cheek was gone, along with

his nose and right eye. The rest of his face was a mixture of dirt
and blood. His lips were pulled back and his teeth were clinched.
Just as I was feeling sorry for him, the Marine showed me the U.S.
Government M1 carbine the gook had used on us. He was wearing
a Timex watch and sporting a new pair of U.S.-made tennis shoes.
So much for feeling sorry for him.

This narrative gives a remarkable — and almost certainly unintentional — insight into the early aspects of rationalizing a personal
kill. Note the writer's recognition of the killer's humanity associated with the use of words such as "he," "him," and "his." But
then the enemy's weapon is noted, the rationalization process
begins, and "he" becomes "the body" and ultimately "the gook."
Once the process begins, irrational and irrelevant supporting evidence is gathered, and the possession of U.S.-made shoes and a
watch becomes a cause for depersonalization rather than identification.

To the reader this rationalization and justification is completely
unnecessary. To the writer this rationalization and justification of
his kill are absolutely essential to his emotional and psychological
health, and their progression is unconsciously revealed in his narrative.

Sometimes the killer is quite aware of his need for and use of
rationalization. Note the conscious rationalization and justification
in this account by scout helicopter pilot D. Bray:

We began to be very efficient executioners, a role we took no real
pride in.

I had mixed feelings about this, but as bad as it was, it was better
than leaving NVA alive to attack American troops somewhere else.
Often orders for the day would be: Find NVA in this or that area
. . . to pick up for interrogation.

We would drift up and down hillsides, following trails and
literally looking under big rocks until we would find several NVA
huddled on the ground, trying to hide. We would radio back to
headquarters as we backed off far enough to arm our rockets.
Orders would be "Wait, we're checking it out." Then the bad

news would come, "Wrong area, Fixer. Are they making any signs
of surrender?"

We would reply, "Negative," and then they would come back
with, "Kill them if you can."

"For God's sake, can't you send someone out to take them
prisoner?"

"There is no one available. Shoot them!"

"Roger," we'd reply, and then we'd cut loose. Sometimes they
would understand and take off running for cover, but usually, they
would just crouch in their holes until our rockets hit. Common
sense told me that the senior officers were right; it was foolish to
send a platoon after every little band of three or four armed men,
but it took all the rationalization I could muster before I could
accept what I was doing.

. . . Distasteful as it was, looking back, I can see that what we
did was the only effective way to counter the NVA tactic of
breaking into such small units that there was no effective way to
go after them.

All of this comes as an introduction to Bray's magazine article in
which he tells of the time when he didn't ask for orders. Instead
he landed his little two-seater helicopter and, at great danger to
himself and his copilot, captured a solitary NVA soldier, rather
than executing him, and subsequently brought the prisoner home
sitting in his copilot's lap.

Here again we see an article that appears to represent a deeply
felt request for understanding by the reader. The average reader
probably sees no need to justify these kills, but the killer does.
The point here is that it is this one incident of which Bray is — I
think justifiably — proud. And it is this incident that he wanted
to tell in a national forum. His message can be seen over and over
in these personal narratives about Vietnam: "Look, we did our
job and we did it well, and it needed doing even though we didn't
like it; but sometimes we just had to go above and beyond what
was expected of us in order to avoid the killing." And maybe by
writing and publishing this article he is telling us that "this time,
the time when I didn't have to kill anybody, this is the time that

I want to tell you about. This is the time that I want to be remembered for."

Sometimes the rationalization can manifest itself in dreams. Ray, a veteran of close combat in the 1989 U.S. invasion of Panama, told me of a recurring dream in which he would talk with the young Panamanian soldier he had killed in close combat. "Why did you kill me?" asked the soldier each time. And in his dreams Ray would attempt to explain to his victim, but in reality he was explaining and rationalizing the act of killing to himself: "Well, if you were in my place, wouldn't you have done the same? . . . It was either you or us." And over the last few years, as Ray worked through the rationalization process in his dreams, the soldier and his questions have gone away.

Here we have seen some aspects of how rationalization and acceptance works, but we need to remember that these are just some aspects of a lifelong process. If the process fails it will result in post-traumatic stress disorder. The failure of the rationalization and acceptance process in Vietnam, and its subsequent impact upon our nation, will be looked at in "Killing in Vietnam," the next section of this book.

Chapter Two

Applications of the Model:

Murder-Suicides, Lost Elections, and

Thoughts of Insanity

An Application: Murder-Suicides and Aggression Responses

An understanding of the killing response stages permits understanding of individual responses to violence outside of combat. For instance, we may now be able to understand some of the psychology behind murder-suicides. A murderer, particularly an individual who kills several victims in a spree of violent passion, may very well be fixated in the exhilaration stage of killing. But once there is a lull, and the murderer has a chance to dwell on what he has done, the revulsion stage sets in with such intensity that suicide is a very common response.

These responses can even occur when aggression intrudes into our day-to-day peacetime lives. They are far more intense when one kills in close combat, but just a fistfight can bring them up. Richard Heckler, a psychologist and a high-level master of the martial art of aikido, experienced the full range of response stages in a fight with a group of teenagers who attacked him in his driveway:

When I turned my back someone shot out of the back seat, grabbed my arm, and spun me around. A bolt of adrenalin surged through me and without a moment's hesitation I backhanded him in the face.

I was suddenly released from all restraints. I'd been assaulted physically, it was now my right to unleash the fury I felt from the beginning. As the driver came towards me I pushed his grab aside and pinned him by the throat against the car. . . . The kid I hit was stumbling around holding his face. I was in full-bloom righteous indignation by this point. Having given myself total permission to set justice in order I turned to settle matters with the kid under my grip.

What I saw stopped me in horror. He looked at me in total and absolute fear. His eyes were glazed in terror; his body shook violently. A searing pain spread through my chest and heart. I suddenly lost my stomach for revenge . . . seeing that boy's terror as I held his throat made me understand what Nietzsche meant when he wrote . . . "Rather perish than hate and fear, and twice rather perish than make oneself hated and feared."

First we see the actual, initial blow being struck reflexively without thinking: "without a moment's hesitation I backhanded him in the face." Then the exhilaration and euphoria stage occurs: "I was suddenly released from all restraints. . . . it was now my right to unleash the fury I felt." And suddenly the revulsion stage sets in: "What I saw stopped me in horror. . . . A searing pain spread through my chest and heart."

This process might even help to explain the responses of nations to killing in warfare. After the Gulf War, President Bush was the most popular president in recent American history. America was in the euphoria stage as it had its parades and congratulated itself on its performance. Then came a kind of moral hangover very much like the revulsion stage, which was just in time for President Bush to lose the election. Could this be pushing the model too far? Perhaps, but the same thing happened to Churchill after World War II, and it almost happened to Truman in 1948. Truman was lucky enough to have his election three years after the war was over, which may have been sufficient time for the nation to begin the rationalization and acceptance stage. This may indeed be stretching the model too far, but perhaps it will give future politicians something to think about when they consider going to war.

"I Thought I Was Insane": Interaction Between Exhilaration and Remorse

When I talk to veterans' groups about the killing response stages their reactions are always remarkable. Any good speaker or teacher recognizes when he has struck a chord in his audience, but the response of veterans to the killing response stage — particularly to the interaction between the exhilaration and the remorse stages — is the most powerful I have ever experienced.

One of the things that appears to occur among men in combat is that they feel the high of the exhilaration stage, and then when the remorse stage sets in they believe that there must be something "wrong" or "sick" about them to have enjoyed it so intensely. The common response is something like: "My God, I just killed a man and I enjoyed it. What is wrong with me?"

If the demands from authority and the threatening enemy are intense enough to overcome a soldier's resistance, it is only understandable that he feel some sense of satisfaction. He has hit his target, he has saved his friends, and he has saved his own life. He has resolved the conflict successfully. He won. He is alive! But a good portion of the subsequent remorse and guilt appears to be a horrified response to this perfectly natural and common feeling of exhilaration. *It is vital that future soldiers understand that this is a normal and very common response to the abnormal circumstances of combat, and they need to understand that their feelings of satisfaction at killing are a natural and fairly common aspect of combat.* I believe that this is the most important insight that can come from an understanding of the killing response stages.

Again, I should emphasize that not all combatants go through all stages. Eric, a USMC veteran, described how these stages occurred in his combat experiences. His first kill in Vietnam was an enemy soldier whom he had just seen urinating along the trail. When this soldier subsequently moved toward him, Eric shot him. "It didn't feel good," he said. "It didn't feel good at all." There was no discernible exhilaration, or even any satisfaction. But later, when he killed enemy soldiers who were "coming over the wire" in a firefight, he felt what he called "satisfaction, a satisfaction of anger."

Eric's case brings out two points. The first is that when you have cause to identify with your victim (that is, you see him participate in some act that emphasizes his humanity, such as urinating, eating, or smoking) it is much harder to kill him, and there is much less satisfaction associated with the kill, even if the victim represents a direct threat to you and your comrades at the time you kill him. The second point is that subsequent kills are always easier, and there is much more of a tendency to feel satisfaction or exhilaration after the second killing experience, and less tendency to feel remorse.

You don't even have to personally kill to experience these response stages and the interaction between the exhilaration and remorse stages. Sol, a veteran of naval combat in World War II, told of his exhilaration when he saw his ship shelling a Japanese-held island. Later, when he saw the charred and mangled Japanese bodies, he felt remorse and guilt, and for the rest of his life he has been trying to rationalize and accept the pleasure he felt. Sol, like thousands of others I have spoken to, was profoundly relieved to realize that his deepest, darkest secrets were no different than those of other soldiers with similar experiences.

One veteran's letter to the editor in response to Jack Thompson's article "Combat Addiction" reveals the desperate need for an understanding of these processes:

> [Jack Thompson's] insight has always astounded me, but this piece was really out of the ordinary. . . . What was really right on target was the combat addiction part. For quite a long time I thought I was insane off and on.

Just a simple understanding of the universality of these emotions helped one man understand that he wasn't really crazy, that he was just experiencing a common human reaction to an uncommon situation. Again, that is the objective of this study: no judgment, no condemnation, just the remarkable power of understanding.

SECTION VII

Killing in Vietnam:
What Have We Done to Our Soldiers?

With the frost of his breath wreathing his face, the new president proclaimed, "Now the trumpet summons us . . . to bear the burden of a long twilight struggle . . . against the common enemies of man: tyranny, poverty, disease, and war itself."

Exactly twelve years later, in January 1973, an agreement signed in Paris would end U.S. military efforts in Vietnam. The trumpet would be silent, the mood sullen. American fighting men would depart with the war unwon. The United States of America would no longer be willing to pay any price.

— Dave Palmer
    Summons of the Trumpet

What happened in Vietnam? Why do between 400,000 and 1.5 million Vietnam vets suffer from PTSD as a result of that tragic war?[1] Just what *have* we done to our soldiers?

Chapter One

Desensitization and Conditioning in Vietnam:

Overcoming the Resistance to Killing

"Nobody Understood": An Incident in a VFW Hall

As I conducted interviews for this study in a VFW hall in Florida in the summer of 1989, a Vietnam vet named Roger started talking about his experiences over a beer. It was still early in the afternoon, but down the bar an older woman already began to attack him. "You got no right to snivel about your little pish-ant war. World War Two was a real war. Were you even alive then? *Huh?* I lost a brother in World War Two."

We tried to ignore her; she was only a local character. But finally Roger had had enough. He looked at her and calmly, coldly, said: "Have you ever had to kill anyone?"

"Well no!" she answered belligerently.

"Then what right have *you* got to tell *me* anything?"

There was a long, painful silence throughout the VFW hall, as would occur in a home where a guest had just witnessed an embarrassing family argument.

Then I asked quietly, "Roger, when you got pushed just now, you came back with the fact that you had to kill in Vietnam. Was that the worst of it for you?"

"Yah," he said. "That's half of it."

I waited for a very long time, but he didn't go on. He only stared into his beer. Finally I had to ask, "What was the other half?"

"The other half was that when we got home, nobody understood."

What Happened over There, and What Happened over Here

As discussed earlier, there is a profound resistance to killing one's fellow man. In World War II, 75 to 80 percent of riflemen did not fire their weapons at an exposed enemy, even to save their lives and the lives of their friends. In previous wars nonfiring rates were similar.

In Vietnam the nonfiring rate was close to 5 percent.

The ability to increase this firing rate, though, comes with a hidden cost. Severe psychological trauma becomes a distinct possibility when psychological safeguards of such magnitude are overridden. Psychological conditioning was applied en masse to a body of soldiers, who, in previous wars, were shown to be unwilling or unable to engage in killing activities. When these soldiers, already inwardly shaken by their inner killing experiences, returned to be condemned and attacked by their own nation, the result was often further psychological trauma and long-term psychic damage.

Overcoming the Resistance to Killing: The Problem

But for the infantry, the problem of persuading soldiers to kill is now a major one. . . . That an infantry company in World War II could wreak such havoc with only about one seventh of the soldiers willing to use their weapons is a testimony to the lethal effects of modern firepower, but once armies realized what was actually going on, they at once set about to raise the average.

Soldiers had to be taught, very specifically, to kill. "We are reluctant to admit that essentially war is the business of killing," Marshall wrote in 1947, but it is readily enough admitted now.

— Gwynne Dyer
   War

At the end of World War II the problem became obvious: Johnny can't kill.

A firing rate of 15 to 20 percent among soldiers is like having a literacy rate of 15 to 20 percent among proofreaders. Once those in authority realized the existence and magnitude of the problem, it was only a matter of time until they solved it.

The Answer

And thus, since World War II, a new era has quietly dawned in modern warfare: an era of psychological warfare — psychological warfare conducted not upon the enemy, but upon one's own troops. Propaganda and various other crude forms of psychological enabling have always been present in warfare, but in the second half of this century psychology has had an impact as great as that of technology on the modern battlefield.

When S. L. A. Marshall was sent to the Korean War to make the same kind of investigation that he had done in World War II, he found that (as a result of new training techniques initiated in response to his earlier findings) 55 percent of infantrymen were firing their weapons — and in some perimeter-defense crises, almost everyone was. These training techniques were further perfected, and in Vietnam the firing rate appears to have been around 90 to 95 percent.[2] The triad of methods used to achieve this remarkable increase in killing are desensitization, conditioning, and denial defense mechanisms.

Desensitization: Thinking the Unthinkable

The Vietnam era was, of course then at its peak, you know, the kill thing. We'd run PT [physical training] in the morning and every time your left foot hit the deck you'd have to chant "kill, kill, kill, kill." It was drilled into your mind so much that it seemed like when it actually came down to it, it didn't bother you, you know? Of course the first one always does, but it seems to get easier — not easier, because it still bothers you with every one that, you know, that you actually kill and you know you've killed.

— USMC sergeant and Vietnam veteran, 1982
  quoted in Gwynne Dyer, *War*

This interview from Dyer's book provides an insight into that aspect of our modern training programs that is clearly and distinctly different from those of the past. Men have always used a variety of mechanisms to convince themselves that the enemy was different, that he did not have a family, or that he was not even human. Most primitive tribes took names that translate as "man" or "human being," thereby automatically defining those outside of the tribe as simply another breed of animal to be hunted and killed. We have done something similar when we call the enemy Japs, Krauts, gooks, slopes, dinks, and Commies.

Authors such as Dyer and Holmes have traced the development of this boot-camp deification of killing as having been almost unheard of in World War I, rare in World War II, increasingly present in Korea, and thoroughly institutionalized in Vietnam. Here Dyer explains exactly how this institutionalization of violent ideation in Vietnam differs from the experiences of previous generations:

> Most of the language used in Parris Island to describe the joys of killing people is bloodthirsty but meaningless hyperbole, and the recruits realize that even as they enjoy it. Nevertheless, it does help to *desensitize* them to the suffering of an "enemy," and at the same time they are being indoctrinated in the most explicit fashion (as previous generations were not) with the notion that their purpose is not just to be brave or to fight well; it is to kill people.

Conditioning: Doing the Unthinkable

But desensitization by itself is probably not sufficient to overcome the average individual's deep-seated-resistance to killing. Indeed, this desensitization process is almost a smoke screen for what I believe is the most important aspect of modern training. What Dyer and many other observers have missed is the role of (1) Pavlovian classical conditioning and (2) Skinnerian operant conditioning in modern training.

In 1904, I. P. Pavlov was awarded the Nobel Prize for his development of the concepts of conditioning and association in dogs. In its simplest form, what Pavlov did was ring a bell just before feeding a dog. Over time, the dog learned to associate the sound of the bell with eating and would salivate when he heard the bell, even if no food was present. The conditioned stimulus was the bell, the conditioned response was salivation: the dog had been conditioned to salivate upon hearing a bell ring. This process of associating reward with a particular kind of behavior is the foundation of most successful animal training. During the middle of the twentieth century B. F. Skinner further refined this process into what he called behavioral engineering. Skinner and the behaviorist school represent one of the most scientific and potentially powerful areas of the field of psychology.

The method used to train today's — and the Vietnam era's — U.S. Army and USMC soldiers is nothing more than an application of conditioning techniques to develop a reflexive "quick shoot" ability. It is entirely possible that no one intentionally sat down to use operant conditioning or behavior modification techniques to train soldiers in this area. In my two decades of military service not a single soldier, sergeant, or officer, nor a single official or unofficial reference, has communicated an understanding that conditioning was occurring during marksmanship training. But from the standpoint of a psychologist who is also a historian and a career soldier, it has become increasingly obvious to me that this is exactly what has been achieved.

Instead of lying prone on a grassy field calmly shooting at a bull's-eye target, the modern soldier spends many hours standing in a foxhole, with full combat equipment draped about his body, looking over an area of lightly wooded rolling terrain. At periodic intervals one or two olive-drab, man-shaped targets at varying ranges will pop up in front of him for a brief time, and the soldier must instantly aim and shoot at the target(s). When he hits a target it provides immediate feedback by instantly and very satisfyingly dropping backward — just as a living target would. Soldiers are highly rewarded and recognized for success in this skill and suffer mild punishment (in the form of retraining, peer pressure, and failure to graduate from boot camp) for failure to quickly and accurately "engage" the targets — a standard euphemism for "kill."

In addition to traditional marksmanship, what is being taught in this environment is the ability to shoot reflexively and instantly and a precise mimicry of the act of killing on the modern battlefield. In behavioral terms, the man shape popping up in the soldier's field of fire is the "conditioned stimulus," the immediate engaging of the target is the "target behavior." "Positive reinforcement" is given in the form of immediate feedback when the target drops if it is hit. In a form of "token economy" these hits are then exchanged for marksmanship badges that usually have some form of privilege or reward (praise, public recognition, three-day passes, and so on) associated with them.

Every aspect of killing on the battlefield is rehearsed, visualized, and conditioned. On special occasions even more realistic and complex targets are used. Balloon-filled uniforms moving across the kill zone (pop the balloon and the target drops to the ground), red-paint-filled milk jugs, and many other ingenious devices are used. These make the training more interesting, the conditioned stimuli more realistic, and the conditioned response more assured under a variety of different circumstances.

Snipers use such techniques extensively. In Vietnam it took an average of 50,000 rounds of ammunition to kill one enemy soldier. But the U.S. Army and USMC snipers in Vietnam expended only 1.39 rounds per kill. Carlos Hathcock, with ninety-three confirmed sniper kills in Vietnam, became involved in police and military sniper training after the war. He firmly believed that snipers should train on targets that look like people — not bull's-eyes. A typical command to one of his students (who is firing from one hundred yards at a life-sized photograph of a man holding a pistol to a woman's head) would be "Put three rounds inside the inside corner of the right eye of the bad guy."

In the same way, Chuck Cramer, the trainer for an Israeli Defense Force antiterrorist sniper course, tried to design his course in such a way that practicing to kill was as realistic as possible. "I made the targets as human as possible," said Kramer.

> I changed the standard firing targets to full-size, anatomically correct figures because no Syrian runs around with a big white square on

his chest with numbers on it. I put clothes on these targets and polyurethane heads. I cut up a cabbage and poured catsup into it and put it back together. I said, "When you look through that scope, I want you to see a head blowing up."

— Dale Dye
   "Chuck Cramer: IDFs Master Sniper"

This is all common practice in most of the world's best armies. Most modern infantry leaders understand that realistic training with immediate feedback to the soldier works, and they know that it is essential for success and survival on the modern battlefield. But the military is not, as a rule, a particularly introspective organization, and it has been my experience that those ordering, conducting, and participating in this training do not understand or even wonder (1) what makes it work or (2) what its psychological and sociological side effects might be. It works, and for them that is good enough.

What makes this training process work is the same thing that made Pavlov's dogs salivate and B. F. Skinner's rats press their bars. What makes it work is the single most powerful and reliable behavior modification process yet discovered by the field of psychology, and now applied to the field of warfare: operant conditioning.

Denial Defense Mechanisms: Denying the Unthinkable

An additional aspect of this process that deserves consideration here is the development of a denial defense mechanism. Denial and defense mechanisms are unconscious methods for dealing with traumatic experiences. Prepackaged denial defense mechanisms are a remarkable contribution from modern U.S. Army training.

Basically the soldier has rehearsed the process so many times that when he does kill in combat he is able to, at one level, deny to himself that he is actually killing another human being. This careful rehearsal and realistic mimicry of the act of killing permit the soldier to convince himself that he has only "engaged" another target. One British veteran of the Falklands, trained in the modern method, told Holmes that he "thought of the enemy as nothing more or less than Figure II [man-shaped] targets." In the same way, an American soldier can convince himself that he is shooting at an E-type silhouette (a man-shaped, olive-drab target), and not a human being.

Bill Jordan, law-enforcement expert, career U.S. Border Patrol officer, and veteran of many a gunfight, combines this denial process with desensitization in his advice to young law-enforcement officers:

> [There is] a natural disinclination to pull the trigger . . . when your weapon is pointed at a human. Even though their own life was at stake, most officers report having this trouble in their first fight. To aid in overcoming this resistance it is helpful if you can will yourself to think of your opponent as a mere target and not as a human being. In this connection you should go further and pick a spot on the target. This will allow better concentration and further remove the human element from your thinking. If this works for you, try to continue this thought in allowing yourself no remorse. A man who will resist an officer with weapons has no respect for the rules by which decent people are governed. He is an outlaw who has no place in world society. His removal is completely justified, and should be accomplished dispassionately and without regret.

Jordan calls this process manufactured contempt, and the combination of denial of, and contempt for, the victim's role in society (desensitization), along with the psychological denial of, and contempt for, the victim's humanity (developing a denial defense mechanism), is a mental process that is tied in and reinforced every time the officer fires a round at a target. And, of course, police, like the military, no longer fire at bull's-eyes; they "practice" on man-shaped silhouettes.

The success of this conditioning and desensitization is obvious and undeniable. It can be seen and recognized both in individuals and in the performance of nations and armies.

The Effectiveness of the Conditioning

Bob, a U.S. Army colonel, knew of Marshall's study and accepted that Marshall's World War II firing rates were probably correct. He was not sure what mechanism was responsible for increasing the firing rate in Vietnam, but he realized that somehow the rate had been increased. When I suggested the conditioning effects of modern training, he immediately recognized that process in himself. His head snapped up, his eyes widened slightly, and he said, "Two shots. Bam-bam. Just like we had been trained in 'quick kill.' When I killed, I did it just like that. Just like I'd been trained. Without even thinking."

Jerry, another veteran who survived six six-month tours in Cambodia as an officer with Special Forces (Green Berets), when asked how he was able to do the things that he did, acknowledged simply that he had been "programmed" to kill, and he accepted it as necessary for his survival and success.

One interviewee, an ex–CIA agent named Duane, who was then working as a high-level security executive in a major aerospace corporation, had conducted a remarkable number of successful interrogations during his lifetime, and he considered himself to be an expert on the process known popularly as brainwashing. He felt that he had been "to some extent brainwashed" by the CIA and that the soldiers receiving modern combat training were being similarly brainwashed. Like every other veteran whom I have discussed the matter with, he had no objections to this, understanding that psychological conditioning was essential to his survival and an effective method of mission accomplishment. He felt that a very similar and equally powerful process was taking place in the shoot–no shoot program, which federal and local law-enforcement agencies all over the nation conduct. In this program the officer selectively fires blanks at a movie screen depicting various tactical situations, thereby mimicking and rehearsing the process of deciding when and when not to kill.

The incredible effectiveness of modern training techniques can be seen in the lopsided close-combat kill ratios between the British and Argentinean forces during the Falklands War and the U.S.

and Panamanian forces during the 1989 Panama Invasion.[3] During his interviews with British veterans of the Falklands War, Holmes described Marshall's observations in World War II and asked if they had seen a similar incidence of nonfirers in their own forces. Their response was that they had seen no such thing occur with their soldiers, but there was "immediate recognition that it applied to the Argentineans, whose snipers and machine-gunners had been very effective while their individual riflemen had not." Here we see an excellent comparison between the highly effective and competent British riflemen, trained by the most modern methods, and the remarkably ineffective Argentinean riflemen, who had been given old-style, World War II–vintage training.

Similarly, Rhodesia's army during the 1970s was one of the best trained in the world, going up against a very poorly trained but well-equipped insurgent force. The security forces in Rhodesia maintained an overall kill ratio of about eight-to-one in their favor throughout the guerrilla war. And the highly trained Rhodesian Light Infantry achieved kill ratios ranging from thirty-five-to-one to fifty-to-one.

One of the best examples in recent American history involved a company of U.S. Army Rangers who were ambushed and trapped while attempting to capture Mohammed Aidid, a Somali warlord sought by the United Nations. In this circumstance no artillery or air strikes were used, and no tanks, armored vehicles, or other heavy weapons were available to the American forces, which makes this an excellent assessment of the relative effectiveness of modern small-arms training techniques. The score? Eighteen U.S. troops killed, against an estimated 364 Somali who died that night.

And we might remember that American forces were never once defeated in any major engagement in Vietnam. Harry Summers says that when this was pointed out to a high-ranking North Vietnamese soldier after the war, the answer was "That may be true, but it is also irrelevant." Perhaps so, but it does reflect the individual close-combat superiority of the U.S. soldier in Vietnam.

Even with allowance for unintentional error and deliberate exaggeration, this superior training and killing ability in Vietnam, Panama, Argentina, and Rhodesia amounts to nothing less than a technological revolution on the battlefield, a revolution that represents total superiority in close combat.

A Side Effect of the Conditioning

Duane, the CIA veteran, told of one incident that provides some insight into a side effect of this conditioning or brainwashing. He was guarding a Communist defector in a safe house in West Germany during the mid-1950s. The defector was a very large, strong, and particularly murderous member of the Stalinist regime then in power. By all accounts he was quite insane. Having defected because he had lost favor among his Soviet masters, he was now beginning to have second thoughts about his new masters and was trying to escape.

Alone for days in a locked and barred house with this man, the young CIA agent assigned to watch him was subject to a series of attacks. The defector would charge at him with a club or a piece of furniture, and each time he would break off the attack at the last minute as Duane pointed his weapon at him. The agent called his superiors over the phone and was ordered to draw an imaginary line on the floor and shoot this unarmed (though very hostile and dangerous) individual if he crossed that line. Duane felt certain that this line was going to be crossed and mustered up all of his conditioning. "He was a dead man. I knew I would kill him. Mentally I *had* killed him, and the physical part was going to be easy." But the defector (apparently not quite as crazy or desperate as he appeared to be) never crossed that line.

Still, some aspect of the trauma of the kill was there. "In my mind," Duane told me, "I have always felt that I had killed that man." Most Vietnam veterans did not necessarily execute a personal kill in Vietnam. But they had participated in dehumanizing the enemy in training, and the vast majority of them *did* fire, or knew in their hearts that they were prepared to fire, and the very fact that they were prepared and able to fire ("Mentally I *had* killed him") denied them an important form of escape from the burden of responsibility that they brought back from that war. Although they had not killed, they had been taught to think the unthinkable and had thereby been introduced to a part of themselves that under ordinary circumstances only the killer knows. The point is that *this program of desensitization, conditioning, and denial defense mechanisms, combined with subsequent participation in a war, may make it possible to share the guilt of killing without ever having killed.*

A Safeguard in the Conditioning

It is essential to understand that one of the most important aspects of this process is that soldiers are *always* under authority in combat. No army can tolerate undisciplined or indiscriminate firing, and a vital — and easily overlooked — facet of the soldier's conditioning revolves around having him fire only when and where he is told to. The soldier fires only when told to by a higher authority and then only within his designated firing lane. Firing a weapon at the wrong time or in the wrong direction is so heinous an offense that it is almost unthinkable to the average soldier.

Soldiers are conditioned throughout their training and throughout their time in the military to fire *only under authority*. A gunshot cannot be easily hidden, and on rifle ranges or during field training any gunshot at inappropriate times (even when firing blank ammunition) must be justified, and if it is not justifiable it will be immediately and firmly punished.

Similarly, most law-enforcement officers are presented with a variety of targets representing both innocent bystanders and gun-wielding criminals during their training. And they are severely sanctioned for engaging the wrong target. In the FBI's shoot–no shoot program, failure to demonstrate a satisfactory ability to distinguish when an officer can and cannot fire can result in revocation of the officer's right to carry a weapon.

Numerous studies have demonstrated that there is not any distinguishable threat of violence to society from the veterans returning to the United States from any of the wars of this century. There are Vietnam vets who commit violent crimes, but statistically there is no greater a population of violent criminals among veterans than there is among nonveterans.[4] What is a potential threat to society is the *unrestrained* desensitization, conditioning, and denial defense mechanisms provided by modern interactive video games and violent television and movies, but that is a topic for the last section in this book, "Killing in America: What Are We Doing to Our Children?"

Chapter Two

What Have We Done to Our Soldiers?
The Rationalization of Killing and
How It Failed in Vietnam

The Rationalization and Acceptance of Killing

> But after the fires and the wrath,
>   But after searching and pain,
> His Mercy opens us a path
>   To live with ourselves again.
>
> — Rudyard Kipling
>   "The Choice"

We have previously examined the killing response stages of concern, killing exhilaration, remorse, and rationalization and acceptance. Let us now apply this model to the Vietnam veteran in order to understand how the process of rationalization and acceptance of killing failed in Vietnam.

The Rationalization Process

Something unique seems to have occurred in the rationalization process available to the Vietnam veteran. Compared with earlier American wars the Vietnam conflict appears to have reversed most

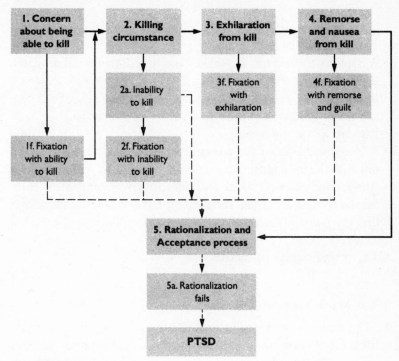

The Killing Response Stages

of the processes traditionally used to facilitate the rationalization and acceptance of killing experiences. These traditional processes involve:

- Constant praise and assurance to the soldier from peers and superiors that he "did the right thing" (One of the most important physical manifestations of this affirmation is the awarding of medals and decorations.)
- The constant presence of mature, older comrades (that is, in their late twenties and thirties) who serve as role models and stabilizing personality factors in the combat environment
- A careful adherence to such codes and conventions of warfare by both sides (such as the Geneva conventions, first established in 1864), thereby limiting civilian casualties and atrocities
- Rear lines or clearly defined safe areas where the soldier can go to relax and depressurize during a combat tour
- The presence of close, trusted friends and confidants who have

been present during training and are present throughout the combat experience
- A cooldown period as the soldier and his comrades sail or march back from the wars
- Knowledge of the ultimate victory of their side and of the gain and accomplishments made possible by their sacrifices
- Parades and monuments
- Reunions and continued communication (via visits, mail, and so on) with the individuals whom the soldier bonded with in combat
- An unconditionally warm and admiring welcome by friends, family, communities, and society, constantly reassuring the soldier that the war and his personal acts were for a necessary, just, and righteous cause
- The proud display of medals

What Made Vietnam Different

In the case of the Vietnam veteran all but the first of these rationalization processes were not only mostly absent, but many of them were inverted and became sources of great pain and trauma to the veteran.

The Teenage War

It's easier if you catch them young. You can train older men to be soldiers; it's done in every major war. But you can never get them to believe that they like it, which is the major reason armies try to get their recruits before they are twenty. There are other reasons too, of course, like the physical fitness, lack of dependents, and economic dispensability of teenagers, that make armies prefer them, but the most important qualities teenagers bring to basic training are enthusiasm and naivete. . . .

The armed forces of every country can take almost any young male civilian and turn him into a soldier with all the right reflexes and attitudes in only a few weeks. Their recruits usually have no more than twenty years' experience of the world, most of it as children, while the armies have had all of history to practice and perfect their technique.

— Gwynne Dyer
War

The combatants of all wars are frightfully young, but the American combatants in Vietnam were significantly younger than in any war in American history. Most were drafted at eighteen and experienced combat during one of the most malleable and vulnerable stages of their lives. This was America's first "teenage war," with the average combatant having not yet seen his twentieth birthday, and these combatants were without the leavening of mature, older soldiers that has always been there in past wars.

Developmental psychologists have identified this stage in an adolescent's psychological and social development as being a crucial period in which the individual establishes a stable and enduring personality structure and a sense of self.

In past wars the impact of combat on adolescents has been buffered by the presence of older veterans who can serve as role models and mentors throughout the process. But in Vietnam there were precious few such individuals to turn to. By the end of the war many sergeants were coming out of "Shake 'n Bake" school and had only a few months more training and maturity than their comrades. Even many officers were coming out of OCS (Officer Candidate School) without any college training whatsoever, and they too had little more training and maturity than their soldiers.

They were teenagers leading teenagers in a war of endless, small-unit operations, trapped together in a real-world reenactment of *The Lord of the Flies* with guns, and destined to internalize the horrors of combat during one of the most vulnerable and susceptible stages of life.

The "Dirty" War

Simultaneously everyone leveled his weapon at him and fired. "Jesus Christ!" somebody gasped behind me as we watched his body reverse course back toward the trees; chunks of meat and bone flew through the air and stuck to the huge boulders. One of our rounds detonated a grenade the soldier carried, and his body smashed to the ground beneath a shower of blood. . . .

The young Viet Cong was a good soldier, even if he was a communist. He died for what he believed in. He was not a gunner for Hanoi, he was a VC. His country was not North Vietnam, he was South Vietnamese. His political beliefs did not coincide with those of the Saigon government, so he was labeled an enemy of the people. . . .

A young Vietnamese girl appeared out of nowhere and sat down next to one of the dead VC. She just sat there staring at the pile of weapons, and slowly rocking herself back and forth. I couldn't tell if she was crying, because she never once looked over at us. She just sat there. A fly crawled along her cheek, but she paid no attention to it.

She just sat there.

She was the 7-year-old daughter of a Viet Cong soldier, and I wondered if she had been conditioned to accept death and war and sorrow. She was an orphan now, and I wondered if there were confusion in her mind, or sadness, or just an emptiness that no one could understand.

I wanted to go over and comfort her, but I found myself walking down the hill with the others. I never looked back.

— Nick Uhernik
  "Battle of Blood"

At a Vietnam Vets Coalition meeting in Florida, one vet told me about his cousin, who was also a vet, who would only say: "They trained me to kill. They sent me to Vietnam. They didn't tell me that I'd be fighting kids." For many, this is the distilled essence of the horror of what happened in Vietnam.

The killing is always traumatic. But when you have to kill women and children, or when you have to kill men in their homes, in front of their wives and children, and when you have to do it not from twenty thousand feet but up close where you can watch them die, the horror appears to transcend description or understanding.

Much of the war in Vietnam was conducted against an insurgent force. Against men, women, and children who were often defending their own homes and who were dressed in civilian clothing. This resulted in a deterioration of traditional conventions and an increase in civilian casualties, atrocities, and resultant trauma. Neither the ideological reasons for the war, nor the target population, was the same as that associated with previous wars.

The standard methods of on-the-scene rationalization fail when the enemy's child comes out to mourn over her father's body or when the enemy is a child throwing a hand grenade. And the North Vietnamese and Vietcong understood this. Among the many excellent narratives gained from personal interviews in Al Santoli's book *To Bear Any Burden* is the story of Troung "Mealy," a former Vietcong agent in the Mekong Delta. "Children were trained," said Mealy, "to throw grenades, not only for the terror factor, but so the government or American soldiers would have to shoot them. Then the Americans feel very ashamed. And they blame themselves and call their soldiers war criminals."

And it worked.

When a soldier shoots a child who is throwing a grenade the child's weapon explodes, and there is only the mutilated body left to rationalize. There is no convenient weapon indisputably telling the world of the victim's lethality and the killer's innocence; there is only a dead child, speaking mutely of horror and innocence lost. The innocence of childhood, soldiers, and nations, all lost in a single act reenacted countless times for ten endless years until a weary nation finally retreats in horror and dismay from its long nightmare.

The Inescapable War

There were no real lines of demarcation, and just about any area was subject to attack. . . . It was an endless war with invisible enemies and no ground gains — just a constant flow of troops in and out of the country. The only observable outcome was an

interminable production of maimed, crippled bodies and countless corpses.

— Jim Goodwin
  Post-Traumatic Stress Disorders

In *The Face of Battle,* John Keegan traces conflicts across the centuries, noting in particular how the duration of a battle and the depth
of the battlefield increased over the years. From a duration of a
few hours and a depth of only a few hundred yards in the Middle
Ages, battle grew to the point where, in this century, the depth
of the danger zone extended for miles into the rear areas, and the
battles could last for months, even blending into one another to
create one endless conflict that would last for years.

In World War I and World War II we discovered that this
endless battle would take a horrendous psychological toll on the
combatant, and we were able to deal with this endless battle by
rotating soldiers into the rear lines. Within Vietnam, the danger
zone increased exponentially, and for ten years we fought a war
unlike any we had experienced before. In Vietnam there were no
rear lines to escape to, there was no escape from the stress of
combat, and the psychological stress of continuously existing at
"the front" took an enormous, if delayed, toll.

The Lonely War

Prior to Vietnam the American soldier's first experience with the
battlefield was usually as a member of a unit that had been trained
and bonded together prior to combat. The soldier in these wars
usually knew that he was in for the duration or until he had
established sufficient points on some type of scale that kept track
of his combat exposure; either way the end of combat for him
was at some vague point in an uncertain future.

Vietnam was distinctly different from any war we have fought
before or since, in that it was a war of individuals. With very few
exceptions, every combatant arrived in Vietnam as an individual
replacement on a twelve-month tour — thirteen months for the
U.S. Marines.

The average soldier had only to survive his year in hell and thus, for the first time, had a clear-cut way out of combat other than as a physical or psychological casualty. In this environment it was far more possible, even natural, that many soldiers would remain aloof, and their bonding would never develop into the full, mature, lifelong relationships of previous wars. This policy (combined with the use of drugs, maintenance of proximity to the combat zone, and establishment of an expectancy of returning to combat) resulted in an all-time-record low number of psychiatric casualties *in Vietnam*.

Military psychiatrists and leaders believed that they had found a solution for the age-old problem of battlefield psychiatric casualties, a problem that, at one point in World War II, was creating casualties faster than we could replace them. Given a less traumatic war and an unconditionally positive World War II–style welcome to the returning veteran, this might have been an acceptable system, but in Vietnam what appears to have happened is that many a combatant simply endured traumatic experiences (experiences that might otherwise have been unbearable) by refusing to come to terms with his grief and guilt and turned instead to the escapist therapy of a "short timer's calendar" and the promise of "only forty-five days and a wake-up."

This rotation policy (combined with the extensive use of psychiatrically and self-prescribed drugs) did create an environment in which the incidence of psychiatric casualties *on the battlefield* was much lower than that of past wars in this century. But a tragic, long-term price, a price that was far too high, was paid for the short-term gains of this policy.

World War II soldiers joined for the duration. A soldier may have come into combat as an individual replacement, but he knew that he would be with his unit for the rest of the war. He was very invested in establishing himself with his newfound unit, and those who were already in the unit had equal cause to bond with this individual, who they knew would be their comrade until the war was over. These individuals developed very mature, fulfilling relationships that for most of them have lasted throughout their lives.

In Vietnam most soldiers arrived on the battlefield alone, afraid, and without friends. A soldier joined a unit where he was an FNG, a "f——ing new guy," whose inexperience and incompetence represented a threat to the continued survival of those in the unit. In a few months, for a brief period, he became an old hand who was bonded to a few friends and able to function well in combat. But then, all too soon, his friends left him via death, injury, or the end of their tours, and he too became a short timer, whose only concern was surviving until the end of his tour of duty. Unit morale, cohesion, and bonding suffered tremendously. All but the best of units became just a collection of men experiencing endless leavings and arrivals, and that sacred process of bonding, which makes it possible for men to do what they must do in combat, became a tattered and torn remnant of the support structure experienced by veterans of past American wars.

That does not mean that no bonds were forged, for men will always forge strong bonds in the face of death, but they were few and all too fleeting, destined never to last longer than a year and usually much less than that.

The First Pharmacological War

One of the major factors that combined with the rotation policy to suppress or delay dealing with psychological trauma was the use of a powerful new family of drugs. Soldiers in past wars often drank themselves into numbness, and Vietnam was no exception. But Vietnam was also the first war in which the forces of modern pharmacology were directed to empower the battlefield soldier.

The administration of tranquilizing drugs and phenothiazines on the combat front first occurred in Vietnam. The soldiers who became psychiatric casualties were generally placed in psychiatric-care facilities in close proximity to the combat zone where these drugs were prescribed by MDs and psychiatrists. The soldiers under their care readily took their "medicine," and this program was touted as a major factor in reducing the incidence of evacuations of psychiatric casualties.[5]

In the same way, many soldiers "self-prescribed" marijuana and, to a lesser extent, opium and heroin to help them deal with the stress they were facing. At first it appeared that this widespread use of illegal drugs had no negative psychiatric result, but we soon came to realize that the effect of these drugs was much the same as the effect of the legally prescribed tranquilizers.

Basically, whether legally or illegally used, these drugs combined with the one-year tour (with the knowledge that all you had to do was "gut out" twelve months to escape) to submerge or delay combat-stress reactions. Tranquilizers do not deal with psychological stressors; they merely do what insulin does for a diabetic: they treat the symptoms, but the disease is still there.

Drugs may help make an individual more susceptible to some forms of therapy, *if* therapy is available. But if drugs are given while the stressor is still being experienced, then they will arrest or supersede the development of effective coping mechanisms, resulting in an increase in the long-term trauma from the stress. What happened in Vietnam is the moral equivalent of giving a soldier a local anesthetic for a gunshot wound and then sending him back into combat.

At their best these drugs only served to delay the inevitable confrontation with the pain, suffering, grief, and guilt that the Vietnam veteran repressed and buried deep inside himself. And at worst they actually increased the impact of the trauma suffered by the soldier.

The Uncleansed Veteran

The traditional cooldown period while marching or sailing home in intact units forms a kind of group therapy that was not available to the Vietnam veteran. This, too, is essential to the mental health of the returning veteran, and this too was denied the American veteran of Vietnam.

Arthur Hadley is a master of military psychological operations (psyops), author of the excellent book *Straw Giant,* and one of this century's great military intellectuals.[6] After his tour as a psyops commander in World War II (for which he was awarded two Silver Stars), Hadley conducted an extensive study on major warrior societies around the world. In this study he concluded that *all* warrior societies, tribes, and nations incorporate some form of

purification ritual for their returning soldiers, and this ritual appears
to be essential to the health of both the returning warrior and the
society as a whole.

Gabriel understands and powerfully illuminates the role of this
purification ritual, and the price of its absence:

> Societies have always recognized that war changes men, that they
> are not the same after they return. That is why primitive societies
> often require soldiers to perform purification rites before allowing
> them to rejoin their communities. These rites often involved wash-
> ing or other forms of ceremonial cleansing. Psychologically, these
> rituals provided soldiers with a way of ridding themselves of stress
> and the terrible guilt that always accompanies the sane after war.
> It was also a way of treating guilt by providing a mechanism through
> which fighting men could decompress and relive their terror with-
> out feeling weak or exposed. Finally, it was a way of telling the
> soldier that what he did was right and that the community for
> which he fought was grateful and that, above all, his community
> of sane and normal men welcomed him back.
>
> Modern armies have similar mechanisms of purification. In
> WWII soldiers en route home often spent days together on troop-
> ships. Among themselves, the warriors could relive their feelings,
> express grief for lost comrades, tell each other about their fears,
> and, above all, receive the support of their fellow soldiers. They
> were provided with a sounding board for their own sanity. Upon
> reaching home, soldiers were often honored with parades or other
> civic tributes. They received the respect of their communities as
> stories of their experiences were told to children and relatives by
> proud parents and wives. All this served the same cleansing purpose
> as the rituals of the past.
>
> When soldiers are denied these rituals they often tend to become
> emotionally disturbed. Unable to purge their guilt or be reassured
> that what they did was right, they turned their emotions inward.
> Soldiers returning from the Vietnam War were victims of this kind
> of neglect. There were no long troopship voyages where they
> could confide in their comrades. Instead, soldiers who had finished
> their tour of duty were flown home to arrive "back in the world"

often within days, and sometimes within hours, of their last combat with the enemy. There were no fellow soldiers to meet them and to serve as a sympathetic sounding board for their experiences; no one to convince them of their own sanity.

Since Vietnam, several different returning armies have applied this vital lesson. The British troops returning from the Falklands could have been airlifted home, but instead they made the long, dreary, and therapeutic South Atlantic crossing with their navy.

In the same way, Israel addressed the need for a cooldown period among their soldiers returning from the nation's extremely unpopular 1982 incursion into Lebanon. They were aware that in the United States there occurred what some have termed a "conspiracy of silence" in discussing the Vietnam War and its moral issues upon its conclusion. Recognizing this problem and the need for psychological decompression, the Israelis did what was probably one of the healthiest things they could have done for the mental welfare of those who participated in their Vietnam. According to Shalit, the withdrawing Israeli soldiers were gathered by unit in meetings in which they could relax for the first time after many months. There they went through a lengthy process of "ventilating their feelings, questions, doubts, and criticisms about all issues: from the failure of military action and planning, to the unnecessary sacrifice of life and the feeling of total failure."

And the U.S. troops deployed to Grenada, Panama, and Iraq left these conflicts in intact units. The continued stability of these units after departing the combat zone ensured that detailed (and psychologically essential) after-action briefings and reviews could be conducted at home stations.

The Defeated Veteran

The Vietnam veteran's belief in the justice of his cause and the necessity for his acts was constantly challenged and ultimately bankrupt when South Vietnam fell to an invasion from the North in 1975. A dim foreshadowing of this form of trauma can be seen in World War I, when the war ended without the unconditional surrender of the enemy, and many veterans bitterly understood that it wasn't really over, over there.

With the collapse of the Soviet Union and the end of the Cold War it might be legitimately argued that we did not lose in Vietnam any more than we lost in the Battle of the Bulge: we got pushed back for a while, but ultimately we won the war. But today such a perspective is small consolation to the Vietnam vet. For the Vietnam veteran there is no walking Flanders Field, no reenactment of D Day, no commemoration of Inchon, or any other celebration by grateful nations whose peace and prosperity was preserved by American blood and sweat and tears. For too many years the Vietnam veterans knew only the defeat of a nation they fought and suffered for and the victory of a regime that many of them believed to be evil and malignant enough to risk dying to fight against.

Ultimately, they have been vindicated. The containment policy that they were an instrument of has been successful. Now the Russians themselves will concede the evils of communism. Hundreds of thousands of boat people attest to the disastrous nature of the North Vietnamese regime. Now the Cold War has ended in victory. And from one perspective we were no more defeated in Vietnam than the U.S. forces were in the Philippines or at the Battle of the Bulge. They lost the battle but they won the war. And the war was worth fighting. Perhaps we can see Vietnam from that perspective now, and I believe that there is truth and healing in that perspective. But for most Vietnam veterans this "victory" comes more than two decades too late.

Unwelcomed Veterans and Unmourned Dead

Two sources of public recognition and affirmation vital to the soldier are the parades that have traditionally welcomed them home from combat and the memorials and monuments that have commemorated and mourned their dead comrades. Parades are an essential rite of passage to the returning veteran in the same way that bar mitzvahs, confirmations, graduations, weddings, and other public ceremonies are to other individuals at key periods of their lives. Memorials and monuments mean to the grieving veteran what funerals and tombstones do to any bereaved loved one. But rather than parades and memorials the Vietnam veteran, who had only done what society had trained and ordered him to do, was greeted by a hostile environment in which he was ashamed to even wear the uniform and decorations that became such a vital part of who he was.

Even the twenty-year-late Vietnam Veterans Memorial had to be constructed in the face of the same indignity and misunderstanding that the veterans had endured for so long. Initially the memorial was not to have the flag and statue traditionally associated with such edifices: instead the monument to our nation's longest war was going to be just a "black gash of shame" with the names of the fallen engraved upon it. It was only after a long and bitter battle that veterans' groups were able to get a statue and a flagpole flying the U.S. flag added to their memorial.

At their own monument, our veterans had to fight to fly the flag that meant so much to them.

The thousands of veterans who wept at "the wall" and marched with tear-streaked faces at welcome-home parades, given two decades after the fact, represented a sincere grieving and a true pain that most Americans did not even know existed. But most of all it represented reconciliation and healing.

The veterans who spurn this reconciliation and "get all they need down at the American Legion" may simply be those who have withdrawn the most deeply into their shells, and as we will see in our look at PTSD, the cost of that shell is significant. But perhaps they have a right to remain in their shells, and it may be that the society that drove them there has no right to expect reconciliation or forgiveness from them.

The Lonely Veteran

The experience of the Vietnam veteran was distinctly different from that of the veterans of previous American wars. Once he completed his tour of duty, he usually severed all bonds with his unit and comrades. It was extremely rare for a veteran to write to his buddies who were still in combat, and (in strong contrast to the endless reunions of World War II veterans) for more than a decade it was even rarer for two or more of them to get together after the war. In *PTSD: A Handbook for Clinicians,* Vietnam vet Jim Goodwin hypothesizes (I think correctly) that "guilt about leaving one's buddies to an unknown fate in Vietnam apparently proved so strong that many veterans were often too frightened to find out what happened to those left behind." Only now, two decades after the fact, are Vietnam veterans beginning to get over this survivor guilt and form veterans' associations and coalitions.

For the Vietnam vet, the postwar years were long, lonely ones. But the Vietnam Veterans Memorial and Memorial Day parades in their honor have fortified and cleansed them, and now they are finally beginning to find the strength and courage to reunite with long lost brothers and welcome one another home.

The Condemned Veteran

On returning from Vietnam minus my right arm, I was accosted twice . . . by individuals who inquired, "Where did you lose your arm? Vietnam?" I replied, "Yes." The response was "Good. Serves you right."

— James W. Wagenbach
   quoted in Bob Greene, *Homecoming*

Even more important than parades and monuments are the basic, day-to-day attitudes toward the returning veteran. Lord Moran felt that public support was a key factor in the returning veteran's psychological health. He believed that Britain's failure to provide her World War I and World War II soldiers the support they needed resulted in many psychological problems.

If Lord Moran could detect a lack of concern and acceptance that had a significant impact on the psychological welfare of World War I and World War II veterans in England, how much greater was the adverse impact of the Vietnam vet's much more hostile homecoming?

Richard Gabriel describes the experience:

The presence of a Viet Nam veteran in uniform in his home town was often the occasion for glares and slurs. He was not told that he had fought well; nor was he reassured that he had done only what his country and fellow citizens had asked him to do. Instead of reassurance there was often condemnation — baby killer, murderer — until he too began to question what he had done and, ultimately, his sanity. The result was that at least 500,000 — perhaps as many as 1,500,000 — returning Viet Nam veterans suffered some degree of psychiatric debilitation, called Post-Traumatic Stress Disorder, an illness which has become associated in the public mind with an entire generation of soldiers sent to war in Vietnam.

As a result of this, Gabriel concludes that Vietnam produced more psychiatric casualties than any other war in American history.

Numerous psychological studies have found that the social support system — or lack thereof — upon returning from combat is a critical factor in the veteran's psychological health. Indeed, social support after war has been demonstrated in a large body of research (by psychiatrists, military psychologists, Veterans Administration mental-health professionals, and sociologists) to be more crucial than even the intensity of combat experienced.[7] When the Vietnam War began to become unpopular the soldiers who were fighting that war began to pay a psychological price for it, even before they returned home.

Psychiatric casualties increase greatly when the soldier feels isolated, and psychological and social isolation from home and society was one of the results of the growing antiwar sentiment in the United States. One manifestation of this isolation, noted by numerous authors such as Gabriel, was an increase in Dear John letters. As the war became more and more unpopular back home, it became increasingly common for girlfriends, fiancées, and even wives to dump the soldiers who depended upon them. Their letters were an umbilical cord to the sanity and decency that they believed they were fighting for. And a significant increase in such letters as well as many other forms of psychological and social isolation probably account for much of the tremendous increase in psychiatric casualties suffered late in that war. According to Gabriel, early in the war evacuations for psychiatric conditions reached only 6 percent of total medical evacuations, but by 1971, the percentage represented by psychiatric casualties had increased to 50 percent. These psychiatric casualty ratings were similar to home-front approval ratings for the war, and an argument can be made that psychiatric casualties can be impacted by public disapproval.

The greatest indignity heaped upon the soldier waited for him when he returned home. Often veterans were verbally abused and physically attacked or even spit upon. The phenomenon of returning soldiers being spit on deserves special attention here. Many Americans do not believe (or do not want to believe) that such events ever occurred. Bob Greene, a syndicated newspaper columnist, was one of those who believed these accounts were probably a myth. Greene issued a request in his column for anyone who had actually experienced such an event to write in and tell of it. He received more than a thousand letters in response, collected in his book, *Homecoming*.

A typical account is that of Douglas Detmer:

> I was spat upon in the San Francisco airport. . . . The man who spat on me ran up to me from my left rear, spat, and turned to face me. The spittle hit me on my left shoulder and on my few military decorations above my left breast pockets. He then shouted at me that I was a "mother f——ing murderer." I was quite shocked and just stared at him. . . .

That combat veterans returning from months of warfare should accept such acts without violence is an indication of their emotional state. They were euphoric over finally returning home alive; many were exhausted after days of travel, shell-shocked, confused, dehydrated, and emaciated from months in the bush, in culture shock after months in an alien land, under orders not to do anything to "disgrace the uniform," and deeply worried about missing flights. Isolated and alone, the returning veterans in this condition were sought out and humiliated by war protesters who had learned from experience of the vulnerability of these men.

The accusations of their tormentors always revolved around the act of killing. When those who had in any way participated in killing activities were called baby killers and murderers, the result was often deep traumatization and scarring as a result of the hostile and accusing "homecoming" from the nation for which they had suffered and sacrificed. And this was the only homecoming they were to receive. At worst: open hostility and spittle. Or at best, as one put it in his letter to Greene, an "indifference that verged on insouciance."

At some level every psychologically healthy human being who has engaged in or supported killing activities believes that his action was "wrong" and "bad," and he must spend years rationalizing and accepting his actions. Many of the veterans who wrote to Greene stated that their letter to him was the first time they had *ever* spoken about the incident to anyone. These returning veterans had shamefully and silently accepted the accusations of their fellow citizens. They had broken the ultimate taboo, they had killed, and at some level they felt that they deserved to be spit upon and punished. When they were publicly insulted and humiliated the trauma was magnified and reinforced by the soldier's own impotent acceptance of these events. And these acts, combined with their acceptance of them, became the confirmation of their deepest fears and guilt.

In the Vietnam veterans manifesting PTSD (and probably in many who don't exhibit PTSD symptoms) the rationalization and acceptance process appears to have failed and is replaced with denial. The typical veteran of past wars, when asked "Did it bother you?" would answer, as a veteran did to Havighurst after World War II, "Hell yes. . . . You can't go through that without being influenced." The Vietnam veteran's defensive response to a nation accusing him of being a baby killer and murderer is consistently, as it was to Mantell and has been so many times to me, "No, it never really bothered me. . . . You get used to it." This defensive repression and denial of emotions appear to have been one of the major causes of post-traumatic stress disorder.

An Agony of Many Blows

American veterans of past wars have encountered all of these factors at one time or another, but never in American history has the combination of psychological blows inflicted upon a group of returning warriors been so intense. The soldiers of the Confederacy lost their war, but upon their return they were generally greeted and supported warmly by those for whom they had fought. Korean War veterans had no memorials and precious few parades, but they fought an invading army, not an insurgency, and they left behind them the free, healthy, thriving, and grateful nation of South Korea as their legacy. No one spat on them or called them murderers or baby killers when they returned. Only the veterans of Vietnam have endured a concerted, organized, psychological attack by their own people. Douglas Detmer shows remarkable insight into the organization and scope of this attack:

> Opponents of the war used every means available to them to make the war effort ineffective. This was partially accomplished by usurping many of the traditional symbols of war and claiming them as their own. Among these were the two-fingered V-for-victory sign, which was claimed as a peace symbol; headlights on Memorial Day used as a call for ending the war, rather than denoting the memory of a lost loved one; utilizing old uniforms as anti-war attire, instead of proud symbols of prior service; legitimate deeds of valor denounced as bully-like acts of murder; and the welcome-home parade replaced with what I experienced.

Never in American history, perhaps never in all the history of Western civilization, has an army suffered such an agony of many blows from its own people. And today we reap the legacy of those blows.

Chapter Three

Post-Traumatic Stress Disorder
and the Cost of Killing in Vietnam

The Legacy of Vietnam: Post-Traumatic Stress Disorder

Before a presentation to the leadership of New York's Jewish War Veterans, in a grand old hotel up in the Catskills, over a bowl of borscht, I met Claire, a woman who knew the meaning of PTSD. She had been a nurse in Burma during World War II and had seen more human suffering than any person should. It had never really bothered her, but when the Gulf War started, she began to have nightmares. Nightmares of an endless stream of torn and mangled bodies. She was suffering from PTSD. A mild case, but PTSD nonetheless.

After another presentation in New York, a veteran's wife asked me to talk with her and her husband. At Anzio he had won the Distinguished Service Cross, our nation's second-highest award for valor, and he continued to fight throughout World War II. Five years ago he retired. Now all he will do is sit around the house and watch war movies, and he is obsessed with the idea that he is a coward. He is suffering from PTSD.

Post-traumatic stress disorder has always been with us, but the long delay time and the erratic nature of its occurrence has made us like the ancient Celts who did not understand the link between sex and pregnancy.

What Is PTSD?

Vietnam was an American nightmare that hasn't yet ended for veterans of the war. In the rush to forget the debacle that became our longest war, America found it necessary to conjure up a scapegoat and transferred the heavy burden of blame onto the shoulders of the Vietnam veteran. It's been a crushing weight for them to carry. Rejected by the nation that sent them off to war, the veterans have been plagued with guilt and resentment which has created an identity crisis unknown to veterans of previous wars.

— D. Andrade

Post-traumatic stress disorder is described by the American Psychological Association's *Diagnostic and Statistical Manual of Mental Disorders* as "a reaction to a psychologically traumatic event outside the range of normal experience." Manifestations of PTSD include recurrent and intrusive dreams and recollections of the experience, emotional blunting, social withdrawal, exceptional difficulty or reluctance in initiating or maintaining intimate relationships, and sleep disturbances. These symptoms can in turn lead to serious difficulties in readjusting to civilian life, resulting in alcoholism, divorce, and unemployment. The symptoms persist for months or years after the trauma, often emerging after a long delay.

Estimates of the number of Vietnam veterans suffering from PTSD range from the Disabled American Veterans figure of 500,000 to Harris and Associates 1980 estimate of 1.5 million, or somewhere between 18 and 54 percent of the 2.8 million military personnel who served in Vietnam.

How Does PTSD Relate to Killing?

Societies which ask men to fight on their behalf should be aware of what the consequences of their actions may so easily be.

— Richard Holmes
Acts of War

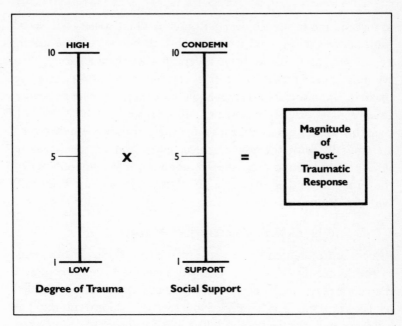

Relationship Between Degree of Trauma and Degree of Social Support in PTSD Causation

In 1988, a major study by Jeanne and Steven Stellman at Columbia University examined the relationship between PTSD manifestations and a soldier's involvement in the killing process. This study of 6,810 randomly selected veterans is the first in which combat levels have been quantified. Stellman and Stellman found that the victims of PTSD are almost solely veterans who participated in high-intensity combat situations. These veterans suffer far higher incidence of divorce, marital problems, tranquilizer use, alcoholism, joblessness, heart disease, high blood pressure, and ulcers. As far as PTSD symptoms are concerned, soldiers who were in noncombat situations in Vietnam were found to be statistically indistinguishable from those who spent their entire enlistment in the United States.

During the Vietnam era millions of American adolescents were conditioned to engage in an act against which they had a powerful resistance. This conditioning is a necessary part of allowing a soldier to succeed and survive in the environment where society has placed him. Success in war and national survival may necessitate killing enemy soldiers in battle. If we accept that we need an army, then we must accept that it has to be as capable of surviving as we can make it. But if society prepares a soldier to overcome his resistance to killing and places him in an environment in which he will kill, then that society has an obligation to deal forthrightly, intelligently, and morally with the psychological event and its repercussions upon the soldier and the society. Largely through an ignorance of the processes and implications involved, this has not happened with the Vietnam veteran.

PTSD and Nonkillers: Accessory to Murder?

After I had presented the essence of the hypotheses in this book to the leadership of a state Vietnam Veterans Coalition, one of the vets said to me, "Your premise [the trauma of killing, enabled by conditioning, and amplified by society's "homecoming"] is valid not only for those who killed, but for those who supported the killing."

This was the state's Veteran of the Year, a lawyer named Dave, who was an articulate, dynamic leader within the organization. "The truck driver who drove the ammo up," he explained, "also drove dead bodies back. There is no definitive distinction between the guy pulling the trigger, and the guy who supported him in Vietnam."

"And," said another veteran, almost whispering, "society didn't make any distinction in who they spat on."

"And," continued Dave, "just like . . . if you came in this room and attacked one of us you would be attacking all of us . . . society, this nation, attacked every one of us."

His point is valid. Everyone in that room understood that he was not talking about the veterans of noncombat situations in Vietnam who, according to Stellman and Stellman, were found to be statistically indistinguishable from those who spent their entire enlistment in the United States.

Dave was referring to the veterans who participated in high-intensity combat situations. They may not have killed, but they were there in the midst of the killing, and they were confronted daily with the results of their contributions to the war.

In study after study two factors show up again and again as critical to the magnitude of the post-traumatic response. First and most obvious is the intensity of the initial trauma. The second and less obvious but absolutely vital factor is the nature of the social support structure available to the traumatized individual. In rapes, we have come to understand the magnitude of the trauma inflicted upon the victim by the defense tactic of accusing the victim during trials and have taken legal steps to prevent and constrain such attacks upon the victim by a defendant's attorneys. In combat, the relationship between the nature of the trauma and the nature of the social support structure is the same.

PTSD in the World War II Veteran

The degree of trauma and the degree of social support work together to amplify each other in a kind of multiplicative relationship. For instance, let us take two hypothetical World War II veterans. One of them was a twenty-three-year-old infantryman who saw extensive combat, killed enemy soldiers at close range, and held his buddy in his arms as he died from close-range enemy small-arms fire. The trauma he endured would probably rate at the very top of the degree-of-trauma scale.

Our other World War II veteran was a twenty-five-year-old truck driver (he might just as easily have been an artilleryman, an airplane mechanic, or a bos'n's mate on a navy supply ship) who served honorably, but never really got up to the front lines. Although he was in an area that took some incoming artillery (or bombing or torpedoes) on a few occasions, he never was even in a situation where it was expected that he would have to shoot at anyone, and no one ever really shot at him. But he did have someone he knew killed by that artillery fire (or bombs or torpedoes), and he did see the constant remains of death and carnage as he moved along behind the advancing Allied lines. He would be placed very low on our degree-of-trauma scale.

When our hypothetical World War II veterans came home after the war they returned as a unit together with the same guys they had spent the whole war with, on board a ship, spending weeks joking, laughing, gambling, and telling tall tales as they cooled down and depressurized in what psychologists would call a very supportive group-therapy environment on the long voyage home. And if they had doubts about what they'd done, or fears about the future, they had a sympathetic group to talk to. Jim Goodwin notes in his book how resort hotels were taken over and made into redistribution stations to which these veterans brought their wives and devoted two weeks to reacquainting themselves with their family on the best possible terms, in an environment in which they were still surrounded by the company of their fellow veterans. Goodwin also observes that the civilian population they were returning to had been prepared to help and understand the returning veteran through movies such as *The Man in the Gray Flannel Suit, The Best Years of Our Lives,* and *Pride of the Marines.* They were victorious, they were justifiably proud of themselves, and their nation was proud of them and let them know it.

Our infantryman was one of the comparatively few World War II vets who participated in a ticker-tape parade in New York. Everyone griped about how what they really wanted to do was put all this "Army BS" behind them, but he would privately admit that marching in front of those tens of thousands of cheering civilians was one of the high points of his life, and today even just the remembrance of it tends to make his chest swell a little with pride.

Our truck driver, like the majority of returning vets, did not participate in a ticker-tape parade, but he would probably say that it made him feel good to know that vets were being honored. And next Memorial Day he did march in his hometown parade as part of the American Legion's commemoration ceremonies. No one was making him do it, but he did it anyway because, well damn it, because he felt like it, and he would keep on doing it every year just like the World War I vets in his town had done as he was growing up.

Both our veterans generally stayed in touch with their World War II buddies, and they linked up with their old comrades in reunions and informal get-togethers. And that was nice, but what was really best about being a veteran was being able to hold your head high and knowing just how much your family, friends, community, and nation respected you and were proud of you. The GI Bill was passed, and if some politician or bureaucrat or organization didn't give the vet the respect he deserved, well, buddy, they would have to answer to the influence and votes of the American Legion and the VFW, who would make damn sure you got treated right.

On our social-support scale, social support provided to these two veterans can be rated as very supportive. Not all returning World War II vets got this kind of support, and it was no bed of roses to return from combat under the best of circumstances, but their nation generally did the best for them that it could.

Remember that the relationship between the degree-of-trauma scale and the social-support scale is multiplicative. These two factors amplify each other. For our infantryman that means that his highly traumatic experience was largely (but perhaps not completely) negated by the very supportive social structure he returned to. Our truck driver, suffering very little trauma and having received a great deal of support, will probably be able to deal with his combat experiences. Our infantryman may tend to medicate himself pretty regularly down at the bar at the American Legion, but like most veterans he will probably continue to function and lead a perfectly healthy life.

PTSD in the Vietnam Veteran

Now let us consider two hypothetical Vietnam veterans, an eighteen-year-old infantryman and a nineteen-year-old truck driver. The infantryman arrived at the combat zone, like most every other soldier in Vietnam, as an individual replacement who didn't know a soul in his unit. Eventually he engaged in extensive close combat. He killed several enemy soldiers, but the hard part was that they were wearing civilian clothes, and one of them, well, damn, he was just a kid, couldn't have been more than twelve. And he had his best buddy die in his arms during a firefight. The trauma he endured definitely rates at the top end of the scale. Maybe fighting kids in civilian clothes, with no rear lines and no chance to ever really rest and get away from the battle, maybe that makes the trauma he endured greater than that of the World War II vet, but at the top of the trauma scale there probably isn't much value in trying to distinguish between shades of black.

The truck driver also arrived alone, but although his job was the same as a World War II truck driver, the environment in which he had to do it had changed. There was no rear area for him, you could never really let your guard down, even when you were off duty, and convoys were one long hell of fear from ambushes and mines. It was like living in the Battle of the Bulge all the time. Convoys into base camps were often like some kind of "Relief of Bastogne," and his truck was always armored and sandbagged in a way that a World War II truck driver would probably never even have considered doing. Fortunately, he never did have to shoot at anybody, but that was always a possibility, and he kept his weapon handy and loaded all the time, and plenty of people were shooting in his general direction on several occasions. Our Vietnam-era truck driver might rate low on the trauma scale, slightly higher than his counterpart in World War II, but not unmanageably so.

Our two Vietnam veterans departed the war the way they had arrived: alone. They departed with a mixture of joy at having survived and shame at having left their buddies behind. Instead of returning to parades, they found antiwar marches. Instead of luxury hotels, they were sent to locked and guarded military bases where they were processed back to civilian life in a few days. Instead of movies about the veteran, his struggles, and his vulnerable emotional state upon reentry into civilian life, the media prepared the American people by calling the returning veterans "depraved fiends" and "psychopathic killers," and beautiful young movie stars led the accusing chant of a nation that echoed through the veteran's soul: "Baby killers . . . murderers . . . butchers . . ."

They were rejected by girlfriends, spit on, and accused by strangers and finally dared not even admit to close friends that they were veterans. They did not show up for Memorial Day parades (which had gone out of style), they did not join the VFW or the American Legion, and they did not participate in any reunions or get-togethers with old comrades. They denied their experiences and buried their pain and grieving beneath a shell.

Some Vietnam vets had families and communities that could insulate them from this, but the vast majority had only to turn on the TV to find themselves being attacked. Even the most average of Vietnam vets endured an absolutely unprecedented degree of societal condemnation. On our social-support scale, our two Vietnam veterans rated at the "condemn" end of the scale.

Remember the multiplicative, amplifying relationship between trauma and social support. For our truck driver the interaction between his limited combat trauma in Vietnam and the societal condemnation that he endured afterward resulted in a total experience that might very well have been more conducive to post-traumatic stress than that experienced by a veteran of close combat in World War II. For our infantry veteran of Vietnam the magnitude of the total trauma experienced is beyond description.

The diffusion of responsibility that happens in combat is a two-way street. It absolves a killer of a part of his guilt, diffusing it to the leaders who gave the order and the truck driver who brought the ammo and hauled back the bodies, but it does so by giving a piece of the killer's guilt to others, and those others must then deal with it just as surely as must the killer. If these "accessories" to killing in combat are accused and condemned, then their slice of the trauma, guilt, and responsibility is amplified, and it will reverberate in their souls as shock and horror.

The Vietnam vet, the average vet who did no killing, is suffering an agony of guilt and torment created by society's condemnation. During and immediately after Vietnam our society judged and condemned millions of returning veterans as accessories to murder. At one level many, even most, of these horrified, confused veterans accepted society's media-driven, kangaroo-court conviction as justice and locked themselves in prisons of the worst kind, prisons in their mind. A prison whose name was PTSD.

I have known these men, both our two "hypothetical" World War II vets and our two Vietnam vets. They are not hypothetical at all. They are real. Their pain is real. Societies that ask men to fight on their behalf should be aware of what the consequences and what the price of their actions may so easily be.

Chapter Four

The Limits of Human Endurance and the Lessons of Vietnam

PTSD and Vietnam: A Nexus of Impact upon Society

For the Vietnam infantryman in the example in the last chapter, the condemnation upon his return amplified the horror of his combat experiences to result in a staggering degree of horror. By the very nature of its unique historical causation, the existence of any significant number of individuals in such a condition is unprecedented in the history of Western civilization.

Although this model only crudely reflects what has happened, it begins to represent the relevant forces.[8] Statistics on the horrible number of suicides among Vietnam vets, on the tragic number of homeless who are Vietnam vets, on divorce rates, drug-use rates, and so on, give evidence that something has occurred that is significantly, startlingly different from that occurring after World War II or any other war our nation has ever encountered.[9]

There is a nexus of events and causation linking the death of enemy soldiers and the spittle of war protesters with a pattern of suicide, homelessness, mental illness, and divorce that will ripple through the United States for generations to come.

The 1978 President's Commission on Mental Health tells us that approximately 2.8 million Americans served in Southeast Asia, and almost 1 million of them saw active combat service or were exposed to hostile, life-threatening situations. If we accept the Veterans Administration's conservative figures of 15 percent incidence of PTSD among Vietnam veterans, then more than 400,000 individuals in the United States suffer from PTSD. Other figures place this number as high as 1.5 million veterans suffering from PTSD as a result of the Vietnam War. Whatever their numbers, there are undoubtedly hundreds of thousands of them, they are four times more likely to be divorced or separated (and those not divorced are significantly more likely to have a troubled marriage), they represent a large proportion of America's homeless population, and as the years go by they are increasingly more likely to commit suicide.

Thus, the long-term legacy of the Vietnam War upon American society is not just hundreds of thousands of troubled veterans, it is also hundreds of thousands of troubled marriages impacting women, children, and future generations. For we know that children of broken families are more likely to be physically and sexually abused, and that children of divorce are more likely to become divorced as adults, and that victims of child abuse are more likely to become child-abusing adults. And this is only one facet of the price this nation will pay for those personal kills in the jungles of Vietnam.

It may indeed be necessary to engage in a war, but we must begin to understand the potential long-term price of such endeavors.

The Legacy and the Lesson

Man did not weave the web of life: he is merely a strand in it. Whatever he does to the web he does to himself.

— Ted Perry (Writing as "Chief Seattle")

We may have enhanced the killing ability of the average soldier through training (that is, conditioning), but at what price? The ultimate cost of our body counts in Vietnam has been, and continues to be, much more than dollars and lives. We can, and have, conditioned soldiers to kill — they are eager and willing and trust our judgment. But in doing so we have not made them capable

of handling the moral and social burdens of these acts, and we
have a moral responsibility to consider the long-term effects of
our commands. Moral direction and philosophical guidance, based
on a firm understanding of the processes involved, must come
with the combat training and deployment of our soldiers.

At the national strategic level, a recognition of the potential
social cost of modern warfare has been obtained at a terrible price,
and a form of moral and philosophical guidance gained from this
experience can be found in the Weinberger doctrine — named
after Caspar Weinberger, secretary of defense for President Reagan.
This doctrine represents an initial attempt to form the kind of
moral direction and philosophical guidance that can be built upon
the lessons of Vietnam. The Weinberger doctrine states that:

- "The United States should not commit forces to combat unless
  our vital interests are at stake."
- "We must commit them in sufficient numbers and with sufficient
  support to win."
- "We must have clearly defined political and military objectives."
- "We must never again commit forces to a war we do not intend
  to win."
- "Before the United States commits forces abroad, the U.S. government should have some reasonable assurance of the support
  of the American people and their elected representatives in the
  Congress. . . . U.S. troops cannot be asked to fight a battle with
  the Congress at home while attempting to win a war overseas.
  Nor will the American people sit by and watch U.S. troops
  committed as expendable pawns on some grand diplomatic
  chessboard."
- "Finally, the commitment of U.S. troops should be as a last
  resort."

A Quest for Further Understanding

The Weinberger doctrine represents, in part, the recognition that
a nation that sends men out to kill must understand the price that
it may have to ultimately pay for these seemingly isolated deeds
in distant lands. If this doctrine and the spirit in which it is intended

prevails, it may prevent a recurrence of the Vietnam experience. But this is just the beginning of a basis for understanding the potentially devastating social costs of modern war at other levels.

Commanders, families, and society need to understand the soldier's desperate need for recognition and acceptance, his vulnerability, and his desperate need to be constantly reassured that what he (or she) did was right and necessary, and the terrible social costs of failing to provide for these needs with the traditional acts of affirmation and acceptance. It is to our national shame that it has taken us almost twenty years to recognize and fulfill these needs with the Vietnam War Memorial and the veterans' parades that have allowed our veterans to "wipe a little spit off their hearts."

The military also must understand the need for unit integrity during and after combat. We are beginning to do so with the army's new personnel system (which assigns and replaces whole units instead of single individuals in combat), and we must continue to do so; and like the British, who took their soldiers home from the Falklands by long, slow sea voyage, we must understand the need for cooldown periods, parades, and unit integrity during the vulnerable period of returning from war. During the 1991 Gulf War it appears that we generally got these things right, but we must make sure that we always do so in the future.

The psychological, psychiatric, medical, counseling, and social work communities must understand the impact of combat kills on the soldier and must attempt to further understand and reinforce the rationalization and acceptance process outlined in this book. In their 1988 research on PTSD Stellman and Stellman, both chemists by training, were the first to conduct a large-scale correlation study on the relationship between combat experience and PTSD. They reported that the "great majority" of veterans turning to mental-health services were not asked about their combat experiences, let alone their personal kills.

Last, we must attempt to understand the basic act of killing, not just in war, but throughout our society.

A Personal Note

"Who the f—— are the two guys up here with the machine gun?" I asked, slinking back over the edge of the cliff.

"That's gotta be Charlie, you asshole ... Blow their ass up and run. . . ."

They didn't know I existed. Low underbrush shielded the edge of the cliff from their view, but I sure as hell saw them. My body started to shake and spasm as I rested my elbow on the hard laterite. I sighted down the barrel and put the front sight under one guy's chest. He was sitting closest to the machine gun, and he would die because of it.

This is one f——ed up way to die, I thought as I squeezed softly on the trigger.

The explosion of the round roared like a cannon in my ear. My target flattened out, and for an instant I couldn't tell if he ducked or had been hit. The doubts disappeared when I saw his foot quiver and his body shudder before he died.

I was so transfixed by his death throes that I never fired a shot at the other guy, who escaped into the thick brush to the south. I jumped over the cliff and ran to reach the dying man, not sure if I wanted to help him or finish him. Something made me have to see him, what he looked like, how he died.

I knelt beside him as his life leaked into the dusty earth. My one shot had hit him in the left chest and ripped through his back. The rest of the patrol was scrambling up the cliff and shouting, but the only sound I heard was the soft bubbling of the dead man's blood as it soaked into the dirt. His eyes were open, and his face was still young. He looked terribly peaceful. His war was over and mine had just begun.

The steady stream of blood from his wound made a widening circle of darkness beneath him, and I felt my innocence deserting me as his life deserted him. I'd come all the way to Vietnam now. I didn't know if I'd ever get out. I still don't.

As the rest of the platoon reached the plateau, I found a bush on the flank of the campfire and retched violently.

— Steve Banko
"Green Grunt Finds Innocence Lost"

Looking back on this narrative from the perspective of this point in the book, I find that there are many factors to be considered.

Our newfound science of killology permits us to identify such key processes as the need to be ordered to kill (demands of authority and diffusion of responsibility), the picking out of the enemy soldier who was closest to the machine gun (target attractiveness and assisting in the rationalization process by picking the greater potential threat of two individuals who represented no immediate threat), and the emotional response of violent revulsion to the act of killing.

But what sticks in my mind is the phrase: "I didn't know if I'd ever get out. I still don't." Those words haunt me.

This is no Ramboesque machismo; this is the actual emotional response of a young American soldier to one of the most horrifying events of his life. As he writes this to a national forum of understanding and sympathetic Vietnam veterans, he and many like him can be free to say that they were sickened by killing — and their writing and its publication become a vital catharsis. I believe that as these veterans write such narratives, they do not mean to say that the war was wrong or that they regret what they did, but that they simply want to be understood.

Understood not as mindless killers, and not as sniveling whiners, but as men. Men who went to do the incomprehensibly difficult job their nation sent them to do and did it proudly, did it well, and all too often did it thanklessly.

As I interviewed veterans during this study, the soldier, the psychologist, and the human being in me were always touched by this desperate, unspoken need for understanding and affirmation. Understanding that they did no more and no less than their nation and their society asked them to do; no more and no less than 200 years of American veterans had honorably done. And affirmation that they were good human beings.

Over and over again I have said, and before I go on to the final section, "Killing in America," I want to say again, I am honored that you have shared this with me. You did all that anyone could ask you to have done, and I am truly proud to have known you. And I hope that I can use your words to help people understand.

SECTION VIII

Killing in America:

What Are We Doing to Our Children?

Chapter One

A Virus of Violence

How simple it now seems for our ancestors to have stood outside
their caves guarding against the fang and claw of predators. The
evil that we must stand vigilant against is like a virus, starting from
deep inside us, eating its way out until we're devoured by and
become its madness.

— Richard Heckler
  In Search of the Warrior Spirit

The Magnitude of the Problem

If we examine the chart showing the relationship between murder,
aggravated assault, and imprisonment in America since 1957, we
see something that should astound us.

"Aggravated assault" is defined in the *Statistical Abstract* (from
which this data was gathered) as "assault with intent to kill or for
the purpose of inflicting severe bodily injury by shooting, cutting,
stabbing, maiming, poisoning, scalding, or by the use of acids,
explosives, or other means." We are also informed that this "ex-
cludes simple assaults."[1]

The aggravated assault rate indicates the incidence of Americans
trying to kill one another, and it is going up at an astounding rate.
Two major factors serve as tourniquets that suppress the bleeding

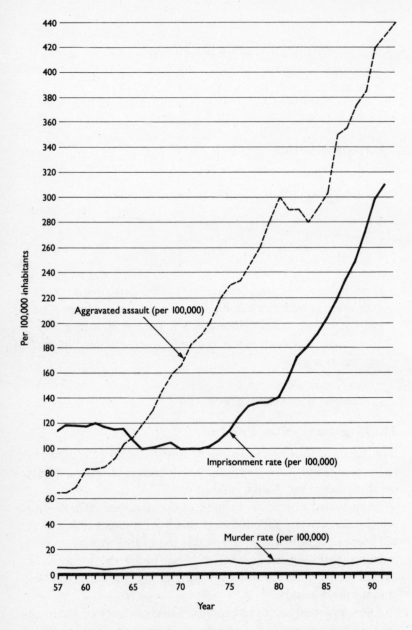

The Relationship Between Aggravated Assault, Murder, and Imprisonment Rates in America Since 1957

that would occur if the number of murders increased at the same rate as aggravated assaults. First is the steady increase in the presumably violent percentage of our population that we imprison. The prison population in America has quadrupled since 1975 (from just over two hundred thousand to slightly more than eight hundred thousand in 1992: nearly a million Americans in jail!). Professor John J. DiIulio of Princeton states unequivocally that "dozens of credible empirical analyses . . . leave no doubt that the increased use of prisons averted millions of serious crimes." If not for our tremendous imprisonment rate (the highest of any major industrialized nation in the world), the aggravated assault rate and the murder rate would both be even higher.

The other major factor that limits the success of these attempts at killing is the continued progress in medical technology and methodology. Professor James Q. Wilson of UCLA estimates that if the quality of medical care (especially trauma and emergency care) were the same as it was in 1957, today's murder rate would be three times higher. Helicopter medevacs, 911 operators, paramedics, and trauma centers are but a few of the technological and methodological innovations that save lives at ever-increasing rates. This more rapid and effective response, evacuation, and treatment of victims is *the* decisive factor in preventing the murder rate from being many times higher than it is now.

It is also interesting to note the dip in aggravated assault rates between 1980 and 1983. Some observers believed this was due to the maturing of the baby-boom generation and the overall aging of America and that violent crime would continue to decrease in succeeding years. However, this did not happen, and, in retrospect, although the aging of our society *should* cause a decrease in violence, a major factor may have been the sharp increase in the imprisonment rate during that period.

But demographers predict that our aging society will again become more youthful as the children of the baby boom have their own teenagers. And just how much longer can America afford to imprison larger and larger percentages of its population? And how much longer can advances in medical technology continue to keep up with advances in the aggravated assault rate?

Like Alice, we are running as fast as we can to stay where we are. America's huge imprisonment rate and desperate application of medical progress are technological tourniquets to stop us from bleeding to death in an orgy of violence. But they do so by dealing with the symptoms of the problem rather than the root cause.

The Cause of the Problem: Taking the Safety Catch off of a Nation

We know, as surely as we know that we are alive, that the whole human race is dancing on the edge of the grave. . . .

The easiest and worst mistake we could make would be to blame our present dilemma on the mere technology of war. . . . It is our attitudes toward war and our uses for it that really demand our attention.

— Gwynne Dyer
War

What *is* the root cause of this epidemic of violence in our society? An application of the lessons of combat killing may have much to teach us about the constraint and control of peacetime violence. Are *the same processes the military used so effectively to enable killing in our adolescent, draftee soldiers in Vietnam being indiscriminately applied to the civilian population of this nation?*

The three major psychological processes at work in enabling violence are classical conditioning (à la Pavlov's dog), operant conditioning (à la B. F. Skinner's rats), and the observation and imitation of vicarious role models in social learning.

In a kind of reverse *Clockwork Orange* classical conditioning process, adolescents in movie theaters across the nation, and watching television at home, are seeing the detailed, horrible suffering and killing of human beings, and they are learning to associate this killing and suffering with entertainment, pleasure, their favorite soft drink, their favorite candy bar, and the close, intimate contact of their date.

Operant conditioning firing ranges with pop-up targets and immediate feedback, just like those used to train soldiers in modern armies, are found in the interactive video games that our children play today. But whereas the adolescent Vietnam vet had stimulus discriminators built in to ensure that he only fired under authority, the adolescents who play these video games have no such safeguard built into their conditioning.

And, finally, social learning is being used as children learn to observe and imitate a whole new realm of dynamic vicarious role models, such as Jason and Freddy of endless *Friday the 13th* and *Nightmare on Elm Street* sequels, along with a host of other horrendous, sadistic murderers. Even the more classic heroes, such as the archetypal law-abiding police detective, is today portrayed as a murderous, unstable vigilante who operates outside the law.

There are more factors involved. This is a complex, interactive process that includes all the factors that enable killing in combat. Gang leaders and gang members demand violent, even killing, activity and create diffusion of individual responsibility; and gang affiliation, loosening family and religious ties, racism, class differences, and the availability of weapons provide forms of real and emotional distance between the killer and the victim. If we look again at our model for killing-enabling factors and apply it to civilian killing, we can see the way in which all of these factors interact to enable violence in America.

All of these factors are important. Drugs, gangs, poverty, racism, and guns are all vital ingredients in a process that has resulted in skyrocketing violence rates in our society. But drugs have always been a problem, just as drugs (alcohol, and so on) have always been present in combat. Gangs have always been present, just as combat has always taken place in organized units. Poverty and racism have always been a part of our society (often much more so than today), just as propaganda, class divisions, and racism have always been manipulated in combat. And guns have always been present in American society, just as they have always been present in American wars.

In the 1950s and 1960s students brought knives to high school, whereas today they bring .22s. But those .22s were pretty much always present at home. And while there is new weapons technology available, fifteen minutes with a hacksaw will make a pistol out of any double-barrel shotgun, a pistol every bit as effective in close combat as any weapon in the world today — this was true one hundred years ago, and it is true today.[2]

The thing we need to ask ourselves is not, Where did the guns come from? They came from home, where they have always been available, or they may have been bought in the street thanks to the drug culture — which deals in illegal weapons as readily as it deals in illegal drugs. But the question we need to ask is, What makes today's children bring those guns to school when their parents did not? And the answer to *that* question may be that the *important* ingredient, the vital, *new, different* ingredient in killing in modern combat *and* in killing in modern American society, is the systematic process of defeating the normal individual's age-old, psychological inhibition against violent, harmful activity toward one's own species. Are we taking the safety catch off of a nation, just as surely and easily as we would take the safety catch off of a gun, and with the same results?

Between 1985 and 1991 the homicide rate for males fifteen to nineteen increased 154 percent. Despite the continued application of an ever-increasing quantity and quality of medical technology, homicide is the number-two cause of death among males ages fifteen to nineteen. Among black males it is number one. The AP wire article reporting this data had a headline announcing, "Homicide Rate Wiping Out Whole Generation of Teens." For once the press was not exaggerating.

In Vietnam a systematic process of desensitization, conditioning, and training increased the individual firing rate from a World War II baseline of 15 to 20 percent to an all-time high of up to 95 percent. Today a similar process of systematic desensitization, conditioning, and vicarious learning is unleashing an epidemic, a virus of violence in America.

The same tools that more than quadrupled the firing rate in Vietnam are now in widespread use among our civilian population. Military personnel are just beginning to understand and accept what they have been doing to themselves and their men. If we

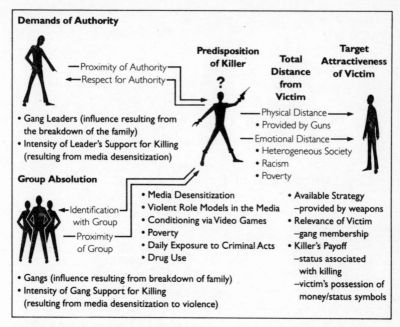

Killing-Enabling Factors in America

have reservations about the military's use of these mechanisms to ensure the survival and success of our soldiers in combat, then how much more so should we be concerned about the indiscriminate application of the same processes on our nation's children?

Chapter Two

Desensitization and Pavlov's Dog at the Movies

I yelled "kill, kill" 'til I was hoarse. We yelled it as we engaged in bayonet and hand-to-hand combat drills. And then we sang about it as we marched. "I want to be an airborne ranger . . . I want to kill the Viet Cong." I had stopped hunting when I was sixteen. I had wounded a squirrel. It looked up at me with its big, soft brown eyes as I put it out of its misery. I cleaned my gun and have never taken it out since. In 1969 I was drafted and very uncertain about the war. I had nothing against the Viet Cong. But by the end of Basic Training, I was ready to kill them.

— Jack, Vietnam veteran

Classical Conditioning in the Military

One of the most remarkable revelations in Watson's book *War on the Mind* is his report of conditioning techniques used by the U.S. government to train assassins. In 1975 Dr. Narut, a U.S. Navy psychiatrist with the rank of commander, told Watson about techniques he was developing for the U.S. government in which classical conditioning and social learning methodology were being used to permit military assassins to overcome their resistance to killing. The method used, according to Narut, was to expose the subjects to "symbolic modeling" involving "films specially designed to show people being killed or injured in violent ways.

By being acclimatized through these films, the men were supposed to eventually become able to disassociate their emotions from such a situation."

Narut went on to say, "The men were taught to shoot but also given a special type of 'Clockwork Orange' training to quell any qualms they may have about killing. Men are shown a series of gruesome films, which get progressively more horrific. The trainee is forced to watch by having his head bolted in a clamp so he cannot turn away, and a special device keeps his eyelids open." In psychological terms, this step-by-step reduction of a resistance is a form of classical (Pavlovian) conditioning called systematic desensitization.

In *Clockwork Orange* such conditioning was used to develop an aversion to violence by administering a drug that caused revulsion while the violent films were shown, until the revulsion became associated with acts of violence. In Commander Narut's real-world training the nausea-creating drugs were left out, and those who were able to overcome their natural revulsion were rewarded, thereby obtaining the opposite effect of that depicted in Stanley Kubrick's movie. The U.S. government denies Commander Narut's claims, but Watson claims that he was able to obtain some outside corroboration from an individual who stated that Commander Narut had ordered violent films from him, and Narut's tale was subsequently published in the London *Times*.

Remember that desensitization is a vital aspect of killing-empowerment techniques used in modern combat-training programs. The experience related by Jack at the beginning of this section is a sample of the desensitization and glorification of killing that has increasingly been a part of combat orientation. In 1974, when I was in basic training, we sang many such chants. One that was only a little bit more extreme than the majority was a running chant (with the emphasis shouted each time the left foot hit the ground):

Iwanna

RAPE,

KILL,

PILLAGE'n'

BURN, annnnn'
EAT dead
BAAA-bies,
Iwanna
RAPE,
KILL . . .

Our military no longer tolerates this kind of desensitization, but for decades it was a key mechanism for desensitizing and indoctrinating adolescent males into a cult of violence in basic training.

Classical Conditioning at the Movies

If we believe that Commander Narut's techniques might work, and if we are horrified that the U.S. government might even *consider* doing such a thing to our soldiers, then why do we permit the same process to occur to millions of children across the nation? For that *is* what we are doing when we allow increasingly more vivid depictions of suffering and violence to be shown as entertainment to our children.

It begins innocently with cartoons and then goes on to the countless thousands of acts of violence depicted on TV as the child grows up and the scramble for ratings steadily raises the threshold of violence on TV. As children reach a certain age, they then begin to watch movies with a degree of violence sufficient to receive a PG-13 rating due to brief glimpses of spurting blood, a hacked-off limb, or bullet wounds. Then the parents, through neglect or conscious decision, begin to permit the child to watch movies rated R due to vivid depictions of knives penetrating and protruding from bodies, long shots of blood spurting from severed limbs, and bullets ripping into bodies and exploding out the back in showers of blood and brains.

Finally, our society says that young adolescents, at the age of seventeen, can *legally* watch these R-rated movies (although most are well experienced with them by then), and at eighteen they can watch the movies rated even higher than R. These are films in which eye gouging is often the least of the offenses that are vividly depicted. And thus, at that malleable age of seventeen and eighteen, the age at which armies have traditionally begun to indoctrinate the soldier into the business of killing, American youth, systematically desensitized from childhood, takes another step in the indoctrination into the cult of violence.

Adolescents and adults saturate themselves in such gruesome and progressively more horrific "entertainment," whose antiheroes — like Hannibal the Cannibal, Jason, and Freddy — are sick, unkillable, unquestionably evil, and criminally sociopathic. They have nothing in common with the exotic, esoteric, and misunderstood Frankenstein and Wolf Man villains of an earlier generation of horror films. In the old horror stories and movies, very real but subconscious fears were symbolized by mythic but unreal monsters, such as Dracula, and then exorcised exotically, such as by a stake through the heart. In contemporary horror, terror is personified by characters who resemble our next-door neighbor, even our doctor. Importantly, Hannibal the Cannibal, Jason, and Freddy are not killed, much less exorcised; they return over and over again.

Even in movies where the killer is not an obvious sociopath, the common formula is to validate violent acts of vengeance by beginning the movie with a vivid depiction of the villain performing horrible acts on some innocents. These victims are usually related in some way to the hero, thereby justifying the hero's subsequent (and vividly depicted) vigilante acts.

Our society has found a powerful recipe for providing killing empowerment to an entire generation of Americans. Producers, directors, and actors are handsomely rewarded for creating the most violent, gruesome, and horrifying films imaginable, films in which the stabbing, shooting, abuse, and torture of innocent men, women, and children are depicted in intimate detail. Make these films entertaining as well as violent, and then simultaneously provide the (usually) adolescent viewers with candy, soft drinks, group companionship, and the intimate physical contact of a boyfriend or girlfriend. Then understand that these adolescent viewers are learning to associate these rewards with what they are watching.

Powerful group processes often work to humiliate and belittle viewers who close their eyes or avert their gaze during these gruesome scenes. Adolescent peer groups reward with respect and admiration those who reflect Hollywood's standard of remaining hardened and undisturbed in the face of such violence. In effect many viewers have their heads bolted in a psychological clamp so they cannot turn away, and social pressure keeps their eyelids open.

Discussing these movies and this process in psychology classes at West Point, I have repeatedly asked my students how the audience responds when the villain murders some innocent young victim in a particularly horrible way. And over and over again their answer was "The audience cheers." Society is in a state of denial as to the harmful nature of this, but in efficiency, quality, and scope, it makes the puny efforts of *Clockwork Orange* and the U.S. government pale by comparison. We are doing a better job of desensitizing and conditioning our citizens to kill than anything Commander Narut ever dreamed of. If we had a clear-cut objective of raising a generation of assassins and killers who are unrestrained by either authority or the nature of the victim, it is difficult to imagine how we could do a better job.

In video stores the horror section repeatedly displays bare breasts (often with blood running down them), gaping eye sockets, and mutilated bodies. Movies rated X with tamer covers are generally not available in many video stores and, if they are, are in separate, adults-only rooms. But the horror videos are displayed for every child to see. Here breasts are taboo if they are on a live woman, but permissible on a mutilated corpse?

When Mussolini and his mistress were publicly executed and hung upside down, the mistress's dress flopped over her head to display her legs and underwear. One woman in the crowd subsequently had the decency to walk up and tuck the corpse's dress between its legs in a show of respect for the dead woman: she may have deserved to die, but she did not deserve to be so degraded after death.

Where did we lose this sense of propriety toward the dignity of death? How did we become so hardened?

The answer to that question is that we, as a society, have become systematically desensitized to the pain and suffering of others. We may believe that tabloids and tabloid TV make us exceedingly conscious of the suffering of others as they spread the stories of victims. But the reality is that they are desensitizing us and trivializing these issues as each year they have to find increasingly more bizarre stories to satisfy their increasingly jaded audiences.

We are reaching that stage of desensitization at which the inflicting of pain and suffering has become a source of entertainment: vicarious pleasure rather than revulsion. We are learning to kill, and we are learning to like it.

Chapter Three

B. F. Skinner's Rats and
Operant Conditioning at the Video Arcade

When I went to boot camp and did individual combat training they said if you walk into an ambush what you want to do is just do a right face — you just turn right or left, whichever way the fire is coming from, and assault. I said, "Man, that's crazy. I'd never do anything like that. It's stupid."

The first time we came under fire, on Hill 1044 in Operation Beauty Canyon in Laos, we did it automatically. Just like you look at your watch to see what time it is. We done a right face, assaulted the hill — a fortified position with concrete bunkers emplaced, machine guns, automatic weapons — and we took it. And we killed — I'd estimate probably thirty-five North Vietnamese soldiers in the assault, and we only lost three killed. . . .

But you know, what they teach you, it doesn't faze you until it comes down to the time to use it, but it's in the back of your head, like, What do you do when you come to a stop sign? It's in the back of your head, and you react automatically.

— Vietnam veteran
    quoted in Gwynne Dyer, *War*

Conditioning Killers in the Military

On the training bases of the major armies of the world, nations struggle to turn teenagers into killers. The "struggle" for the mind of the soldier is a lopsided one: armies have had thousands of years to develop their craft, and their subjects have had fewer than two decades of life experience. It is a basically honest, age-old, reciprocal process, especially in today's all-volunteer U.S. Army. The soldier intuitively understands what he or she is getting into and generally tries to cooperate by "playing the game" and constraining his or her own individuality and adolescent enthusiasm, and the army systematically wields the resources and technology of a nation to empower and equip the soldier to kill and survive on the battlefield. In the armed forces of most modern armies this application of technology has reached new levels by integrating the innovations of operant conditioning into traditional training methods.

Operant conditioning is a higher form of learning than classical conditioning. It was pioneered by B. F. Skinner and is usually associated with learning experiments on pigeons and rats. The traditional image of a rat in a Skinner box, learning to press a bar in order to get food pellets, comes from Skinner's research in this field. Skinner rejected the Freudian and humanist theories of personality development and held that *all* behavior is a result of past rewards and punishments. To B. F. Skinner the child is a tabula rasa, a "blank slate," who can be turned into anything provided sufficient control of the child's environment is instituted at an early enough age.

Instead of firing at a bull's-eye target, the modern soldier fires at man-shaped silhouettes that pop up for brief periods of time inside a designated firing lane. The soldiers learn that they have only a brief second to engage the target, and if they do it properly their behavior is immediately reinforced when the target falls down. If he knocks down enough targets, the soldier gets a marksmanship badge and usually a three-day pass. After training on rifle ranges in this manner, an automatic, conditioned response called automaticity sets in, and the soldier then becomes conditioned to respond to the appropriate stimulus in the desired manner. This process may seem simple, basic, and obvious, but there is evidence to indicate that it is one of the key ingredients in a methodology that has raised the firing rate from 15 to 20 percent in World War II to 90 to 95 percent in Vietnam.

Conditioning at the Video Arcade

In video arcades children stand slack jawed but intent behind machine guns and shoot at electronic targets that pop up on the video screen. When they pull the trigger the weapon rattles in their hand, shots ring out, and if they hit the "enemy" they are firing at, it drops to the ground, often with chunks of flesh flying in the air.

The important distinction between the killing-enabling process that occurs in video arcades and that of the military is that the military's is focused on the enemy soldier, with particular emphasis on ensuring that the U.S. soldier acts only under authority. Yet even with these safeguards, the danger of future My Lai massacres among soldiers drawn from such a violent population must not be ignored, and, as we saw in the section "Killing and Atrocity," the U.S. armed forces are taking extensive measures to control, constrain, and channel the violence of their troops in future conflicts. The video games that our children conduct their combat training on have no real sanction for firing at the wrong target.

This is not an attack on all video games. Video games are an interactive medium. They demand and develop trial-and-error and systematic problem-solving skills, and they teach planning, mapping, and deferment of gratification. Watch children as they play video games and interact with other children in their neighborhood. To parents raised on a steady diet of movies and sitcoms, watching a child play Mario Brothers for hours on end may not be particularly gratifying, but that is just the point. As they play they solve problems and overcome instructions that are intentionally inadequate and vague. They exchange playing strategies, memorize routes, and make maps. They work long and hard to attain the gratification of finally winning a game. And there are no commercials: no enticements for sugar, no solicitation of violent toys, and no messages of social failure if they do not wear the right shoes or clothes.

We might prefer to see children reading or getting exercise and interacting with the *real* real world by playing outside, but video games are definitely preferable to most television. But video games can also be superb at teaching violence — violence packaged in the same format that has more than quadrupled the firing rate of modern soldiers.

When I speak of violence enabling I am not talking about video games in which the player defeats creatures by bopping them on the head. Nor am I talking about games where you maneuver swordsmen and archers to defeat monsters. On the borderline in violence enabling are games where you use a joystick to maneuver a gunsight around the screen to kill gangsters who pop up and fire at you. The kind of games that are very definitely enabling violence are the ones in which you actually hold a weapon in your hand and fire it at human-shaped targets on the screen. These kinds of games can be played on home video, but you usually see them in video arcades.

There is a direct relationship between realism and degree of violence enabling, and the most realistic of these are games in which great bloody chunks fly off as you fire at the enemy.

Another, very different type of game has a western motif, in which you stand before a huge video screen and fire a pistol at actual film footage of "outlaws" as they appear on the screen. This is identical to the shoot–no shoot training program designed by the FBI and used by police agencies around the nation to train and enable police officers in firing their weapons.

The shoot–no shoot program was introduced nearly twenty years ago in response to the escalating violence in our society that was resulting in an increase in deaths among police officers who hesitated to shoot in an actual combat situation. And, of course, we recognize it as another form of operant conditioning that has been successful in saving the lives of both law-enforcement officers and innocent bystanders, since the officer faces severe sanctions if he fires in an inappropriate circumstance. Thus the shoot–no shoot

program has served successfully to both enable *and* constrain violence among police officers. Its video arcade equivalent has no
such sanctions to constrain violence. It only enables.

The worst is yet to come. Just as movies have become succes-
sively more realistic in their depiction of violence and death, so
too have video games. We are now entering an era of virtual
reality, in which you wear a helmet that has a video screen before
your eyes. As you turn your head the screen changes just as though
you were within the video world. You hold a gun in your hand
and fire it at the enemies who pop up around you, or you hold
a sword and hack and stab at the enemies around you.

Alvin Toffler, author of *Future Shock,* says, "This manipulation
of reality may provide us with exciting games, entertainment, but
it will substitute not a virtual reality, but a pseudo reality, so subtly
deceptive as to raise the levels of public suspicion and disbelief
beyond what any society can tolerate." This new "pseudo reality"
will make it possible to replicate all the gore and violence of
popular violent movies, except now you are the one who is the
star, the killer, the slayer of thousands.

Through operant conditioning B. F. Skinner held that he could
turn *any* child into *anything* he wanted to. In Vietnam the U.S.
armed forces demonstrated that Skinner was at least partially correct
by successfully using operant conditioning to turn adolescents into
the most effective fighting force the world has ever seen. And
America seems intent on using Skinner's methodology to turn us
into an extraordinarily violent society.

Chapter Four

Social Learning and Role Models in the Media

The basic training camp was designed to undermine all the past concepts and beliefs of the new recruit, to undermine his civilian values, to change his self-concept — subjugating him entirely to the military system.

— Ben Shalit
   The Psychology of Conflict and Combat

Classical (Pavlovian) conditioning can be done with earthworms, and operant (Skinnerian) conditioning can be conducted on rats and pigeons. But there is a third level of learning that pretty much only primates and humans are capable of, and that is what is called social learning.

This third level of learning, in its most powerful form, revolves primarily around the observation and imitation of a role model. Unlike operant conditioning, in social learning it is not essential that the learner be directly reinforced in order for learning to take place. What is important in social learning is to understand the characteristics that can lead to the selection of a specific individual as a role model.

The processes that make someone a desirable role model include:

• *Vicarious reinforcement.* You see the role model being reinforced in a manner that you can experience vicariously.

- *Similarity to the learner.* You perceive that the role model has a key trait that makes him/her similar to you.
- *Social power.* The role model has the power to reward (but does not necessarily do so).
- *Status envy.* You envy the role model's receipt of rewards from others.

An analysis of these processes can help us understand the role of the drill sergeant as a role model in violence enabling in military training, and it can help us understand why a new type of violent role model is so popular among America's youth.

Violence, Role Models, and Drill Sergeants in Basic Training

From this time on *I* will be your *mother,* your *father,* your *sister, and* your *brother. I* will be your best friend and your worst enemy. *I* will be there to *wake* you up in the morning, and *I* will be there to *tuck* you in at night. You will *jump* when I say *"frog"* and when I tell you to *s——* your only *question* will be *"What color."* IS THAT CLEAR?

— Drill Sergeant G., Fort Ord, California, 1974

Lives there a veteran who cannot close his eyes and vividly visualize his drill sergeant? Over the years a hundred bosses, teachers, professors, instructors, sergeants, and officers have directed various aspects of my life, but none has had the impact that Drill Sergeant G. had on that cold morning in 1974.

The armies of the world have long understood the role of social learning in developing aggression in their soldiers. In order to do this their venue has been basic training, and their instrument has been the drill sergeant. The drill sergeant is a role model. He is the ultimate role model. He is carefully selected, trained, and prepared to be a role model who will inculcate the soldierly values of aggression and obedience. He is also the reason that military service has always been a positive factor for young people from delinquent or disadvantaged backgrounds.

He is invariably a decorated veteran. The glory and recognition bestowed on him are things that the trainees deeply envy and desire. Within the young soldiers' new environment the drill sergeant has enormous and pervasive authority, giving him social power. And the drill sergeant looks like his charges. He wears the uniform. He has the haircut. He obeys orders. He does the same things. But he does all of them well.

The lesson that the drill sergeant teaches is that physical aggression is the essence of manhood and that violence is an effective and desirable solution for the problems that the soldier will face on the battlefield. But it is very important to understand that the drill sergeant also teaches obedience. Throughout training the drill sergeant will not tolerate a single blow or a single shot executed without orders, and even to point an empty weapon in the wrong direction or to raise your fist at the wrong time merits the harshest punishment. No nation will tolerate soldiers who do not obey orders on the battlefield, and the failure to obey orders in combat is the surest route to defeat and destruction.

This is a centuries-old, perhaps *millennia*-old, process that is essential to ensuring that our soldiers survive and obey in combat. In the Vietnam era the drill sergeant communicated a glorification of killing and violence of an intensity never before seen. We did it intentionally. We did it calculatingly. And as long as we have armies we must continue to provide some form of appropriate role model if we want our sons and daughters to survive on future battlefields.

Role Models, the Movies, and a New Kind of Hero

If such "manipulation of the minds of impressionable teenagers" is a necessary evil, accepted only reluctantly and with reservations for combat soldiers, how should we feel about its indiscriminate application to the civilian teenagers of this nation? For that is what we are doing through the role models being provided by the entertainment industry today. But while the drill sergeant teaches and models aggression in obedience to law and authority, the aggression taught by Hollywood's new role models is unrestrained by any obedience to law. And while the drill sergeant has a profound one-time impact, the aggregate effect of a lifetime of media may very well be even greater than that of the drill sergeant.

It has long been understood that movies can have a negative effect on a society through this role-modeling process. For example, the movie *Birth of a Nation* has been widely and plausibly credited with the revival of the Ku Klux Klan. But in general, throughout its golden age Hollywood intuitively understood its potential for doing harm and acted responsibly by providing positive role models for society. In the war movies, westerns, and detective movies of the past, heroes only killed under the authority of the law. If not, they were punished. In the end the villain was never rewarded for his violence, and he always received justice for his crimes. The message was simple: No man is above the law, crime does not pay, and for violence to be acceptable it must be guided by the constraints of the law. The hero was rewarded for obeying the law and channeling his desire for vengeance through the authority of the law. The viewer identified with the hero and was vicariously reinforced whenever the hero was. And the audience members left the theater feeling good about themselves and sensing the existence of a just, lawful world.

But today there is a new kind of hero in movies, a hero who operates outside the law. Vengeance is a much older, darker, more atavistic, and more primitive concept than law, and these new antiheroes are depicted as being motivated and rewarded for their obedience to the gods of vengeance rather than those of law. One of the fruits of this new cult of vengeance in American society can be seen in the Oklahoma City bombing, and if we look into the mirror provided by the television screen, the reflection we see is one of a nation regressing from a society of law to a society of violence, vigilantes, and vengeance.

And if America has a police force that seems unable to constrain its violence, and a population that (having seen the videotape of Rodney King and the LAPD) has learned to fear its police forces, then the reason can be found in the entertainment industry. Look at the role models, look at the archetypes that police officers have grown up with. Clint Eastwood's Dirty Harry became the archetype for a new generation of police officers who were not constrained by the law, and when Hollywood's new breed of cop was rewarded for placing vengeance above the law, the audience was also vicariously rewarded for this same behavior.

Feeding their audience a steady stream of vicarious reinforcement through such vengeful, lawless role models, these movies prepare our society for the acceptance of a truly hideous and sociopathic brand of role model. The essence of this new brand of role model is a brutal and usually supernaturally empowered murderer who is depicted as graphically torturing and murdering innocent victims.

In these movies there is usually no real attempt to paint the victims as being criminals; it is generally acceptable to justify their deaths as deserved due to the snobbery or social slights they have inflicted on others (as in the classic horror movie *Carrie,* which has spawned dozens more, cast from the same mold) or due to their membership in some social group or class held in scorn by the bulk of the youthful target audience. In these movies the viewers receive reinforcement by vicariously killing the people in their lives who have socially snubbed or otherwise "dissed" (shown disrespect to) them. And, in real life, the youth and the gangs of America escalate violence in our nation as they learn to take the law into their own hands and mete out "justice" to those who "diss" them.

At a lower level are the vicarious role models who kill without even the tissue of any apparent justification whatsoever. Having been desensitized by the kinds of movies outlined above, a portion of our population is then willing to accept role models who kill entirely without reason. The vicarious reinforcement here is not even vengeance for supposed social slights, but simply slaughter and suffering for its own sake and, ultimately, for the sake of power.

Notice the sequence in this downward spiral of vicarious role models. We began with those who killed within the constraints of the law. Somewhere along the line we began to accept role models who "had" to go outside the law to kill criminals who we know "deserved to die," then vicarious role models who killed in retribution for adolescent social slights, and then role models who kill completely without provocation or purpose.

At every step of the way we have been vicariously reinforced by the fulfillment of our darkest fantasies. This new breed of role models also has social power: the power to do whatever they want in a society depicted as evil and deserving of punishment. These role models transcend the rules of society, which results in great "status" to be envied by a portion of society that has come to adore this new breed of celebrity. And of course we have observed a similarity to the learner in the role model's rage. A rage felt by most human beings toward the slights and perceived crimes inflicted upon them by their society, but which is particularly intense in adolescence.

The increase in divorces, teenage mothers, and single-parent families in our society has often been noted and lamented, but a little-noted side effect of this trend has been to make America's children even more susceptible to this new breed of violent role models. In the traditional nuclear family there is a stable father figure who serves as a role model for young boys. Boys who grow up without a stable male figure in their lives are desperately seeking a role model. Strong, powerful, high-status role models such as those offered in movies and on television fill the vacuum in their lives. We have taken away their fathers and replaced them with new role models whose successful response to every situation is violence. And then we wonder why our children have become ever more violent.

Chapter Five

The Resensitization of America

Throughout this book we have observed the relevant factors in military training. Men are recruited at a psychologically malleable age. They are distanced from their enemy psychologically, taught to hate and dehumanize. They are given the threat of authority, the absolution and pressure of groups. Even then they are resistant and have trouble killing. They shoot in the air; they find nonviolent tasks to occupy them. And so they still need to be conditioned. The conditioning is astoundingly effective, but there is a psychological price to pay.

In this last section we have applied what we have learned about killing on the battlefield in order to gain an understanding of killing in our society. Violent movies are targeted at the young, both men and women, the same audience the military has determined to be most susceptible for its killing purposes. Violent video games hardwire young people for shooting at humans. The entertainment industry conditions the young in exactly the same way the military does. Civilian society apes the training and conditioning techniques of the military at its peril.

Add to this the dissolution of the family. Children from all economic strata no longer have a censor, counsel, or role model at home. They turn to their peers as authority figures. In some cases they find a family in gangs.

And then there are factors that provide psychological distance in our society. American society is increasingly divided along lines of race, gender, and so on. It has become compartmentalized. People in ghettos rarely leave their own areas — the larger world, the larger country is foreign land. The reverse is true with middle and upper classes. They travel everywhere except for impoverished areas — which they avoid anxiously. It is quite easy to maintain this distance. They ride in their cars; they live in the suburbs and eat in nice restaurants. The separation is not as strident as the soldier who learns to think of his enemy as an animal or refer to him as a "gook," but there is distance.

The only connecting point in our society is the media. The media, which should act to bring us together, serves to pull us apart: conditioning and teaching violence, nurturing our darkest instincts, and feeding the nation with violent stereotypes that foster our deepest fears.

We are most assuredly on the road to ruin, and we need desperately to find the road home from this dark and fearful place to which we have traveled.

The Road to Ruin

And in that state of nature, no arts; no letters; no society; and which is worst of all, continual fear and danger of violent death; and the life of man, solitary, poor, nasty, brutish, and short.

— Thomas Hobbes
Leviathan

Some would claim that modern, ultraviolent movies and their video-game equivalents examined here serve as a form of sublimation that will make violence and war obsolete. "Sublimation" is a term coined by Sigmund Freud referring to the turning of unacceptable urges and desires toward something socially desirable: taking the dark, unacceptable drives of the id and diverting them toward the sublime. Thus someone with a desire to slice open bodies may become a surgeon, or someone with an unacceptable urge toward violence may channel it toward sports, the military, or law enforcement. But watching movies is *not* sublimation.

The entertainment industry is not providing a socially acceptable channeling of energy. Indeed, very little energy is generally spent in the passive reception of television and movies. And this hardly qualifies as a socially acceptable or desirable channel for energies. Unless it has become socially desirable to kill outside the authority of the law, or to murder innocent victims — which, in the twisted world of the entertainment industry, it has.

If violence in television and movies were a form of sublimation, and if it were at all effective, then per capita violence should be going down. Instead it has multiplied nearly seven times in the span of the same generation in which this supposed sublimation has become available. It is not sublimation, or even neutral entertainment. It is classical conditioning, operant conditioning, and social learning, all focused toward the violence enabling of an entire society.

When our 1992 Olympic hockey team displayed a degree of lawlessness, violence, and aggression never before seen in such competitions, we should have begun to wonder. When the mother of one high school cheerleader was convicted of hiring a hit man to murder her daughter's competitor for the cheerleader squad, and when the "bodyguard" for one Olympic figure skater attempted to eliminate the competition by maiming an opponent, we should have begun to understand that this is a society that is increasingly conditioned to turn to violence as the answer to all of its difficulties.

And the Road Home: The Resensitization of America

Male power, male dominance, masculinity, male sexuality, male aggression are not biologically determined. They are conditioned. . . . What is conditioned can be deconditioned. Man can change.

— Catherine Itzin
Pornography: Women, Violence and Civil Liberties

So what is the answer? Which is the road home from this dark and fearful place to which we have traveled?

Perhaps it is time to begin the "resensitization" of America.

When the framers of the U.S. Constitution wrote the Second Amendment, guaranteeing the right to keep and bear arms, they never dreamed that the concept of "arms" could someday include weapons of mass destruction that can vaporize whole cities. In the same way, until late in this century, no one ever dreamed that the right to free speech could include mechanisms of mass conditioning and desensitization. During the 1930s our society began for the first time to consider the need to control access to high explosives, and today even the most rabid defender of Second Amendment rights would not argue for private ownership of rental trucks full of high explosives, artillery, nerve gas, or nuclear arms. In the same way, perhaps the time has come for society to consider the price being paid for the implications of technology on some First Amendment rights.

There is no more need to constrain the print media than there is to control bowie knives, tomahawks, or flintlock rifles, but there might just be a justification for controlling the technology that goes beyond print media and flintlocks. The more advanced the technology, the greater the need for control. In the realm of weapons technology that means controlling explosives, artillery, and machine guns, and it may mean that the time has come to consider controlling assault rifles or pistols. In the realm of media technology, that may mean that the time has come to consider controlling TV, movies, and video games.

Technology has leapfrogged in a variety of ways that change the context of violence in our society. Today technology has enabled distribution of a much wider variety of entertainment: movies, television, videos, video games, multimedia and interactive television, specialized magazines, and the Internet. The result is that entertainment is now a private act. In many cases this is good, but in many other cases it has had the potential for developing, feeding, and sustaining individual pathologies. We have a two-hundred-year-old tradition of protecting the right to free speech and the right to bear arms. Obviously, though, our founding fathers did not have these factors (let alone operant conditioning!) in mind when they wrote the Constitution.

Media critic Michael Medved believes that some form of censorship (either self-censorship or the formal, legal kind) is in the cards, and that this might not be so bad, pointing out that the age of censorship in Hollywood was also the age of greatest artistry, yielding movies such as *Gone with the Wind* and *Casablanca*. As Simon Jenkins put it in a London *Times* editorial:

> Censorship is external regulation and therefore professional anathema. Yet such sanction is the community's natural response to what it feels might threaten its stability, be it adulterated food, dangerous drugs, guns or films that incite social evils. Film-makers, like all artists, claim a license from such sanction. They are observers outside of society looking in. But the license is held on lease. It is not freehold. It can be withdrawn.

But the road to resensitization is probably not through formal censorship. There may be a legitimate place for new laws and legal constraints in our future, but oppression of one sort can never truly be relieved by other forms of oppression, and in today's video society it would be difficult to completely squelch all manifestations of violence enabling. However, we may be able to find compromises that can put us back on the road toward becoming the kind of society that most of us want, while still respecting the rights of one another. What is needed is not censorship, at least not censorship in any legal or legislative sense.

There is a sound argument for changing the way we view and apply First Amendment rights, but I do not advocate it. I do, however, believe that the time has come for our society to censure (not censor) those who exploit violence for profit. In A. M. Rosenthal's words we must "turn entirely away from those ugly people, defeating them by refusing them tolerance or respectability."

What we must realize is that our society is trapped in a pathological spiral with all vectors pulling inward toward a tighter and tighter cycle of violence and destruction.

The prescription for resensitization is as complex and interactive as has been the path to our current dark state. Guns, drugs, poverty, gangs, war, racism, sexism, and the destruction of the nuclear family are just a few of the factors that can act to cheapen human life. The current debates over euthanasia, abortion, and the death penalty indicate that we are divided over the ethics of life and death. To greater or lesser degrees each of these factors helps to pull us toward destruction, and any comprehensive war on crime needs to consider all of them. But these factors have always been there. The *new* factor that is at work today is the same factor that increased the firing rate from 15 to 20 percent in World War II to 90 to 95 percent in Vietnam. The new factor is desensitization and killing enabling in the media.

Television programmers have always tried to claim the "best of two uncomfortably contradictory worlds," as Michael Medved puts it. It is really not new or profound to point out that television executives have for years claimed that they are not capable of influencing our actions or changing behavior, but for decades America's major corporations have paid them billions of dollars for a paltry few seconds or a minute to do just that. To sponsors, media executives claim that just a few well-placed seconds can control how America will spend its hard-earned money. But to Congress and other watchdog agencies they argue that they are not responsible for causing viewers to change the way they will respond to any emotionally charged, potentially violent circumstance that they may subsequently find themselves in. This in spite of the fact that, as of 1994, there have been more than two hundred studies demonstrating the correlation between television and violence.[3]

This body of scientific evidence against the media is overwhelming. In March 1994, Professor Elizabeth Newson, head of the child-development unit at Nottingham University, in England, released a report signed by twenty-five psychologists and pediatricians. They wrote:

> Many of us hold our liberal ideals of freedom of expression dear, but now begin to feel that we were naive in our failure to predict the extent of damaging material and its all-too-free availability to children. By restricting such material from home viewing, society must take on a necessary responsibility in protecting children from this, as from other forms of child abuse.

By calling for legislation to limit the availability of "video nasties," Professor Newson and her colleagues raised a storm of controversy in Britain. They also became the latest in a series of scientists to publicly join the ever-swelling ranks of those who are convinced by the scientific research linking violence in the media to violent crime.

In the spring 1993 issue of *The Public Interest,* Dr. Brandon Canterwall, professor of epidemiology at the University of Washington, summarized the overwhelming nature of this body of evidence. His report focused on the effect of television when it was introduced to rural, isolated communities in Canada and when English-language TV broadcasts were permitted in South Africa in 1975, having previously been banned by the Afrikaans-speaking government. In each case, violent crime among children increased spectacularly.

Canterwall points out that aggressive impulses, like most human phenomena, are distributed along a bell-shaped curve, and the significant effect of any change will occur at the margins. He notes:

> It is an intrinsic effect of such "bell curve" distribution that small changes in the average imply major changes at the extremes. Thus, if an exposure to television causes 8 percent of the population to shift from below-average aggression to above-average aggression, it follows that the homicide rate will double.

In statistical terms, an increase in the aggressive predisposition of 8 percent of the population is very small. Anything less than 5 percent is not even considered to be statistically significant. But in human terms, the impact of doubling the homicide rate is enormous. Canterwall concludes:

> The evidence indicates that if, hypothetically, television technology had never been developed, there would today be 10,000 fewer homicides each year in the United States, 70,000 fewer rapes, and 700,000 fewer injurious assaults. Violent crime would be half what it is.

The evidence is quite simply overwhelming. The American Psychological Association's commission on violence and youth concluded in 1993 that "there is *absolutely no doubt* that higher levels of viewing violence on television are correlated with increased acceptance of aggressive attitudes and increased aggressive behavior."

Ultimately, in the face of all this evidence, the deglamorization and condemnation of violence in the media are inevitable. It will be done in simple self-defense as our society rises up against the enabling of the violent crimes that are destroying our lives, our cities, and our civilization. When it occurs this process will probably be similar to the deglamorization of drugs and tobacco that has occurred in recent years, and for much the same reasons.

Throughout history nations, corporations, and individuals have used noble-sounding concepts such as states' rights, lebensraum, free-market economics, and First or Second Amendment rights to mask their actions, but ultimately what they are doing is for their own personal gain and the result — intentional or not — is killing innocent men, women, and children. They participate in a diffusion of responsibility by referring to themselves as "the tobacco industry" or "the entertainment industry," and we permit it, but they are ultimately individuals making individual moral decisions to participate in the destruction of their fellow citizens.

The ever-ascending tide of violence in our society must be stopped. Each act of violence breeds ever-greater levels of violence, and at some point the genie can never be put back in the bottle. The study of killing in combat teaches us that soldiers who have had friends or relatives injured or killed in combat are much more likely to kill and commit war crimes. Each individual who is injured or killed by criminal violence becomes a focal point for further violence on the part of their friends and family. Every destructive act gnaws away at the restraint of other men. Each act of violence eats away at the fabric of our society like a cancer, spreading and reproducing itself in ever-expanding cycles of horror and destruction. The genie of violence cannot really ever be stuffed back into the bottle. It can only be cut off here and now, and then the slow process of healing and resensitization can begin.

It can be done. It has been done in the past. As Richard Heckler observes, there is a precedent for limiting violence-enabling technology. It started with the classical Greeks, who for four centuries refused to implement the bow and arrow even after being introduced to it in a most unpleasant way by Persian archers.

In *Giving Up the Gun,* Noel Perrin tells how the Japanese banned firearms after their introduction by the Portuguese in the 1500s.

The Japanese quickly recognized that the military use of gunpowder threatened the very fabric of their society and culture, and they moved aggressively to defend their way of life. The feuding Japanese warlords destroyed all existing weapons and made the production or import of any new guns punishable by death. Three centuries later, when Commodore Perry forced the Japanese to open their ports, they did not even have the technology to make firearms. Similarly, the Chinese invented gunpowder but elected not to use it in warfare.

But the most encouraging examples of restraining killing technology have all occurred in this century. After the tragic experience of using poisonous gases in World War I the world has generally rejected their use ever since. The atmospheric nuclear test ban treaty continues after almost three decades, the ban on the deployment of antisatellite weapons is still going strong after two decades, and the United States and the former USSR have been steadily reducing the quantity of nuclear weapons for over a decade. As we have de-escalated instruments of mass destruction, so too can we de-escalate instruments of mass desensitization.

Heckler points out that there has been "an almost unnoticed series of precedents for reducing military technology on moral grounds," precedents that show the way for understanding that we do have a *choice* about how we think about war, about killing, and about the value of human life in our society. In recent years we have exercised the choice to move ourselves from the brink of nuclear destruction. In the same way, our society can move away from the technology that enables killing. Education and understanding are the first step. The end result may be that we will come through these dark years as a healthier, more self-aware society.

To fail to do this leaves us with only two possible results: to go the route of the Mongols and the Third Reich, or the route of Lebanon and Yugoslavia. No other result is possible if successive generations continue to grow up with greater and greater desensitization to the suffering of their fellow human beings. We must put the safety catch back on our society.

We have to understand, as we have never understood before, why it is that men fight and kill and, equally important, why it is that they will not. Only on the basis of understanding human behavior can we hope to influence it. The essence of this book has been that there is a force within man that will cause men to rebel against killing even at the risk of their own lives. That force has existed in man throughout recorded history, and military history can be interpreted as a record of society's attempt to force its members to overcome their resistance in order to kill more effectively in battle.

But that force for life, Freud's Eros, is balanced by the Thanatos, the death force. And we have seen how pervasive and consistent has been the battle between these two forces throughout history.

We have learned how to enable the Thanatos. We know how to take the psychological safety catch off of human beings almost as easily as you would switch a weapon from "safe" to "fire." We must understand where and what that psychological safety catch is, how it works, and how to put it back on. That is the purpose of killology, and that has been the purpose of this book.

Notes

Introduction: Killing and Science

1. I would like to note that some friends (such as the noted historian Bill Lind, author of the superb book *Retroculture*) disagree with this representation of Victorian sexual repression, but I have yet to meet a single individual who disagrees with the analysis of our modern repression outlined here, and that is the pertinent point.

2. There is not even a name for the specific study of killing. "Necrology" would be the study of the dead, and "homicidology" would have undesired connotations of murder. Perhaps we should consider coining the simple and precise term "killology" for this study, just as "suicidology" and "sexology" are terms that have been recently created for the legitimate study of these precise fields.

Section I: Killing and the Existence of Resistance

1. There has been considerable controversy concerning the quality of Marshall's research in this area. Some modern writers (such as Harold Leinbaugh, author of *The Men of Company K*), are particularly vociferous in their belief that the firing rate in World War II was significantly higher than Marshall represented it to be. But we shall see that at every turn my research has uncovered information that would corroborate Marshall's basic thesis, if not his exact percentages. Paddy Griffith's studies of infantry regimental killing rates in Napoleonic and U.S. Civil War battles; Ardant du Picq's surveys; the research of soldiers and scholars such as Colonel Dyer, Colonel (Dr.) Gabriel, Colonel (Dr.) Holmes, and General (Dr.) Kinnard; and the observations of World War I and World War II veterans like Colonel Mater and Lieutenant Roupell — all of these corroborate General Marshall's findings.

Certainly this subject needs more research and study, but I cannot conceive of any motive for these researchers, writers, and veterans to misrepresent the truth. I can, however, understand and appreciate the very noble emotions that could cause men to be offended by anything that would seem to besmirch the honor of those infantrymen who have sacrificed so much in our nation's (or any nation's) past.

The latest volley in this ongoing battle was on the side of Marshall. His grandson, John Douglas Marshall, in his book *Reconciliation Road* put forth one of the most interesting and convincing rebuttals. John Marshall was a conscientious objector in the Vietnam War and was completely disowned by his grandfather. He had no cause to love his grandfather, but he concludes in his book that most of what S. L. A. Marshall wrote "still stands, while much of the way he lived deserves criticism."

2. The universal distribution of automatic weapons is probably responsible for much of this large number of shots fired per kill. Much of this firing was also suppressive fire and reconnaissance by fire. And much of it was by crew-served weapons (e.g., squad machine guns, helicopter door gunners, and aircraft-mounted miniguns firing thousands of rounds per minute), which, as mentioned before, almost always fire. But even when these factors are taken into consideration, the fact that so much fire occurred and that so many individual soldiers were *willing* to fire indicate that something different and unusual was happening in Vietnam. This subject is addressed in detail later in this book, in the section entitled "Killing in Vietnam."

3. This is an important concept. In both this section and in later sections we will observe the vital role of groups (including nonkillers) and leaders as we look at "An Anatomy of Killing."

4. Marshall also observed that if a leader came close to an individual and ordered him to fire, then he would do so, but as soon as the obedience-demanding authority departed, the firing would stop. However, the focus in this section is upon the average soldier armed with a rifle or musket and his apparent unwillingness to kill in combat. The impact of obedience-demanding authority and the effect of group processes on crew-served weapons, i.e., machine guns, which almost always fire, and key weapons (i.e., flamethrowers and automatic rifles), which usually fire, are both addressed in "An Anatomy of Killing."

5. I too have graduated from many a U.S. Army leadership school, including basic training, advanced individual training, the XVIII Airborne Corps NCO Academy, Officer Candidate School, the Infantry Officer Basic Course, Ranger school, the Infantry Officer Advanced Course, the Combined Arms and Services Staff School, and the Command and General Staff College at Fort Leavenworth. Not at any time in any of these schools do I remember this problem being mentioned.

Section II: Killing and Combat Trauma

1. The information in this section has been taken largely from Gabriel's *No More Heroes*, which in turn was taken largely from the *Diagnostic and Statistical Manual* of the American Psychiatric Association and from *Military Psychiatry: A Comparative Perspective*, an anthology that he edited.

2. The cause of PTSD is associated primarily with the nature of the support structure the soldier receives upon returning to society from combat. This section is primarily concerned with the nature and etiology of psychiatric casualties occurring *during* combat. Post-traumatic stress disorder is a distinctly

different type of psychiatric illness that will be addressed in detail in the section of this study entitled "Killing in Vietnam."

3. It is important to note here that, although the lack of battlefield psychiatric casualties among medical personnel has held true in all wars about which I have data, Vietnam was very different in that the incidence of post-traumatic stress disorder appears to have been *higher* among medical personnel. I believe that this was due to the unique nature of what happened *after* the veteran returned from that war, and we will look at this in greater detail in the section "Killing in Vietnam."

4. Frankl (1959), Bettelheim (1960), and Davidson (1967) are but a few of the many who have studied the psychological impact of this environment.

5. For example, Weinberg (1946), Weinstein (1947, 1973), and Spiegel (1973).

6. This is an excerpt from World War I veteran James H. Knight-Adkin's "No Man's Land," a powerful poem that does a superb job of communicating some of the horror of the soldier's dilemma:

No Man's Land is an eerie sight
At early dawn in the pale gray light . . .
And never a living soul walks there
To taste the fresh of the morning air;
Only some lumps of rotting clay,
that were friends or foemen yesterday . . .

But No Man's Land is a goblin sight
When patrols crawl over at dead o' night;
Boche or British, Belgian or French,
You dice with death when you cross the trench.
When the "rapid," like fireflies in the dark,
Flits down the parapet spark by spark,
And you drop for cover to keep your head
With your face on the breast of the four months' dead.

The man who ranges in No Man's Land
Is dogged by shadows on either hand
When the star-shell's flare, as it bursts o'erhead,
Scares the gray rats that feed on the dead,
And the bursting bomb or the bayonet-snatch
May answer the click of your safety-catch,
For the lone patrol, with his life in his hand,
Is hunting for blood in No Man's Land.

Section III: Killing and Physical Distance

1. For an understanding of how it was possible for Nazis and Assyrians to kill at this "extreme" end of the spectrum, see Section V, "Killing and Atrocities."

2. Quoted from an article by R. K. Brown. These are extracts from after-action

reports describing the activities of Sergeant First Class (retired) Adelbert F. Waldron who, during his tour of duty as a sniper using a starlight scope and a noise suppressor (silencer) on his match- (competition-) grade M14 rifle, was credited with 113 confirmed kills and 10 blood trails in five months in Vietnam. Waldron's fame spread, and he was given the nom de guerre Daniel Boone. Apparently, the VC were also impressed with his skill and put a fifty-thousand-dollar price on his head. Twelve hours after Army Intelligence discovered that Waldron had been identified and a bounty offered for his scalp, he was on a plane out of Vietnam.

3. This has been mentioned elsewhere, but it bears repeating that the universal distribution of automatic weapons in Vietnam is probably responsible for much of this large number of shots fired per kill. Much of this firing was also suppressive fire and reconnaissance by fire. And much of it was by crew-served weapons (e.g., squad machine guns, helicopter door gunners, and aircraft-mounted mini-guns firing thousands of rounds per minute), which, as mentioned before, almost always fire. But even when these factors are taken into consideration, the fact that so much fire occurred and that so many individual soldiers were *willing* to fire indicates that something different and unusual was happening in Vietnam. This subject is addressed in detail later in this book in the section "Killing in Vietnam."

4. A detailed analysis of these stages of a kill can be found in the section entitled "The Killing Response Stages."

5. Stewart concludes the article with this sentence. The object of his tale, the climax. The point of this lengthy article appears to be this line that communicates the extent of his empathy for his victim and gives him a little peace: "that hard look had left his eyes before he died." The message we can take away from this is that he cared deeply what this dying VC thought of him, and what the reader thinks of him. If we look for it, over and over again in these killing narratives we will find this underlying message of (1) the writer's empathy for his kill and (2) a deep concern for what the reader thinks of the writer. We will address these needs in much greater detail in the section "Killing in Vietnam."

6. But the Greeks refused to use "unmanly" projectile weapons, and the uniquely designed javelins and pilums cast in volleys by Roman soldiers — combined with the Romans' superior training in thrusting the sword, their maneuverability on the battlefield, and their use of leaders — ultimately permitted the professional Roman legions to defeat the citizen-soldiers of the Greek phalanx.

7. Yet even with all their emphasis on stabbing wounds, it appears that many Roman soldiers still slashed and hacked at the enemy, for we read constantly of enemy soldiers who suffer multiple slash wounds as a result of their encounters with the Roman legions. In his *Commentaries on the Gallic War,* Caesar mentions how after a battle the enemy, "at length, worn out with wounds, . . . began to retreat."

8. It is interesting to note that the new U.S. Army M16 bayonet is a very wicked-looking, saw-backed device.

9. Some would claim that writing of such esoteric killing techniques in a public forum is an inappropriate act, since they now become "thinkable." In some martial arts organizations the release of such "secret" or "high-level" techniques can result in disciplining and censure. This whole subject of modeling violence and making the unthinkable thinkable is addressed in the section "Killing in America." In actuality it must also be noted that the construction of the skull and eye socket make it difficult to get into the brain, and I believe that, in consideration of the potential audience, the benefit associated with using this example in this context far outweighs any potential harm.

10. Permit me to caveat all of this just a little. Freud made similar observations as to the latent homosexuality of men who smoked large cigars, but as a cigar smoker himself Freud was quick to add that "sometimes a cigar is just a cigar." In the same way let me simply add, as a soldier and a gun owner, that sometimes a gun is . . . just a gun.

Section IV: An Anatomy of Killing

1. Helping a veteran in such a situation involves encouraging him to share his experience, confronting the word "murder," and discussing the Bible's or Torah's view on killing.

Encouraging Him to Share This Experience with His Wife. In this case I suggested that he do this by asking her to read William Manchester's *Goodbye, Darkness* and then use a remarkably similar incident in that book as a point of departure to discuss his experience. (The need for the vet to share with his wife and the value of a book to serve as point of departure are recurring themes in this kind of counseling. Early drafts of this book have served just such a purpose on several occasions.)

Encouraging Him to Confront His Use of the Word "Murder." It was not murder, it was self-defense, and if it happened in the street tomorrow no charges would be pressed. His answer, as it is so often when the veteran represses and never discusses these situations, was "I never looked at it that way." (This is a common and repeated theme in such counseling.)

Discussing What the Bible or the Torah Says about Killing. I encouraged him to study the matter further or discuss it with a clergyman of his faith. This is another common and important theme. There is a body of belief in America that it is not "good" to be a soldier. Much of this antimilitary bias is founded on the commandment "Thou shalt not kill," but within the realm of Christianity there is great disagreement on this matter, and it is not nearly that simple. For the sake of therapy among soldiers I have found that there is great value in presenting the other side of the theological debate about killing.

In Exodus, chapter 20, we find the Ten Commandments. Almost four hundred years ago the King James Version translated the Sixth Commandment as "Thou shalt not kill." When the translators wrote that, no one ever dreamed that "God's word" would be taken so out of context as to interpret this commandment to mean that the death penalty or killing on the battlefield is wrong. In this century, with only one exception, every major modern translation has translated this commandment as "Thou shall not murder." In chapter 21 of the same book of the Bible (on the same page as the Ten Commandments in most Bibles) the death penalty is commanded when it says: "He that smiteth a man, so that he die, shall surely be put to death" (Exodus 21:12). The Hebrew word used in the original text of the Sixth Commandment refers to killing for your own personal gain; it has nothing to do with killing under authority. And this is not the first or the last time that the death penalty is commanded by God. In Genesis 9:6, when he got off the ark, Noah was commanded by God, "Whosoever sheddeth man's blood, by man shall his blood be shed."

King David was a "man after God's own heart," and he was also a man of war. The Bible praises David for killing Goliath in battle, and as a king he is praised:

"Sol killed his thousands, but David has killed his tens of thousands." Killing in war, under authority, is presented as honorable and acceptable throughout the Bible. It was only when King David committed murder, in killing Uriah, that he got into trouble with God. The Old Testament is full of such righteous warrior leaders. David, Joshua, and Gideon are just a few of the hundreds of soldiers mentioned in the Old Testament who found favor in God's eyes for their labors on the battlefield. In Proverbs 6:17, the Bible says that God "*hates* . . . shedders of *innocent* blood [emphasis added]." But there is nothing but honor in the Bible for the soldier who kills in just combat.

In the New Testament the story is the same. When the rich young man came to Jesus he was told that he must give away everything he had in order to follow Jesus. But in Matthew 8:10, when the Roman centurion came to him, Jesus said, "I have not found so great a faith, no, not in Israel." And in Acts, chapter 10, the first non-Jewish Christian was designated by God, and he was Cornelius . . . *a Roman centurion*. God sent Peter to convert him, and it appears to have been a bit of a shock to Peter (and all the other disciples) that a non-Jew could be a Christian, but he never questioned that a *soldier* should have the honor of being the first one. Most of chapter 10 of the Book of Acts is devoted to Peter's sermon to the centurion Cornelius and his guidance as to how to be a Christian, but never once does Peter, or *anyone else, anywhere in the Bible*, state that it is incompatible to be a soldier and a Christian. Indeed, exactly the opposite is communicated over and over again.

In Luke 22:36, just minutes before his arrest and subsequent crucifixion, Jesus commanded his disciples that "he that hath no sword, let him sell his garment, and buy one." They had three swords among them, and when the soldiers came to arrest Jesus, Peter drew his. But Jesus commanded him to put it away, saying, "He that lives by the sword shall die by the sword," meaning that if the sword is your law, you *should* die by the sword — the sword wielded by the agents of the government, and in Romans 13:4 Paul wrote that the government "beareth not the sword in vain."

Thus there is a foundation for the argument that (1) "Thou shalt not kill" is a poor translation taken grossly out of context and (2) this has been responsible for doing great emotional harm to our veterans. The position outlined above has been, and continues to be, the one accepted by much of Catholic and Protestant Christianity for two millennia. This has been the philosophical justification for the church's support for fighting to free the slaves in the Civil War and fighting Germany and Japan in World War II. Today many churches hold that those who have died for our nation are exemplifying Jesus' love and Jesus' sacrifice for every one of us, for Jesus said, "Greater love has no man than this, that he give his life for his friends."

2. An interview with a veteran who was a retired law-enforcement officer led me to realize that moral distance is the dominant factor that enables violence and the rationalization of violence among police forces. When I described the distance processes to him he pointed out that the establishment and maintenance of what I was calling moral distance are essential to the mental health of police officers, and on a good force it is *the* primary enabling process. If, on the other hand, the racial and ethnic hatred of cultural distance begins to set in, then there are problems, and a kind of moral rot can cut into the soul of the police force.

3. It is interesting to observe how many of these "punishment" motivators were, in retrospect, less than legitimate. We really never did find out what caused the sinking of the *Maine,* and it might very well have been an accident. The *Lusitania* was carrying war munitions, and the Germans did give us fair warning. And the Gulf of Tonkin Incident appears to have been almost completely fabricated by President Johnson. In most of these cases, though, the politicians were motivated to use these incidents as a rally to excite the popular imagination in order to get involved in a war that they (the politicians) thought was morally legitimate.

The great British statesman Benjamin Disraeli observed that the role of such "passion" issues would always be a key aspect of a democracy's entry into war. "If," said Disraeli,

> you establish a democracy, you must in due season reap the fruits of a democracy. . . . You will in due season have wars entered into from passion, and not from reason; and you will in due season submit to peace . . . which will diminish your authority and perhaps endanger your independence. You will, in due season, with a democracy find that your property is less valuable and that your freedom is less complete.

4. B. F. Skinner's operant conditioning theory and its application to killing will be looked at in greater detail in subsequent sections. His theory is basically that aspect of psychology which most people associate with the lab rat conditioned to press a bar for food. From Skinner's research has arisen a body of psychological thought and theory that is probably matched only by Freud's in its influence.

5. Modern snipers are enabled by group processes, since they are almost always teamed with a spotter who provides mutual accountability and turns the sniper into a crew-served weapon. In addition, snipers are enabled by (1) the physical distance at which they fire, (2) the mechanical distance created by viewing the enemy through a scope, and (3) a temperament predisposed to the job, due to their careful selection by command and self-selection through their willingness to volunteer for the job.

6. But of course the Rhodesians won all the battles and lost the war — as did the U.S. forces in Vietnam. I would submit that in both cases this is because the "enemy" was willing to absorb these horrendous losses, while the Americans and the Rhodesians were not. This is partially a reflection on the impact of moral distance, but it is also a matter of political will and the effectiveness of democracies versus totalitarian forms of government in times of war, and *that* is a factor that is generally outside the realm of consideration of this study.

7. Like most personality disorders, this one is a continuum that contains many individuals who, while they would not meet the full diagnostic criteria, are on the borderline of antisocial personality disorder. The *DSM-III-R* tells us that some individuals "who have several features of the disorder [but not enough to be diagnosed with it] achieve political and economic success," and some successful combatants may also fit into this category.

8. Terry Pratchett, in his book *Witches Abroad*, captured (in a metaphoric sense that Jung would have loved) the essence of the power of archetypal roles and their ability to entrap and warp lives:

> Stories exist independently of their players. If you know that, the knowledge is power.
>
> Stories, great flapping ribbons of shaped space-time, have been blowing and uncoiling around the universe since the beginning of time. And they have evolved. The weakest have died and the strongest have survived and they have grown fat on the retelling . . . stories, twisting and blowing through the darkness.
>
> And their very existence overlays a faint but insistent pattern on the chaos that is history. Stories etch grooves deep enough for people to follow in the same way that water follows certain paths down a mountainside. And every time fresh actors tread the path of the story, the groove runs deeper.

Pratchett calls this "the theory of narrative causality," and he is quite correct in noting that in its most extreme form the archetype, or the "story," can have a dysfunctional influence on lives. "Stories don't care who takes part in them," says Pratchett. "All that matters is that the story gets told, that the story repeats. Or, if you prefer to think of it like this: stories are a parasitical life form, warping lives in the service only of the story itself."

This is especially true if (1) society invests and entraps an individual in a role — for example, the role of the hero who bathes in blood and gore while slaying the "dragon," and then (2) society cuts the story short and refuses to continue to play its part in the age-old drama/story of the returning warrior. Which is exactly what America did to her returning Vietnam veterans. But that is a story for a later chapter.

9. Synthesizing various models and variables into a single paradigm may assist in providing a more detailed understanding of the soldier's response to killing circumstances on the battlefield. It may even be possible to develop an equation that can represent the total resistance involved in a specific killing circumstance.

The variables represented in our equation include:

• **Probability of Personal Kill** = total probability of execution of specific personal kill (This is an estimation of the total psychological leverage available to enable the execution of a specific personal kill in a specific circumstance.)
• **Demands of Authority** = (intensity of demand for killing) × (legitimacy of obedience-demanding authority) × (proximity of obedience-demanding authority) × (respect for obedience-demanding authority)
• **Group Absolution** = (intensity of support for killing) × (number in immediate killing group) × (identification with killing group) × (proximity of killing group)
• **Total Distance from Victim** = (physical distance from victim) × (cultural distance from victim) × (social distance from victim) × (moral distance from victim) × (mechanical distance from victim)
• **Target Attractiveness of Victim** = (relevance of victim) × (relevance of available strategies) × (payoff in killer's gain + payoff in victim's loss)
• **Aggressive Predisposition of Killer** = (training/conditioning of the killer) × (past experiences of the killer) × (individual temperament of killer)

An equation that would permit us to tie in all of these factors and determine the resistance to a specific personal kill would look something like this:

> Probability of Personal Kill =
> (demands of authority) × (group absolution) ×
> (total distance from victim) ×
> (target attractiveness of victim) ×
> (aggressive predisposition of killer)

Let us say that the baseline for all of these factors is 1. A baseline of 1 works well, since in our multiplicative equation this number would be neutral; any factor under 1 would influence all other factors downward, and any factor over

1 would interact to influence all other factors upward. Since these processes are all multiplicative, an extraordinarily low factor in any one area (such as .01 in aggressive predisposition) would have to be overcome through very high ratings in other factors. On the other hand, all other factors being equal, an extremely high rating in demands of authority (as seen in Milgram's studies) or a high aggressive predisposition (as would be likely if the killer had recently had a buddy or a family member killed by the "enemy") would result in a high probability of a personal kill or even the unrestrained killing resulting in war crimes and other atrocities.

Like most factor analyses, this one has probably not identified all of the factors that would influence this situation, but this model is certainly vastly more effective than anything we have had before — since, to the best of my knowledge, none has ever existed before. Much work is needed to truly quantify these factors, but I would hypothesize that the threshold for a personal kill in wartime would be lower than that in peacetime. In a peacetime killing (murder) the threshold would probably be significantly higher, but the basic factors might still generally apply. Certainly this model would apply to gang killings and most random street violence, but the most common form of murder is that committed by acquaintances and family members upon one another, and I believe that the psychological mechanics of that kind of killing are quite different from what we are studying here.

Section V: Killing and Atrocities

1. The only other time I have heard this process spoken of was by one particularly astute and unusually introspective British wing commander from the Gulf War. He noted that the RAF ground crews who supported his squadron felt like "impostors" because they had lived in a hotel, did not personally approach the enemy, and had not yet endured any Iraqi Scud missile attacks. However, they were only a few hundred meters from the U.S. National Guard unit that was subsequently hit by a Scud attack at considerable loss of life. "I hope," he said, "that you will not misunderstand if I tell you that my ground crews felt a little better about themselves when the Americans were hit." Again, instead of being diminished by friendly losses, they were strangely magnified and empowered by them.

2. This is the only place in this entire book where I have used a quote from fiction. I do so in this instance because Conrad's Kurtz is an unparalleled representation of a man who is entrapped in the power of atrocity. This was superbly embellished and built upon in Marlon Brando's portrayal of Kurtz in *Apocalypse Now*. In that movie Kurtz's representation of how he was ensnared by the power of the Vietcong's use of atrocity represents a singularly powerful insight into the dark attraction of atrocity.

Section VI: The Killing Response Stages

1. The "obedience versus sympathy" and "cultural versus biological norm" conflicts, which may be at the root of this killing trauma, have been explored by Eibl-Eibesfeldt. He delves deeply into this area and relates how soldiers in firing squads have been traditionally drugged with alcohol and issued the random blank bullet to permit some form of denial. Even so, they often later needed psychological counseling. Eibl-Eibesfeldt also tells of the atonement rituals traditionally used in primitive tribes after killing the enemy.

Eibl-Eibesfeldt does not, however, examine the need for, and quality of, ritual atonement methods for dealing with the trauma of a personal kill in *modern* warfare. These modern atonement processes, and how they failed in Vietnam, are an important part of what we must attempt to examine and understand. But first we must complete our dissection of the stages of a personal kill.

2. A fixation is sometimes defined as too much pain or pleasure associated with a specific stimuli. Classical examples of Freudian fixations include individuals who are fixated by the delight of nursing and the trauma of being weaned (oral fixation) or individuals who have become fixated by traumatic toilet training (anal fixation).

3. Many veterans cut themselves off entirely from their emotions at the time of killing. They tell me (sincerely, I believe) that they feel now and felt then absolutely nothing. This is discussed elsewhere, but it is very important at this point to distinguish between these individuals who have denied and repressed their emotions and those who can truly enjoy killing without any resultant remorse.

4. But all would defend his right to reflect openly on the war as he saw it, in a forum of his peers. It is very much to the credit of *Soldier of Fortune,* the magazine in which this article was published, that for twenty years this was essentially the *only* national forum in which Vietnam veterans could write such deeply emotional, open, and often unpopular reminiscences of their war. The editors added that "(?)" to the title of this article as their subtle means of distancing themselves from the author's statements, and let it go at that. The route of recovery from all combat trauma is through rationalization and acceptance, and this lifelong self-exploration process that I have termed "rationalization and acceptance" is exactly what occurs when veterans write, and read, these first-person narratives. I believe that writing and reading these narratives provide an extremely powerful form of therapy for these men. And I must deeply respect the courage and fortitude it took to both write and publish such accounts over the last twenty years.

Note that here the "thrill of the kill" is placed before the "terrible bitterness of losing a friend," the latter being a trauma that is intentionally downplayed in relationship to the pleasure that the writer found in combat. It must be emphasized that such a fixation does not make an individual a "bad" person. On the contrary, it was men like this, with a thirst for adventure and addiction to excitement, who pioneered our nation, and it is men such as this whom our country depends upon as the backbone of our military force in time of war. And, again, there are numerous sound studies that demonstrate that the returning veteran represents no greater threat to society than already existed in the society. As always, the objective must be not to judge, but simply to understand.

Section VII: Killing in Vietnam

1. The 1978 President's Commission on Mental Health tells us that approximately 2.8 million Americans served in Southeast Asia. If we accept the Veterans Administration's conservative figures of 15 percent incidence of PTSD among Vietnam veterans, then more than 400,000 individuals in the United States suffer from PTSD. Independent estimates of the number of Vietnam veterans suffering from PTSD range from the Disabled American Veterans figure of 500,000 to Harris and Associates 1980 estimate of 1.5 million. These figures would mean that somewhere between 18 and 54 percent of the 2.8 million military personnel who served in Vietnam are suffering from PTSD.

2. This improvement is so astounding that a few modern observers have publicly questioned Marshall's World War II findings. But to do that means that you have to go on and question his Korean War findings and his Vietnam findings (which have been independently verified by Scott). To do so also refutes the findings of every other author who has looked deeply into this matter, including Holmes, Dyer, Keegan, and Griffith. It is possible these modern writers are partially motivated by a difficulty in believing that they and "their" soldiers exist to do something that is so offensive and horrible that they must be conditioned to do it. See the earlier section "Killing and the Existence of Resistance" for a more detailed discussion of this topic.

3. There was too little close combat in the Gulf War to really make any conclusions of this sort.

4. Stouffer, in "The American Soldier: Combat and Its Aftermath" (in *Studies in Social Psychology in World War II,* vol. 2), says that "Personal readjustment problems of varying degrees of intensity are disclosed by the [World War II] veterans in this study. But the typical veteran pictured in some quarters as a bitter, hardened individual does not emerge from this survey." Charles C. Moskos Jr., in *The American Enlisted Man,* looked at the Vietnam veteran and found that, compared with when they entered the army, these men returned to civilian life more mature and better suited to contribute to society.

The situation, however, is not all that simple. Since Stouffer's and Moskos's studies, we have become aware of the impact of PTSD on Vietnam veterans. It would appear there is no evidence to indicate that, when compared with a nonveteran of the same age, the average Vietnam vet has any greater potential for committing murder, assaults, or robbery. What the epidemic of PTSD among Vietnam vets *has* caused is a significant increase in suicides, drug use, alcoholism, and divorce.

5. See Gabriel's *No More Heroes* for more information about these drugs and their physical and mental effects. Gabriel also spends a great deal of time assessing the potential impact of these drugs on killing and their potential effects on the trauma of killing. Those interested in a more detailed assessment of the impact of psychopharmacology in Vietnam should look at *Military Psychiatry: A Comparative Perspective,* which Gabriel edited and drew from extensively for *No More Heroes.*

6. No, the term is not necessarily an oxymoron.

7. Fry and Stockton (1982), Keane and Fairbank (1983), Strech (1985), Lifton (1974), Brown (1984), Egendorf, Kadushin, Laufer, Rothbart, and Sloan (1981), and Levetman (1978) are just a few of the psychiatrists, military psychologists, Veterans Administration mental-health professionals, and sociologists who have identified lack of social support after returning from combat as a critical factor in the development of PTSD.

8. Research is proceeding in this area, and we may someday be able to actually calibrate these numbers. In 1992, twelve cadets from the U.S. Military Academy at West Point spent their summer at the VA Medical Center in Boston. They were participating as part of their Individual Academic Development Program under my supervision, and their mission was to interview veterans about their combat experiences in order to begin to establish a database of information and interviews specifically about killing processes. The cadets involved then evaluated and assessed the data gathered in these summer interviews as a part of subsequent directed individual studies courses under my supervision.

This database continues to grow and will, hopefully, expand further based upon input from veterans as a result of this book. The long-term objective is to be able to begin a detailed analysis of the processes associated with killing, to include the degree of importance and influence represented by the various factors in the killing-enabling model; the validity of the killing response stages; and the interaction between combat trauma (specifically killing experiences) and social support and their relationship to the resulting magnitude of post-traumatic stress response. Individuals who are willing to provide data for this study are invited to write the author care of the publisher.

9. As mentioned before, Stouffer's and Moskos's studies indicate that returning veterans are generally better members of society. There is also no evidence to indicate that a Vietnam vet is more likely than a nonvet to commit crimes of violence. What the epidemic of PTSD among Vietnam vets *has* caused is a statistically significant increase in suicides, drug use, alcoholism, and divorce.

I should note that most Vietnam vets have done quite well for themselves. There is, therefore, a backlash movement among some Vietnam veterans who are tired of the current label, who have had no difficulty themselves (perhaps due to repression and denial, or an unusually strong support structure upon return combined with their own personal psychic strength in the face of the stresses that they have endured), and these individuals sometimes have little patience for the veterans who are having problems.

In the face of this current conflict among veterans I would contribute the observation that the world is big enough, and people are complex enough, that probably both sides are correct.

Section VIII: Killing in America

1. There is some confusion about crime reporting in America, generally due to the fact that there are two crime reports produced each year by the U.S. government. One report is compiled by the FBI based on all crimes reported by law-enforcement agencies across the nation. In recent years this report has reflected a steady *decrease* in overall crime and a steady *increase* in violent crime, as reflected in the graph on page 300.

In 1994 the FBI report reflected a 0.4 percent *decrease* in the per capita aggravated assault rate. This is the first decrease in this area in nearly a decade. But the same report also reflected a 2.2 percent *increase* in the per capita murder rate, and criminologists offer little hope for a long-term decrease in violent crime. "We haven't even begun to see the problem with teenagers that we will see in the next ten years," says Dr. Jack Levin, sociology and criminology professor at Northeastern University in Boston. "There will be a 23 percent increase in the teenage population over the next generation, and as a result, we're going to see the murder rate rise precipitously."

The other annual crime report is based on a national survey of crime victims and reports its findings according to the number of crimes per household. In recent years this report has *also* reflected a steady increase in violent crime. The results of this survey have been questioned by some experts, and it may be that this report is underreporting crime as the nature and number of American "households" increase due to the breakdown of the nuclear family. The data in this report also have potential for error (probably in the direction of underreporting), since they are based on a subjective assessment on the part of the increasingly jaded population being surveyed. Nevertheless, in 1994 this survey reflected a 5.6 percent increase in violent crime.

The fact that the crime victim survey reflected a significant increase in violent crime in the same year that the FBI reported a small decrease supports a school of thought which holds that the FBI report has also been increasingly underreporting crime. This theory holds that law-enforcement agencies will become more and more swamped as the incidence of violent crime increases. As a result of this, both an exhausted police force and a jaded population (which is also increasingly fearful of criminal retribution) will raise the threshold of what is reported. There is evidence to indicate that in many high-crime areas attacks and assaults that would have received immediate attention thirty years ago (for example, drive-by shootings in which no one is hit and beatings in which no one is killed) are routinely ignored today.

As the inner cities continue to sink into lawlessness and anarchy it may well be that an increasing proportion of violent crimes will continue to go unreported and unnoticed. As a result of this, both crime reports will increasingly fail to reflect the full magnitude of the problem of violent crime in America.

2. Another common red herring in this area involves the increasing "deadliness" of modern small arms. This is simply a myth.

For example, the high-velocity, small-caliber (5.56 mm/.223 caliber) ammunition used in most assault rifles today (e.g., the M16, AR-15, Mini-14, etc.) was designed to wound rather than kill. The theory is that wounding an enemy soldier is better than killing him because a wounded soldier eliminates three people: the wounded man and two others to evacuate him. These weapons do inflict great (wounding) trauma, but they are illegal for hunting deer in most states due to their ineffectiveness at quickly and effectively killing game.

Similarly, since World War II the weapon that we associated with criminals was generally a .45 automatic, which was also the current military side arm. In recent years the criminal weapon of choice has reflected the military's transition to the 9 mm pistol, which has a smaller, faster round, which many experts argue is considerably less effective at killing.

What these new smaller ammunitions (5.56 mm for rifle and 9 mm for pistol) *do* make possible is greater magazine capacity, and this has increased the effectiveness of weapons in one way, while decreasing it in another way.

The point is that there has *not* been any significant increase in the effectiveness of the weapons available today. The shotgun is still the single most effective weapon for killing someone at close range, and it has been available and basically unchanged for more than one hundred years. Medical technology, computer technology, and entertainment technology have all advanced at quantum rates, but the technology of close-range killing has been essentially unchanged throughout the last century.

3. But the situation is more complex. Correlation does not prove causation. To *prove* that TV causes violence you must conduct a controlled, double-blind experiment in which, if you are successful, you will *cause* people to commit murder. Clearly to perform such an experiment with human beings is unethical and largely impossible. This same situation is the foundation for the tobacco industry's continued argument that no one has ever "proven" that cigarettes "cause" cancer.

There comes a point when, in spite of this type of reasoning, we must accept that cigarettes do cause cancer. Similarly, there comes a point at which we must accept the verdict of 217 correlation studies.

Bibliography

Selected Books

Appel, J. W., and G. W. Beebe. Aug. 18, 1946. Preventive psychiatry: an epidemiological approach. *Journal of the American Medical Association* 131, 1469–75.

Ardant du Picq, C. 1946. *Battle studies.* Harrisburg, Pa.: Telegraph Press.

Aurelius, M. 1964. *Meditations.* Trans. M. Staniforth. New York: Viking Penguin Books. (Original work completed 180.)

Bartlett, F. C. 1937. *Psychology and the soldier.* Cambridge: Cambridge University Press.

Berkun, M. 1958. Inferred correlation between combat performance and some field laboratory stresses. Research Memo (Fighter II). Arlington, Va.: Human Resources Research Office.

Bettleheim, B. 1960. *The informed heart.* New York.

Blackburn, A. B., W. E. O'Connell, and B. W. Richman. 1984. Post-traumatic stress disorder, the Vietnam veteran, and Adlerian natural high therapy. *Individual Psychology: Journal of Adlerian Theory, Research & Practice* 40 (3), 317–32.

Bolte, C. G. 1945. *The new veteran.* New York: Reynal and Hitchcock.

Borowski, T. 1962. *This way for the gas, ladies and gentlemen.* New York, Viking/Penguin.

Brennan, M. 1985. *Brennan's war.* New York: Pocket Books.

Broadfoot, B. 1974. *Six war years 1939–1945.* New York: Doubleday.

Brooks, J. S., and T. Scarano, 1985. Transcendental meditation in the treatment of post-Vietnam adjustments. *Journal of Counselling and Development* 64 (3), 212–15.

Clausewitz, C. M. von. 1976. *On war.* Ed. 2nd trans. M. Howard and P. Paret. Princeton, N.J.: Princeton University Press.

Cooper, J. 1985. *Principles of personal defense.* Boulder, Colo.: Paladin Press.

Crump, L. D. 1984. Gestalt therapy in the treatment of Vietnam veterans experiencing PTSD symptomatology. *Journal of Contemporary Psychotherapy* 14 (1), 90–98.

Davidson, S. 1967. A clinical classification of psychiatric disturbances of Holocaust survivors and their treatment. *The Israel Annals of Psychiatry and Related Disciplines* 5, 96–98.

Dinter, E. 1985. *Hero or coward: pressures facing the soldier in battle.* London: Frank Cass and Company.

Dyer, G. 1985. *War*. London: Guild Publishing.

Eibl-Eibesfeldt, I. 1975. *The biology of peace and war: men, animals, and aggression*. New York: Viking Press.

Fromm, E. 1973. *The anatomy of human destructiveness*. New York: Holt, Rinehart and Winston.

Fussell, P. 1989. *Wartime*. New York: Oxford University Press.

Gabriel, R. A. 1986. *Military psychiatry: a comparative perspective*. New York: Greenport Press.

————. 1987. *No more heroes: madness and psychiatry in war*. New York: Hill and Wang.

Geer, F. C. 1983. Marine-machine to poet of the rocks: poetry therapy as a bridge to inner reality: some exploratory observations. *Arts in Psychotherapy* 10 (1), 9–14.

Glass, A. J. 1957. *Observations on the epidemiology of mental illness in troops during warfare*. Symposium on Prevention and Social Psychiatry. Washington, D.C.: Walter Reed Army Institute of Research.

————. 1953. Psychiatry in the Korean campaign. A historical review. *U.S. Armed Forces Medical Journal* 4 (11), 1563–83.

Glenn, R. W. Apr. 1989. Men and fire in Vietnam. *Army: Journal of the Association of the United States Army*, 18–27.

Goodwin, Jim. 1988. *Post-traumatic stress disorders: a handbook for clinicians*. Disabled American Veterans.

Gordon, T. 1977. *Enola Gay*. New York: Simon and Schuster.

Gray, J. G. 1970. *The Warriors: Reflections on Men in Battle*. London.

Greene, B. 1989. *Homecoming: when the soldiers returned from Vietnam*. New York: G. P. Putnam's Sons.

Griffith, P. 1989. *Battle tactics of the civil war*. New Haven, Conn.: Yale University Press.

Grossman, D. A. May 1984. Moral approach only the start: the bottom line in P.O.W. treatment. *Army: Journal of the Association of the United States Army*, 15–16.

Harris, F. G. 1956. Experiences in the study of combat in the Korean theater. Vol II. Comments on a concept of psychiatry for a combat zone. *WRAIR Research Report* 165–66. Washington, D.C.: Walter Reed Army Institute of Research.

Havighurst, R. J., W. H. Eaton, J. W. Baughman, and E. W. Burgess. 1951. *The American veteran back home*. New York: Longmans, Green and Co.

Heckler, R. S. 1989. *In search of the warrior spirit*. Berkeley, Calif.: North Atlantic Books.

Hendin, H. 1983. Psychotherapy for Vietnam veterans with posttraumatic stress disorders. *American Journal of Psychotherapy* 37 (1), 86–99.

Holmes, R. 1985. *Acts of war: the behavior of men in battle*. New York: Free Press.

Hooker, R. D. 1993. *Maneuver warfare: an anthology*. Novato, Calif.: Presidio Press.

Ingraham, L., and F. Manning. Aug. 1980. Psychiatric battle casualties: the missing column in the war without replacements. *Military Review* 21.

Junger, E. 1929. *The storm of steel.* London.

Keegan, J. 1976. *The face of battle.* Suffolk, England: Chaucer Press.

Keegan, J., and R. Holmes. 1985. *Soldiers.* London: Guild Publishing.

Keillor, G. 1994. "Hog Slaughter." *A Prairie Home Companion.* Prod. Minnesota Public Radio.

Kupper, H. I. 1945. *Back to life.* New York: American Book–Stratford Press.

Lawrence, T. E. 1926. *Seven pillars of wisdom.* New York: Doubleday.

Leonhard, R. 1991. *The art of maneuver: maneuver-warfare theory and airland battle.* Novato, Calif.: Presidio Press.

Lind, W. S. 1985. *Maneuver warfare handbook.* Boulder, Colo.: Westview Press.

———. Retro-culture. Unpublished manuscript.

Lord, F. A. 1976. *Civil war collector's encyclopedia.* Harrisburg, Pa.: The Stackpole Co.

Lorenz, K. 1963. *On aggression.* New York: Bantam Books.

McCormack, N. A. 1985. Cognitive therapy of posttraumatic stress disorder: a case report. *American Mental Health Counselors Association Journal* 7 (4), 151–55.

Manchester, W. 1981. *Goodbye, darkness.* London: Penguin Books.

Mantell, D. M. 1974. *True Americanism: green berets and war resisters; a study of commitment.* New York: Teachers College Press.

Marin, P. Nov. 1981. Living in moral pain. *Psychology Today,* 68–80.

Marshall, J. D. 1994. *Reconciliation Road.* New York: Syracuse University Press.

Marshall, S. L. A. 1978. *Men Against fire.* Gloucester, Mass.: Peter Smith.

Masters, J. 1956. *Road past Mandalay.* New York: Viking Press.

Mauldin, B. 1945. *Up front.* New York: H. Wolff.

McIntyre, B. F. 1963. *Federals on the Frontier.* Tilky, N.M. ed. Austin, Tex.: University of Texas Press.

Metelmann, H. 1964. *Through hell for Hitler: a dramatic first hand account of fighting for the Wehrmacht.* London: Harper Collins.

Milgram, S. 1963. Behavioral study of obedience. *Journal of Abnormal and Social Psychology* 67, 371–78.

Miller, M. J. 1983. Empathy and the Vietnam veteran: touching the forgotten warrior. *Personnel & Guidance Journal* 62 (3), 149–54.

Montagu, A. 1976. *The nature of human aggression.* New York: Oxford University Press.

Moran, L. 1945. *Anatomy of courage.* London: Constable and Company.

Moskos, Charles C., Jr. 1970. *The American Enlisted Man.* New York: Russell Sage Foundation.

Murry, Simon. 1978. *My five years in the French Foreign Legion.* New York: Times Books.

Ryan, C. 1966. *The last battle.* New York: Popular Library.

Sager, G. 1968. *The forgotten soldier.* New York: Harper and Row.

Santoli, A. 1985. *To bear any burden.* New York: E. P. Dutton.

Shalit, B. 1988. *The psychology of conflict and combat.* New York: Praeger Publishers.

Spiegel, H. X. 1973. Psychiatry with an infantry battalion in North Africa. In *Neuropsychiatry in World War II,* ed. W. S. Mullens and A. J. Glass. Vol. 2, *Overseas theaters.* Washington, D.C.: U.S. Government Printing Office, 111–26.

Stellman, J. M., and S. Stellman. 1988. Post traumatic stress disorders among American Legionnaires in relation to combat experience: associated and contributing factors. *Environmental Research* 47 (2), 175–210.

Stouffer, S. A., et al. 1949. *The American Soldier.* 5 vols. Princeton, N.J.: Princeton University Press.

Swank, R. L., and W. E. Marchand. 1946. Combat neuroses: development of combat exhaustion. *Archives of Neurology and Psychology* 55, 236–47.

Waller, W. 1944. *The veteran comes back.* New York: Dryden Press.

Watson, P. 1978. *War on the mind: the military uses and abuses of psychology.* New York: Basic Books.

Wecter, D. 1944. *When Johnny comes marching home.* Cambridge, Mass.: Riverside Press.

Weinberg, S. K. 1946. The combat neuroses. *American Journal of Sociology* 51, 465–78.

Weinstein, E. A. 1973. The fifth U.S. Army Neuropsychiatric Center — "601 st." In *Neuropsychiatry in World War II,* ed. W. S. Mullens and A. J. Glass. Vol. 2, *Overseas theaters.* Washington, D.C.: U.S. Government Printing Office, 127–42.

———. 1947. The function of interpersonal relations in the neurosis of combat. *Psychiatry* 10, 307–14.

Personal Narratives from *Soldier of Fortune* Magazine

Anderson, R. B. Nov. 1988. Parting shot: Vietnam was fun (?), 96.

Banko, S. Oct. 1988. Sayonara Chery-San, 26.

Barclay, G. Apr. 1984. Rhodesia's hand-picked professionals, 30.

Bray, D. Aug. 1989. Prowling for POWs, 35,75.

Doyle, E. Aug. 1983. Three battles, part 2: the war down South, 39.

Dye, D. A. Sept. 1985. Chuck Cramer: IDF's master sniper, 60.

Freeman, J. Summer 1976. Angola fiasco, 38.

Horowitz, D. Jan. 1987. From Left to Right, 103.

Howard, J. June 1979. SOF interviews Chris Dempster, 64.

John, Dr. Nov. 1984. American in ARDE, 70.

Kathman, M. Aug. 1983. Triangle tunnel rat, 44.

McKenna, B. Oct. 1986. Combat weaponcraft, 16.

McLean, D. Apr. 1988. Firestorm, 68.

Morris, J. May 1982. Killers in retirement, 29.

———. Dec. 1984. Make Pidgin Talk, 44.

Norris, W. Nov. 1987. Rhodesia's fireforce commandos, 64.

Roberts, C. May 1989. Master sniper's one shot saves, 26.

Stewart, H. March 1978. Tet 68: rangers in action — Saigon, 24.

Stuart-Smyth, A. May 1989. Congo horror: peacekeeper's journey into the heart of darkness, 66.

Thompson, J. Oct. 1985. Combat weaponcraft, 22.

————. June 1988. Hidden enemies, 21.

Tucker, D. Jan. 1978. High risk/low pay: freelancing in Cambodia, 34.

Uhernik, N. Oct. 1979. Battle of blood: near the end in Saigon, 38.

The author is grateful for permission to include the following previously copyrighted material:

Many of the quotes within this book are from personal interviews with the author. As mentioned in the acknowledgements, another major source for this book has been *Soldier of Fortune* magazine. In the environment of condemnation and accusation that existed immediately after the Vietnam War, *SOF* was the only national forum in which Vietnam veterans could attain some degree of closure by writing of their experiences in a sympathetic and nonjudgmental environment.

I would ask those who would prejudge this material as "mindless machismo" to observe the true nature of these narratives. Many of these veterans tell of instances in which they did not kill the enemy even when they had every reason and justification to do so; and many tell of the shock and trauma associated with having killed, and the guilt and anguish which followed their experiences. I want to thank Colonel (retired) Alex McColl, at *Soldier of Fortune,* for his support and assistance in using these quotes (a detailed listing of which can be found in the bibliography) and I would like to thank all of the authors of these and every other work quoted in this book, and all of those whom I have had the priviledge to interview as a part of this study. This book — indeed this entirely new field of study, which I have termed killology — would not be possible were it not for those who have gone before us, the veterans and authors on whose shoulders this study stands.

Index